Exploring the
Apocrypha

from a Latter-day Saint Perspective

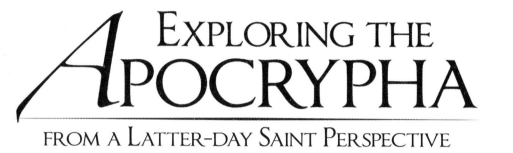

EXPLORING THE
APOCRYPHA

FROM A LATTER-DAY SAINT PERSPECTIVE

JARED W. LUDLOW

CFI
An imprint of Cedar Fort, Inc.
Springville, Utah

ISBN 13: 978-1-4621-2195-3

Published by CFI, an imprint of Cedar Fort, Inc.
2373 W. 700 S., Springville, UT 84663
Distributed by Cedar Fort, Inc., www.cedarfort.com

LIBRARY OF CONGRESS CATALOGING-IN-PUBLICATION DATA

Names: Ludlow, Jared W., author.
Title: Exploring the Apocrypha from an LDS perspective / Jared W. Ludlow.
Description: Springville, Utah : CFI, An imprint of Cedar Fort, Inc., [2018]
  | Includes bibliographical references and index.
Identifiers: LCCN 2018002838 (print) | LCCN 2018004027 (ebook) | ISBN
  9781462128907 (epub, pdf, mobi) | ISBN 9781462121953 | ISBN
  9781462121953 (perfect bound : alk. paper)
Subjects: LCSH: Bible. Apocrypha--Introductions. | Bible.
  Apocrypha--Criticism, interpretation, etc. | Mormon Church--Doctrines. |
  Church of Jesus Christ of Latter-day Saints--Doctrines.
Classification: LCC BS1700 (ebook) | LCC BS1700 .L83 2018 (print) | DDC
  229/.061--dc23
LC record available at https://lccn.loc.gov/2018002838

Cover design by Jeff Harvey
Cover design © 2018 Cedar Fort, Inc.
Edited by Emily Chambers and Justin Greer
Typeset by Kaitlin Barwick

Printed in the United States of America

10 9 8 7 6 5 4 3 2 1

Printed on acid-free paper

To my wife, Margaret, and five wonderful children:
Jared Jr., Joshua, Joseph, Marissa, and Melia.

Thank you for many great experiences together in the past,
and I look forward to more in the future.

CONTENTS

PREFACE

WHEN A READER TURNS THE PAGE FROM THE LAST CHAPTER OF
Malachi in the Old Testament to the first page of Matthew in the
New Testament, he has skipped a period of approximately four
hundred years. This simple turn of a page oversteps an important
era of Jewish development that led to sectarian groups such as the
Pharisees, Sadducees, and Essenes, as well as set the stage for the
rise of Christianity. The study of the roots of Christianity leads to
encountering a variety of texts not found in the Bible, and the discovery of the Dead Sea Scrolls has only added to the intrigue of this early
literature. The Apocrypha is one list or collection of books related
to the Old Testament that forms an important backdrop to early
Christianity. Found in some faith traditions' canons, like those of
the Roman Catholics and Eastern Orthodox Christians, these books
tell us more about the events and religious thought of the first centuries BC and AD. Despite the fact that many of them are set during
earlier Old Testament events, purporting to give us more stories about
figures like Daniel and Ezra, they were part of a burgeoning Greek
tradition and likely written much later. They are extremely valuable
to understanding more about this historical time period as well as the
creativity and religious thought of early Jews and Christians.

This study is an introduction to the Apocrypha, giving an LDS
perspective on what the Apocrypha meant to the early restored

Church and the role it can play in our own spiritual lives. After a few introductory chapters on the development of the Apocrypha and its use by Joseph Smith and early members, this book provides a brief overview of each book in the Apocrypha. Since some denominations vary in which books should be included in the Apocrypha, we will follow the list found in the Bible used by Joseph Smith (the Phinney Bible) which led him to ask the Lord whether he should translate the Apocrypha as part of what came to be known as the Joseph Smith Translation (JST). This particular list is common among Protestant Bibles that include the Apocrypha.

Besides possible spiritual edification, the Apocrypha provides an important window to a period of Greek influence on the Jews shortly before the time of Jesus. As Jews grappled with the issue of what to do with Greek thought, language, and religion, various responses emerged. Many stories found in the Apocrypha highlight the tension and accommodations made to live nearer to or among Gentiles. Although ultimately the Apocrypha would be excluded from later Jewish canons, its influence, especially from the wisdom sayings of Sirach, can be seen in rabbinic writings. The accounts of the Maccabees influenced early Christian martyrs and continue to inspire Jewish strength and independence. The Apocrypha is still considered scripture by a majority of Christians around the world. Joseph Smith recorded the word of the Lord regarding reading the Apocrypha in Doctrine and Covenants 91:5, stating that "whoso is enlightened by the Spirit shall obtain benefit therefrom." It is my hope that this introduction to the Apocrypha will stimulate learning about this important work from ancient times and provide possible avenues for readers' personal study of these religious texts in order to "obtain benefit" from them.

This work has been a great opportunity for me to dig deeper into the rich literature of the Apocrypha. I appreciate my wife's support in my scholarly endeavors. A special thanks is owed to Andy Mickelson, who carried a huge load in the research for this book.

1

Apocrypha: What Is It and Where Did It Come From?

The Apocrypha has elicited curiosity and interest from its very inception. The name itself, meaning "obscure" or "hidden things," adds to its intrigue. So what is the Apocrypha, where did it come from, and why should we read it? This book explores these questions by introducing the content of the Apocrypha to a Latter-day Saint audience while highlighting passages that may be of particular doctrinal interest to LDS readers. Joseph Smith and early church members interacted with the Apocrypha, but not to a great extent (see Chapter 2). Yet there is still an invitation in the Doctrine and Covenants to explore the Apocrypha because "whoso is enlightened by the Spirit shall obtain benefit therefrom" (D&C 91:5).

The Apocrypha (capital *A*), as opposed to the broader category of apocryphal texts (lowercase *a*), is basically a closed list of books with some variance among Christian denominations. It has had a most interesting canonical history. When the Hebrew Bible (the Old Testament) was translated into Greek, the resulting manuscript tradition came to be known as the Septuagint. Besides the Greek translations of Hebrew books, some additional stories were included that were popular among Greek-speaking Jews living in diaspora (living outside the land of Israel, predominantly in Greek-speaking regions), many of which dealt with events after the time of Ezra and Malachi. Essentially, the Apocrypha, with the exception of one Old Latin text, consists of the additional books or stories found in the Septuagint, but not in the original Hebrew Bible.

An ancient document, *The Letter of Aristeas*, claims to record the production of the Septuagint.[1] The text purports to be a letter from Aristeas, a Greek official in the court of Ptolemy Philadelphus II (the Greek Ptolemaic ruler in Egypt from 285 to 246 BC) to an interested friend, Philocrates. Ptolemy II wanted copies of all the books in the world for his grand library in Alexandria. Demetrius, his librarian, suggested that the library should include a copy of the "laws of the Jews," to which Ptolemy II agreed. He sent an epistle (and a sizable amount of treasure) to the Jewish high priest in Jerusalem and requested the services of seventy-two learned Jewish elders (six from each tribe) to come to Egypt to translate their scriptures into Greek.[2] Upon the arrival of the Jewish elders in Alexandria, the king entertained the men at his palace for seven days and asked them a variety of theological and philosophical questions, to which they admirably responded.[3] The Jewish envoys were then given stately accommodations on the nearby isle of Pharos and began the task of translation. (Aristeas was one of the seventy-two translators.) A final version of the Greek text was completed in exactly seventy-two days,[4] after which it was read to the Jewish community of Alexandria, who declared that it had "been made rightly and reverently, and in every respect accurately."[5] They decreed that a curse would follow anyone who altered the translated text in any way.

As fascinating as *The Letter of Aristeas* is, its account of the Septuagint's translation cannot be taken at face value. Aside from numerous historical inaccuracies,[6] the strongly apologetic tone marks it as a work written to glorify the Jewish people and the Jewish law.[7] But scholars believe that, despite its biases and factual errors, *The Letter of Aristeas* does reflect some truths about the translation of the Septuagint. For example, it is widely believed that the Septuagint was translated in the Egyptian city of Alexandria[8]—but for different reasons than those given by Aristeas. Instead of being written to enrich the Ptolemaic library, it was likely written to meet the needs of Jews living outside of Israel for whom Hebrew was becoming increasingly a "foreign" language. After the conquest of Alexander the Great (334–326 BC), Greek became the *lingua franca* throughout the Mediterranean world. For Jews living in Hellenistic cities like Alexandria and Antioch, Greek was the language of everyday life. It is likely that knowledge of Hebrew was limited to the highly educated. Thus, a Greek translation of the Hebrew scriptures was not just necessary for making God's word accessible to Gentiles; it was also necessary to give Diaspora Jews access to their own religious heritage. Alexandria, as both a center of Greek learning and a center of Jewish Diaspora life, was an ideal place for the birth of this translation, which likely occurred during the third century BC.[9]

However, this initial project was simply the beginning of the process of translating the Old Testament into Greek. *The Letter of Aristeas* is not specific as to which books of the Hebrew Bible were translated at that time, but scholars believe that initially only the Torah, the five books of Moses (known as the Pentateuch), was translated. The other books of the Hebrew Bible were translated gradually, likely by many separate individuals on a book-by-book basis, during the centuries that followed.[10] This may seem odd to us in modern times, but it is understandable when we remember that there was no firmly established "Bible" during this period: each book circulated as an individual scroll.[11] We do know that by the time of the New Testament all the books of the Old Testament had been translated, as Paul and others regularly referred to scriptures from throughout the Septuagint when they preached.[12]

In addition to the translated books of the Old Testament, some additional books and stories began to be circulated among Greek-speaking Jews; many were original Greek compositions written by early Jewish authors or groups. These new compositions formed what came to be known as the Apocrypha. They were written after the books of Ezra and Malachi, which were regarded as the latest writings of the Hebrew Bible (around 400 BC), though some were attributed to biblical figures or set during biblical events. Two of them are internal expansions of Esther and Daniel. Two texts are "histories" of the Maccabees detailing the events in Judea during the second century BC. Like the earlier books of the Septuagint, these works circulated as individual scrolls to be read by Jews throughout the ancient world.

The collection of the books of the Apocrypha can be divided into three categories:

Biblical Expansions

- The Additions to the Book of Esther
- Daniel Stories: Song of the Three Young Men, Susanna, Bel and the Dragon
- First Book of Esdras (Greek form of the name *Ezra*)
- Second Book of Esdras (the only Apocrypha text not from the Greek Septuagint but found in several Old Latin manuscripts)
- Prayer of Manasseh
- Baruch and Letter of Jeremiah

Heroic Stories

- Tobit
- Judith
- 1 Maccabees
- 2 Maccabees

Wisdom Literature

- Wisdom of Solomon
- Ecclesiasticus or the Wisdom of Jesus ben Sirach

Altogether, the Apocrypha (found in many versions of the Bible, including some earlier printed King James Versions) consists of 183 additional chapters (the New Testament has 260),[13] making it a substantial contribution to the Judeo-Christian religious literature of its day. For modern readers, the Apocrypha can be a valuable tool for helping us understand the political, cultural, and religious background of Jesus Christ and his contemporaries.

The original language of composition of these texts has been debated, although more certainty is possible with some texts. They are commonly divided into three main groups of writings:

1. Works whose Greek style shows that they were composed in Greek: additions B and E to the Book of Esther; Wisdom of Solomon; 2 Maccabees; 3 Maccabees; 2 Esdras 1–2, 15–16; 4 Maccabees; and probably the Prayer of Manasseh.

2. Works for which the discovery of Hebrew or Aramaic manuscripts of their texts—particularly, but not only, as part of the discoveries at Qumran—has confirmed the view that they were composed in one or other of these languages: Tobit, Ecclesiasticus, and Psalm 151.

3. Works for which composition in Hebrew or Aramaic seems very probable, or is at least suspected, even though we lack textual proof of this: Judith, the additions to the Book of Esther (except for additions B and E), Baruch, the Letter of Jeremiah, the additions to the Greek Book of Daniel, 1 Maccabees, and 1 Esdras.

• In addition, 2 Esdras 3–14 was also probably composed in Hebrew, but neither the original Hebrew nor the Greek translation of this have survived, and we are dependent on the evidence of the versions made from the Greek, particularly the Latin version.[14]

As Jewish and Christian groups began debating these texts' usefulness and place within their respective canons, they labeled them *apocrypha*, or "things that are hidden." For various groups of early Jews and Christians, this label held either positive or negative connotations depending on the authority they granted these writings. If viewed positively, they were held with reverence as hidden gems that had been specially revealed to the wise (following the principle of not casting pearls before swine).[15] These texts were like the hidden or sealed books in apocalyptic writings (for example, John's *Revelation*) that were reserved to be opened and come forth at a future time. If viewed negatively, these texts were seen as unworthy of attention and even dangerous, so they should be buried, hidden, and forgotten.[16] These texts also deserve the designation *apocrypha* because their origins are hidden and thus the authority of the authors is in question.[17]

The broader category of apocryphal texts (lowercase *a*) included many more texts than those listed above. These included texts called by modern scholars "Pseudepigrapha," a term that "has evolved from *pseudepigrapha*, a transliteration of a Greek plural noun that denotes writings 'with false superscription.'"[18] Despite being associated with Old Testament figures, these stories were likely written much later by individuals who falsely ascribed them to respected patriarchs and prophets. These include texts like the Apocalypse of Abraham, the Testaments of the Twelve Patriarchs, the books of Enoch, the Life of Adam and Eve, and dozens of others.[19] Some of these were found among the Dead Sea Scrolls, which indicates that they probably carried some authority among certain early Jewish groups. They were translated into a variety of languages and passed down through Christian groups. Some of these texts influenced early Christian writings; some were even quoted in the New Testament itself.[20]

The later authors probably did not use the name of earlier figures for their own gain by creating a hoax or as literary forgery, but instead to put forth teachings under the authority or by adopting the persona of earlier, more well-known figures.[21] It was a "pious fraud," presented in a time when revelation was believed to have ceased, by hoisting their texts on earlier prophetic figures in order to effect change.[22] The false attribution of the text could have happened with the original story or secondarily by a copyist who thought the text went back to an earlier figure (and, incidentally, by attributing it to an earlier authoritative figure, actually helped preserve it by raising its stature—because otherwise people may not have wanted to read or copy it). Another possibility for these texts is that some stories may have been actual oral or written accounts of biblical figures that were passed down until found in these later manuscripts, but they had never become part of the canonical Old Testament. Thus, there could be historical kernels of stories or teachings of earlier figures now found in later written texts alongside additional new material. It is also possible that later readers of the Old Testament who saw gaps in the text or felt uncomfortable with something in a story created additional stories (or altered existing ones) about Old Testament figures—a possible motive for Apocrypha authors as well.

The Place of the Apocrypha in Scripture

Although there is nothing intrinsically different about the texts that came to be collected in the Apocrypha compared with other Jewish and Christian texts of the day, it is nonetheless a fact that these particular texts started showing up in scriptural lists and became part of some religious groups' canons while most other Pseudepigrapha and apocryphal texts did not. It would be impossible to relate here every facet of the Apocrypha's roller-coaster ride through over 2,000 years of canonical history, but it is helpful to see at least the general role the Apocrypha has played in various religious denominations. By doing so, we will also see how it led to the LDS decision to exclude the Apocrypha from our canon (the Standard Works), but why the Apocrypha was known by Joseph Smith and was still mentioned in the Doctrine and Covenants.

As was mentioned above, the discovery of several apocryphal books among the Dead Sea Scrolls indicates that these texts were popular among some Jews of the Second Temple period.[23] While they didn't hold the same stature as their older counterparts, they were certainly read by educated Jews throughout the Near East, and some may even have been used in synagogues. Yet despite their Jewish origin and popularity, in the end these books were permanently excluded from the Jewish canon in the first centuries AD. Following the destruction of the Jerusalem Temple in AD 70, Jewish sages, meeting in places like Yavneh (*Jamnia* in Greek) near the Mediterranean coast, debated religious issues, such as what books should be accepted as canonical. Perhaps as a reaction against Greek influence that had become so prevalent among some Jews in previous centuries, many Jews rejected these Greek texts even though they held important Jewish history and thought. These Jews determined that prophecy had ended at the time of Malachi, so although these additional texts provided historical information on later periods, they were not deemed prophetic.[24] Perhaps the later Jewish insistence on the end of prophecy in 400 BC was a reaction against Christian belief that God continued to interact with mankind up to and through the time of the New Testament.[25] Although no specific list of authoritative books exists from the first centuries AD, several texts mention that 22 or 24 texts were authoritative.[26] The rabbis often used the term "outside books" to exclude certain texts from the canon and discourage the reading of them because they might get confused with the Torah. Yet quotations from books in the Apocrypha, especially the Wisdom of Jesus ben Sirach, still show up in rabbinic writings and are permitted for the use of instruction. The Maccabees continued to be read as part of Jewish history—especially because Maccabees recounts the beginnings of the Jewish festival Hanukkah. But the books in the Apocrypha are not part of liturgical readings in synagogues, nor are they considered authoritative like the Hebrew Bible books.

All of this helps explain why, despite having been written by Jews for a Jewish audience, the books of the Apocrypha were largely preserved and passed down by Christians. During the first two centuries AD, all the books of the Septuagint (including the Apocrypha) seemed to have been accepted as part of the Christian Bible. Early Christian writers and leaders such as Clement of Rome, Irenaeus, Tertullian, Cyprian, Clement of Alexandria, and Origen quoted from and accepted the books of the Apocrypha as scripture.[27] Origen in particular makes a strong case for early Christian acceptance of the Old Testament Apocrypha: he cites them as scripture in the same way he cites other Old Testament books, and he particularly identifies Tobit, Judith, the Additions to Esther, Ecclesiasticus, and the Wisdom of Jesus ben Sirach to be divinely inspired.[28] He included them in his critical edition of the Old Testament, the Hexapla, which was then later used by Eusebius to create Bibles for the city of Constantinople; these Bible manuscripts were then used to create even more Bibles, each containing the Apocrypha.[29] The earliest complete manuscripts of Greek Bibles from the fourth through fifth centuries AD include the Apocrypha interspersed among the other Old Testament books, although with different contents and ordering, which seems to indicate fluidity related to these texts at that time.[30]

The debate about the authoritative nature of the Apocrypha grew among later Christians: though many groups kept these texts in their canon, some questioned their authority and whether they should be used to determine doctrine or practice, or simply read as uplifting literature. The fourth century was a particularly divisive period; Eastern Church leaders tended to not accept the books in the Apocrypha as canonical, yet they would still cite from them as they did from canonical texts.[31] A few centuries later, the Byzantine Christians reverted to the attitude of the earlier Church in accepting the Apocrypha. In the Council in Trullo held at Constantinople under Justinian II (AD 692), eastern bishops adopted the decisions of earlier councils to accept the Apocrypha as canonical. Selections from the Apocrypha were widely used in sermons, homilies, and church writings.[32] Eastern Orthodox Christians tended to accept all the books of the Apocrypha and some additional ones, including

3 Maccabees, Psalm 151, and 4 Maccabees (in an appendix). The Greek Orthodox Church, for example, accepted these books during the Synod of Jerusalem of 1672, but they usually referred to them as "things which are read" (Greek *anagignōskomena*). "The affirmation of the validity of the 'Deuterocanonical' writings by the Synod was more a commendation than a dogmatic pronouncement, so that opinion regarding their canonical status in the Church has varied."[33] Some of the earliest complete Syriac Bibles from the sixth century found among the West-Syrian Orthodox traditions contain the writings from the Apocrypha and even more additional texts (like 2 Baruch, 4 Ezra, and 4 Maccabees). The Ethiopian Orthodox Church includes many of the same books from the Apocrypha, but differs in that it did not receive them from the Greek Bible (Septuagint) but from their own manuscripts in Classical Ethiopic (Ge'ez). Throughout their history, they have considered some of these books as "undisputed," "disputed," or "noncanonical."

The Western Church (Catholic), on the other hand, heartily accepted the Apocrypha as canonical in early regional councils under Augustine's leadership (held in the cities of Hippo in AD 393 and Carthage in AD 397).[34] Augustine had realized that not all churches recognized this fuller canon, so he instructed his readers to base the authority of these texts on two criteria: whether the more important churches regarded it as scripture and if the majority of the churches did so.[35] Augustine hoped that being more broad-minded on this issue would promote greater unity with the Greek-speaking churches in the East. Some church figures, however, took a different view. For example, the Catholic theologian Jerome did not accept the books of the Apocrypha and did not want to include them in his famous Latin translation of the Bible, the Vulgate.[36] Under pressure from Church leaders, he reluctantly included them—but with descriptions of their dubious nature. (Those in the Catholic Church who took issue with the Apocrypha tended to have connections with the East, such as Jerome, who had lived out his days in Bethlehem.)

Some Christians, especially the Catholics, termed the books from the Apocrypha as *deutero*-canonical, not because they were *secondary* or inferior in status, but *secondary* in chronology by coming into the canon and being formalized by ecclesiastical authorities later than the Old Testament books.[37] The final status for these books in the Catholic Church was determined at the Council of Trent in 1546. At this council, all the books were deemed canonical except 2 Esdras and the Prayer of Manasseh, which were placed in an appendix at the end of the New Testament to be read only for edification, not doctrine.[38] Following the list of all the canonical books, Catholic Bibles included the statement: "If anyone does not accept as sacred and canonical the aforesaid books in their entirety and with all their parts, as they have been accustomed to be read in the Catholic Church . . . let him be anathema."[39] Still, in the face of continuing challenges from prominent Catholics, the Catholic Church felt the need to reassert the canonicity of the Apocrypha in the Vatican Council of 1870 by upholding the decree of the Council of Trent.

Many Protestants rejected the Apocrypha as canon, yet often the Apocrypha was still printed with their Bibles until about 1650, usually in its own section (the Prayer of Manasseh and 1 and 2 Esdras were treated as apocryphal). Luther, for example, thought some of the books from the Apocrypha were profitable and good to read (while others were ignored), but he felt they should not form the basis for doctrine and were not considered equal to the Holy Scriptures.[40] The Church of England's sixth article declared that the books in the Apocrypha could be read for examples of life and instruction in manners,[41] but a later Westminster Conference declared that the Apocrypha was not to be approved and its books were simply examples of human writing.[42]

A more discriminating statement about their value was offered in 1520 by Andreas Bodenstein of Karlstadt (*De Canonicis Scripturis Libellus*): some works (Wisdom of Solomon, Sirach, Tobit, Judith, 1 and 2 Maccabees) outside the Hebrew canon are 'holy writings' and their content 'is not to be despised' (sections 114, 118), while others (1 and 2 Esdras, Baruch, Prayer of Manasseh, Prayer of Azariah, Song of the Three Young Men, Susanna, Bel and the Dragon) are so problematic that they are 'worthy of a censor's ban.' Thus, despite the inclusion of 'Apocrypha' in a number of Protestant translations, sentiments comparable to those of Karlstadt were widely held (e.g., the Belgic Confession 1561, the Synod of Dort 1619–19, Westminster Confession 1647) and have led to the removal of these writings in many translations of the Bible until today.[43]

Therefore, it is rare today to see the Apocrypha included in Protestant Bibles except perhaps in Study Bibles.

Despite the Apocrypha's checkered canonical history, there can be no doubt that it has impacted Christian and Jewish cultures. In Jewish practice, Hanukkah has become a central festival and the Maccabees form a part of Jewish identity. In the Christian world, the Apocrypha has influenced poets, artists, hymn-writers, dramatists, composers, and even explorers such as Christopher Columbus, who used a passage in 2 Esdras about the earth being composed of six parts land to seek financial support for his journey westward. Even in early Christian sites like the catacombs of Rome, depictions of Apocrypha scenes have been found. But what has been the role and impact of the Apocrypha for Latter-day Saints? The next chapter will address this question.

NOTES

1. For a commonly used translation of this text (as well as other works of Jewish Pseudepigrapha), see James H. Charlesworth, ed., *The Old Testament Pseudepigrapha* (2 vols.; Garden City, NY: Doubleday & Company, 1985).

2. Both ancient and modern commentators are quick to correlate the seventy-two Jewish elders chosen to translate the law with the seventy Jewish elders who accompanied Moses up Mount Sinai when he first

received the law; in fact, later tradition cites the number of translators as seventy, to make the stories even more harmonious. Michael Law writes, "If the Ptolemaic Library were to include the Jewish Law, an accurate version was necessary. This outstanding version was to be completed by seventy-two translators, six from each of the twelve tribes, and it is no accident that the feature of seventy-two translators is close to the number of the seventy elders who went with Moses to Sinai (sections 28–32; cf. Exodus 24:1, 9). The Septuagint, the *Letter of Aristeas* implies, is a new revelation." Timothy Michael Law, *When God Spoke Greek: The Septuagint and the Making of the Christian Bible* (New York: Oxford University Press, 2013), 37.

3. Stories of Jews impressing foreign rulers with their wisdom is an element common in many Old Testament texts; the stories of Joseph in Egypt and Daniel in Babylon are but two examples. Banquets in which kings philosophize with others are also common in ancient literature—perhaps drawing upon the tradition of Greek *symposia*. "Authors in antiquity often made such banquets the setting for wise and witty talk and for learned answers to the weighty matters posed by kings. Here at each of the seven banquets the king addresses questions to ten or eleven of the seventy-two translators and compliments each on his prompt and sagacious response. The topic of conversation is the theory and practice of kingship. The seventy-two answers provide many variations on a few basic themes. Each answer climaxes with a reference to 'God' or 'divine' activity." George W.E. Nickelsburg, *Jewish Literature between the Bible and the Mishnah* (2nd ed.; Minneapolis: Fortress Press, 2005), 196.

4. Philo of Alexandra, writing during the early first century AD, adds the detail that each of the translators went about their translation efforts in separate rooms, yet miraculously produced identical texts, giving their work the weight of divine inspiration. This helps demonstrate the great importance of the Septuagint to Greek-speaking Jews of Philo's time. See Jennifer M. Dines, *The Septuagint* (ed. Michael A. Knibb; New York: T&T Clark, 2004), 67–70.

5. R. J. H. Shutt, "Letter of Aristeas (Third Century B.C.–First Century A.D.)," in *The Old Testament Pseudepigrapha* (2nd vol.; ed. J. H. Charlesworth; Garden City, NY: Doubleday & Company, 1985), 33.

6. "The most glaring [inaccuracy] is the presence of Demetrius of Phalerum who had been banished by Philadelphus soon after his accession and who is never referred to elsewhere as royal librarian. There are also several improbabilities: the apparently non-Jewish Aristeas's working knowledge of Judaism; Philadelphus's relation of equality with Eleazer, and his excessive enthusiasm for all things Jewish; a hundred thousand

Jewish slaves being emancipated to secure the translation of the Hebrew scrolls." Dines, *The Septuagint*, 31.

7. The glowing descriptions of Jerusalem's temple and priests, as well as the lavish praise heaped upon the Jewish envoys and the Law of Moses, make the apologetic intentions of the author transparent. Such an approach may have had several purposes. The account was likely meant to bolster the fidelity of Diaspora Jews to their religion, but it also held a message for their Gentile neighbors. As Larry Helyer argues, "[t]he letter is not intended for internal consumption alone; it is intended to impress pagans with the excellencies of Judaism. Such a system of belief would be an attractive option for one's own life—so the implied argument of the letter. We thus have a document that aggressively promotes the superiority of Judaism vis-à-vis paganism." Larry R. Helyer, *Exploring Jewish Literature of the Second Temple Period: A Guide for New Testament Students* (Downers Grove, IL: IVP Academic, 2002), 279.

8. Although Aristeas claims that the seventy-two translators of the Septuagint were Jews from Jerusalem, R. Timothy McLay notes that "the language of the Greek Pentateuch [first five books of the Bible] is consistent with what is known of the Greek language that was common in third-century Egypt." R. Timothy McLay, *The Use of the Septuagint in New Testament Research* (Grand Rapids, MI: William B. Eerdmans Publishing, 2003), 102.

9. "That the Greek Pentateuch was produced at the very latest in the second century BCE [BC] is proven by the linguistic evidence of the translation, by the citations of the Greek Pentateuch in other Hellenistic authors and in later Septuagint books dated to the second century, and by manuscripts dating also to the second century. Other places of origin, such as the Egyptian cities of Leontopolis or Memphis or even parts of North Africa (e.g. Cyrene) and Asia Minor (e.g. Ephesus) have been put forth as options but none are as convincing as the city of Alexandria. The Greek Pentateuch contains enough hints of Egyptian origin to rule out non-Egyptian sites, and Alexandria is the most plausible given its status as the center of Greek culture during this period." Law, *God Spoke Greek*, 35–36.

10. Although the dating and Alexandrian provenance of the Pentateuch's translation is generally agreed upon, such consensus does not exist with the other books. As Jobes and Silva surmise, "[t]he historical and prophetic books of the Hebrew Bible were probably translated into Greek during the following century, but we do not know where or by whom." Karen H. Jobes and Moises Silva, *Invitation to the Septuagint* (Grand Rapids, MI: Baker Academic, 2000), 34.

11. "The books of the Hebrew Bible were originally translated independently into Greek by different translators over several centuries. What we call books were at that time written on individual scrolls. Typically no longer than thirty-five feet, a single scroll could not contain the Greek version of the Hebrew Bible in its entirety, and so each book was usually written on a separate scroll. A different format, the codex, came into use in the second century of the Christian era. This format made it possible to bind originally separate texts (which would fill many scrolls) into one volume, giving a false impression of homogeneity. Just because the texts were bound together, one should not infer that they shared a common origin. In fact, there was no one uniform Greek version of the entire Hebrew Bible—just individual scrolls that had been copied from other scrolls throughout the ages." Jobes and Silva, *Invitation*, 31.

12. "[T]he LXX played a vital part in the life of the earliest church. Although the members of the first community of believers in Jerusalem were all Jews (or proselytes to Judaism; cf. Acts 6:5) and spoke Aramaic or Hebrew, many also spoke Greek and were familiar with the LXX. As the Church moved out of its Jewish enclave in Jerusalem and then made the huge breakout into the Gentile world, primarily under the impetus of the Pauline mission, the LXX became the basic Bible of these house churches. When one examines Paul's letters and studies his use of the OT in them, it quickly becomes apparent that this was the version he cited." Helyer, *Exploring Jewish Literature,* 283. For a more specific discussion on Paul's quotations of Old Testament scripture, see Jared W. Ludlow, "Paul's Use of Old Testament Scripture," in *How the New Testament Came to Be*, ed. Kent P. Jackson and Frank F. Judd Jr., (Provo and Salt Lake City, UT: Brigham Young University Religious Studies Center and Deseret Book, 2006), 227–242.

13. For comparison purposes: the Old Testament has 929 chapters, 23,214 verses, and 592,439 words. The New Testament has 260 chapters, 7,959 verses, and 181,253 words. The Apocrypha has 183 chapters, 6,081 verses, and 152,185 words.

14. Michael A. Knibb, "Language, Translation, Versions, and Text of the Apocrypha," in *The Oxford Handbook of Biblical Studies*, ed. J.W. Rogerson and Judith M. Lieu (Oxford: Oxford University Press, 2006), 160. Knibb's entire article (159–183) gives a helpful overview of the transmission of the Apocrypha through the ages. Timothy Law also follows a similar separation of Apocrypha texts into three linguistic groups. See Law, *God Spoke Greek,* 60–61.

15. The positive sense of the term *apocrypha* may be influenced by "the widespread notion of 'hidden' or 'sealed' books in Greco-Roman and especially Jewish antiquity (Dan. 8:26; 12:4, 9–10; *Sib. Or.* 11.163–71;

4 Ezra 12:37; 14:5–6; 14:44–47; *2 Bar.* 20:3–4; 87:1; implied in *Jub.* 1:5; *1 Enoch* 82:1–3; 107:3; *2 Enoch* 35:1–3). In a number of Jewish apocalyptic writings, authors sometimes presented themselves (or, rather, those ancient figures whose names they were using) as having been instructed by God or an angel to 'seal' or 'hide' their works. This fictional instruction functioned as a way of explaining how such works attributed to such ancient authors had not been in circulation until the present. The existence of these books was a 'secret' until the time when they actually appeared. A closely related idea is the instruction that a writer 'seal' the book so that its contents will not be accessible until the appropriate time." From Loren T. Stuckenbruck, "Apocrypha and Pseudepigrapha," in *The Eerdmans Dictionary of Early Judaism*, ed. John J. Collins and Daniel C. Harlow (Grand Rapids, MI/Cambridge, UK: William B. Eerdmans Publishing Company, 2010), 148.

16. This term for the heretical texts that should be avoided was already used "as early as the late second century C.E. [AD] by Irenaeus who, in his *Against Heresies* (1.20.1), referred to the existence of 'an unspeakable number of apocryphal and spurious writings' that confuse the foolish and ignorant. Similarly, Origen in the third century C.E. [AD] declared that certain writings are called *apocryphae* because 'many things in them are corrupt and contrary to true faith' (*Commentary on Song of Songs*; cf. also *Commentary on Matthew*). The equation of 'secret' books with deception, though applied by Irenaeus (and Origen) to inauthentic traditions about Jesus, would in time be applied to 'pseudepigraphal' Jewish compositions as well." From Stuckenbruck, "Apocrypha and Pseudepigrapha," 148.

17. For example, one of several Catholic writers who viewed the Apocrypha with suspicion was Isidore of Seville, who stated that these books "are called this [apocrypha], a word which means 'secret,' because they come with doubts attached to them. Their origins are hidden, or they were not known to the Fathers from whom the authority of the most true and most certain scriptures has come down to us through a well-known succession. And although some truth is found in these works, nonetheless they have no canonical authority because there is much in them that is false. Therefore, prudent people rightly judge that these books are not to be accepted as having been written by the people whose names are attached to them." Quoted in Thomas O'Loughlin, "Inventing the Apocrypha: The Role of Early Latin Canon Lists," *Irish Theological Quarterly* 74:53 (2009): 53–54.

18. "[Old Testament Pseudepigrapha] etymologically denotes writings falsely attributed to ideal figures featured in the Old Testament. Contemporary scholars employ the term 'pseudepigrapha' not because it denotes

something spurious about the documents collected under that title, but because the term has been inherited and is now used internationally." J. H. Charlesworth, "Introduction for the General Reader," in *The Old Testament Pseudepigrapha. Vol 1* (ed. J. H. Charlesworth; Garden City, NY: Doubleday & Company, 1985), xxv.

19. As was mentioned in the discussion of *The Letter of Aristeas*, James H. Charlesworth's two-volume work *The Old Testament Pseudepigrapha* provides both excellent introductions to and translations of these texts.

20. For example, Jude 1:14–15 quotes from 1 Enoch 1:9. 2 Timothy 3:8 alludes to the legend of the magicians Jannes and Jambres, who opposed Moses. Jude 1:9 preserves a tradition early Christian writers equated with The Assumption of Moses.

21. "While many discount the value of the pseudepigrapha due to their spurious claims to authorship, it would seem that ancient readers weren't bothered with the authenticity of the authorial claims like modern readers may be. Two pseudepigrapha in particular, 1 Enoch and Jubilees, were read as authoritative scripture at Qumran, and they have always been scripture in the Ethiopian Orthodox Church." Law, *God Spoke Greek*, 59.

22. See this discussion, originally put forth by R.H. Charles, from an LDS perspective in the excellent article by Stephen E. Robinson, "Lying for God: the Uses of the Apocrypha," in *Apocryphal Writings and the Latter-day Saints*, ed. C. Wilfred Griggs (Provo, UT: Religious Studies Center, Brigham Young University, 1986), 133–54. Robinson argues, "I believe that Charles was absolutely correct in understanding pseudonymity as an intentional deceit practiced to gain normative standing for new ideas, and the polemic purposes to which the apocrypha were put seem to bear this out. The apocryphal literature was employed in basically four ways: to fill in the gaps in the scriptural account, to attack opposing theologies, to defend against the attacks of others, and to bring about or to legitimize theological change."

23. "Four works from the Apocrypha have been identified from the Qumran library: Tobit, Ecclesiasticus (Sirach), Letter of Jeremiah and Psalm 151." Helyer, *Exploring Jewish Literature*, 189.

24. It is also possible that many apocryphal texts, being only a couple of centuries old, just had not been given enough time to reach authoritative status when early rabbis sought to establish a set canon. "Some of the Apocrypha were composed in Greek and thus left aside, but they might also have been considered too new for inclusion. There was a premium on antiquity in the Greco-Roman world in which the Bible was finalized and recently written books were no match for the prestige and presumed sanctity of books written long before." Law, *God Spoke Greek*, 60.

25. "The closing of the Jewish canon may be seen as part of the Jewish reaction to knowledge of the books of the New Testament and the increasing influence of Christianity. The Tosefta, for instance, polemicizes against the holiness of Christian writings, characterizing them as heretical books . . . Joshua Bloch argued that Rabbi Akiba coined the term 'outside books' not to refer to apocalyptic or heretical books but 'to stigmatize as un-Jewish' the books of the Nazarenes or Christians. Thus the ban against books of the New Testament involved the imprecation that any Jew who read them aloud in the synagogue would not have a place in the world-to-come." Timothy H. Lim, *The Formation of the Jewish Canon* (New Haven: Yale, 2013), 183.

26. The difference in number reflects whether some short texts were combined with others, but it was never such a large number as to include the texts of the Apocrypha.

27. For an excellent compilation of early Christian commentary on the books of the Apocrypha, see Sever J. Voicu, ed., *Apocrypha*, (vol. 15 of *Ancient Christian Commentary on Scripture*, ed. Thomas C. Oden: Downers Grove, IL: InterVarsity Press, 2010). The editors of this volume are quick to point out that early Christians expressed a certain reserve towards the books of the Apocrypha, distinguishing them from the regular canon but nonetheless preserving them and citing them in their writings. For another view: "The evidence for the use of the Old Testament Apocrypha by patristic writers is stronger. Early Christian writers frequently appealed to characters such as Tobit and the Maccabean martyrs in these books as examples of morality or courage. They also found in them relevant material about angels (Tobit), immortality and resurrection (Wisdom, 2 Maccabees), and the doctrine of *creatio ex nihilo* (2 Macc. 7:8). Material from the book of Sirach was often quoted and adapted by Greek and Latin Christian writers, because that book was regarded as a repository of human wisdom and as relevant for Christians as well as Jews." Daniel J. Harrington, "Apocrypha, Old Testament," in *The Eerdmans Dictionary of Early Judaism*, ed. John J. Collins and Daniel C. Harlow (Grand Rapids and Cambridge: William B. Eerdmans Publishing Company, 2010), 350.

28. Law, *When God Spoke Greek*, 124.

29. See David L. Dungan, *Constantine's Bible: Politics and the Making of the New Testament* (Minneapolis: Fortress Press, 2007), 51.

30. Two of the earliest major codices of the Bible, the uncials B (Vatican Codex) and A (Alexandrian Codex) had the books in the following order: 1 Esdras follows Chronicles (in Cod. A it comes after Judith); Judith and Tobit follow Esther; Additions to Esther, Baruch and Epistle of Jeremiah, and Additions to Daniel add integral parts to their respective

books; Wisdom and Ecclesiasticus are after the other wisdom books (but in Cod. A all the wisdom books come together at the end of the whole list); I and II Maccabees do not occur in Cod. B, but in Cod. A they come after the Esdras books and before the Wisdom books. There were two exceptions: II Esdras was not in any manuscript of the Septuagint; the Prayer of Manasseh figured among the canticles appended to the Psalms.

31. "It was in the fourth century [AD], particularly where the scholarly standards of Alexandrian Christianity were influential, that these doubts began to make their mark officially. The view which now commended itself fairly generally in the Eastern church, as represented by Athanasius, Cyril of Jerusalem, Gregory of Nazianzus and Epiphanius, was that the deuterocanonical books should be relegated to a subordinate position outside the canon proper . . . Yet it should be noted (a) that no such scruples seem to have troubled adherents of the Antiochene School, such as John Chrysostom and Theodoret; and (b) that even those Eastern writers who took a strict line with the canon when it was formally under discussion were profuse in their citations from the Apocrypha on other occasions." J. N. D. Kelly, *Early Christian Doctrines* (New York: Harper & Brothers, 1958), 54–55.

32. For an excellent compilation of early Christian commentary on the books of the Apocrypha, see Sever J. Voicu, ed., *Apocrypha*, (vol. 15 of *Ancient Christian Commentary on Scripture*, ed. Thomas C. Oden: Downers Grove, IL: InterVarsity Press, 2010). The editors of this volume are quick to point out that early Christians expressed a certain reserve towards the books of the Apocrypha, distinguishing them from the regular canon but nonetheless preserving them and citing them in their writings.

33. Loren T. Stuckenbruck, "Apocrypha and Pseudepigrapha," in *The Eerdmans Dictionary of Early Judaism*, ed. John J. Collins and Daniel C. Harlow (Grand Rapids, MI/Cambridge, U.K.: William B. Eerdmans Publishing Company, 2010), 145.

34. The majority of the apocryphal works were declared scripture by various synods in 382, 393, 394, 397, and 419. See Thomas O'Loughlin, "Inventing the Apocrypha: The Role of Early Latin Canon Lists," *Irish Theological Quarterly* 74:53 (2009): 56–61.

35. See David A. deSilva, *Introducing the Apocrypha: Message, Context, and Significance* (Grand Rapids, MI: Baker Academic, 2002), 37.

36. "[A]t the end of the fourth century, Jerome announced his doctrine of '*hebraica veritas*,' according to which only books translated from a Hebrew original were recognized as authentically inspired. Jerome, however, did not dare exclude the deuterocanonical books from the Vulgate, since by his time they had gained a high level of acceptance

among Christians." "Introduction to the Apocrypha," in *Apocrypha* (ed. Sever J. Voicu: vol. 15 of *Ancient Christian Commentary on Scripture*, ed. Thomas C. Oden: Downers Grove, IL: InterVarsity Press, 2010), xxi. "In a letter (107.12) written in the year 403, he [Jerome] instructs a certain Laeta to have her daughter 'avoid all apocryphal writings' because they cannot be read for 'the truth of the doctrines they contain,' they 'are not actually written by those to whom they are ascribed,' and they have 'many faults' that 'have been introduced into them.' This negative assessment of 'apocrypha' did not mean Jerome denied them all religious value; but it takes 'great prudence (*grandis . . . prudentiae*) to find gold in the mire (*in iuto*)." From Stuckenbruck, "Apocrypha and Pseudepigrapha," 147.

37. "Greek term meaning literally 'second(ary) canon.' As used by Roman Catholics since the Council of Trent (1545–63), Deuterocanonical designates books or parts of books not in the Hebrew Bible (the 'proto' canon) but present in the Greek OT (LXX) and accepted as inspired both by early church fathers and the Council. In academic parlance the term *Deuterocanonical* is increasingly employed as more accurately describing the OT Apocrypha." From Richard N. Soulen and R. Kendall Soulen, *Handbook of Biblical Criticism*. Third Edition (Louisville: Westminster John Knox Press, 2001), 46.

38. The Fourth Session of the Council of Trent declared the following: "[The Synod,] following the examples of the orthodox Fathers, receives and venerates with an equal affection of piety and reverence, all the books both of the Old and of the New Testament . . . And it has thought it meet that a list of the sacred books be inserted in this decree, lest a doubt may arise in any one's mind, which are the books that are received by this Synod. They are as set down below: of the Old Testament: Genesis, Exodus, Leviticus, Numbers, Deuteronomy; Josue, Judges, Ruth, four books of Kings, two of Paralipomenon, the first book of **Esdras**, and the second which is entitled Nehemias; **Tobias**, **Judith**, Esther, Job, the Davidical Psalter, consisting of a hundred and fifty psalms; the Proverbs, Ecclesiastes, the Canticle of Canticles, **Wisdom**, **Ecclesiasticus**, Isaias, Jeremias, with **Baruch**; Ezechiel, Daniel; the twelve minor prophets, to wit, Osee, Joel, Amos, Abdias, Jonas, Micheas, Nahum, Habacuc, Sophronias, Aggaeus, Zacharias, Malachias; **two books of the Machabees, the first and the second**." Philip Schaff, ed., *The Creeds of Christendom* (rev. by David S. Schaff, 3rd ed.: Grand Rapids, MI: 1996), 2:80–81; bold font added to some books from the Apocrypha.

39. Schaff, *The Creeds*, 2:82.

40. "What books did Luther include in his Scripture? For the Old Testament, everyone knew that Jerome had designated the writings in the Greek Old Testament (the Septuagint), but not in the Hebrew Old Testament,

as 'apocrypha' (meaning uncanonical). Luther followed the same procedure." Like books in the New Testament he found questionable, Luther "put these writings in a separate group at the end of his German translation . . . with the warning not to found any doctrines upon them." Dungan, *Constantine's Bible*, 136.

41. Article VI of the Thirty-Nine Articles of Religion of the Church of England contains these statements: "In the name of the Holy Scripture we do understand those canonical Books of the Old and New Testament, of whose authority was never any doubt in the Church . . . And the other Books (as [Jerome] saith) the Church doth read for example of life and instruction of manners: but yet doth it not apply to them to establish any doctrine." Schaff, ed., *The Creeds*, 3:490–91.

42. Chapter III of the Westminster Confession of Faith begins with this sentence: "The books commonly called Apocrypha, not being of divine inspiration, are no part of the Canon of the Scripture; and therefore are of no authority in the Church of God, nor to be any otherwise approved, or made use of, than other human writings." Schaff, *The Creeds*, 3:602.

43. Stuckenbruck, "Apocrypha and Pseudepigrapha," 144.

2

Joseph Smith and the Latter-day Saint Use of the Apocrypha[1]

On a spring morning in 1833, Joseph Smith finished the Old Testament portion of his revision of the Bible (usually known as the Joseph Smith Translation—JST; he had previously completed the New Testament). Joseph Smith's Protestant Bible (King James Version, Phinney edition) included the Apocrypha, so the Prophet asked the Lord if he should likewise revise the Apocrypha as part of this revelatory project.[2] The Lord's response, recorded on March 9, 1833, is now included in the Doctrine and Covenants as section 91:

> 1 Verily, thus saith the Lord unto you concerning the Apocrypha— There are many things contained therein that are true, and it is mostly translated correctly;
>
> 2 There are many things contained therein that are not true, which are interpolations by the hands of men.
>
> 3 Verily, I say unto you, that it is not needful that the Apocrypha should be translated.
>
> 4 Therefore, whoso readeth it, let him understand, for the Spirit manifesteth truth;
>
> 5 And whoso is enlightened by the Spirit shall obtain benefit therefrom;

6 And whoso receiveth not by the Spirit, cannot be benefited. Therefore it is not needful that it should be translated. Amen.

This section of the Doctrine and Covenants provides a few key principles for the LDS treatment of the Apocrypha:

- First, the Apocrypha was not to be translated as part of the JST, and, consequently, it is not part of the LDS canon.[3]
- There are things in the Apocrypha that are true, but there are also many false interpolations of men.
- Whoever is going to read the Apocrypha should read it by the Spirit; in this way, they can benefit from their study as the Spirit manifests truth.

So, do we find later instances of Joseph Smith or his fellow Church leaders discussing or preaching from the Apocrypha? Was section 91 the end of the Apocrypha in the LDS Church? A quick review of early Church literature shows other instances where the Apocrypha was still part of LDS discussion, although, unsurprisingly, not a major focus.[4]

In perhaps the earliest outside reference (dated June 25, 1833) to the new revelation recorded in section 91, the Church leaders in Kirtland wrote a letter back to W. W. Phelps and others in Zion responding to some of their queries. They stated that "respecting the Apochraphy [sic] the Lord said to us that there were many things in it which were true and there were many things in it which were not true and to those who desired, it should be given by the spirit to know true from the false, we have received some revelations within a short time back which you will obtain in due time."[5] This letter alludes to "some revelations" that would be shared with them in "due time," and since it is basically echoing the same content as section 91, it may be pointing towards this section and the fact that it had not been widely disseminated yet. In this response, they are now sharing some of this newly received knowledge from the revelation behind Section 91. In another experience that seems to have echoes of section 91, Edward Stevenson recounts how "the

Prophet also looked over our large Bible and remarked that much of the Apocrypha was true, but it required the Spirit of God to select the truth out of those writings."[6]

At the sealing of the Nauvoo Temple's unfinished capstone was another mention of the Apocrypha with the early Saints, not so much for the Apocrypha's content but simply for its being part of the Bible. In Samuel Miles's later recollection of the event, he made the following claim:

> I was present when the books, writings, etc., were deposited in the southeast cornerstone of the Nauvoo Temple. Joseph was there overseeing the selection made for deposit. Perhaps two hundred persons were collected around the place. When a Bible was presented for deposit it was thought necessary that it should be complete— containing the Apocrypha. As there seemed to be none within reach, except large, highly-prized family Bibles, Brother Reynolds Cahoon volunteered to go to his home, which was nearby and cut out the Apocrypha from his large family Bible, which was accepted and the Bible thus made complete.[7]

In this case, it seems Joseph Smith placed enough respect on the Apocrypha to include it in the "complete Bible" that was going to be deposited in the Nauvoo Temple.

For an example where the content of the Apocrypha played a more active role, we can turn to early Church periodicals. It is not always clear how involved Joseph Smith was with these publications, but presumably he at least gave approval for most of the published articles. One of the earliest quotations from the Apocrypha in Church literature comes from *The Evening and the Morning Star* in 1832. In a brief article giving commentary on Hosea 3, 2 Maccabees is quoted to give important information on sacred objects like the Urim and Thummin. The article introduces 2 Maccabees as that "which the wisdom of man has seen fit to call Apocrypha."[8] It then quotes chapter 2, verses 1–8, which describe the prophet Jeremiah's exhortations to those about to be deported to Babylon and Jeremiah's taking "the tent and the ark and the altar of incense" to Mount Nebo, where they were sealed up in a cave-dwelling. Those who tried to mark the way to the cave could not find it later, and Jeremiah declared that the place would remain unknown until the time God gathers his people together again and discloses these things. This passage was thus quoted in the Church periodical to show that some of these sacred objects were kept safe by the Lord, but that they would come forth again when the final gathering occurred, which was then underway.

A later piece referring to the Apocrypha was published twice, first in the *Gospel Reflector*, a publication by the presiding elder in Philadelphia, B. Winchester, in 1841; and then later that year it was republished in *Times and Seasons*.[9] It focuses on some of the prophecies from the book of Esdras in the Apocrypha. The first part of the article sets forth the value of Esdras's writings: "Perhaps there are none of the writings of the ancient prophets that are more accurate, and distinct in pointing out future events, than the writings of the prophet Esdras."[10] It addresses the concern of whether his writings were inspired, given that they were written in Greek, rather than in Hebrew like the other prophets (a concern, incidentally, first brought up by early Jews who rejected the Greek books from their canon). The author felt that this was the same figure as Ezra of the Old Testament, so his writings were worth reading. "We have reasons for believing that Ezra, whose writings are acknowledged to be pure, and Esdras are the same person, or that the two names are synonymous. The difference in the name, no doubt, arose from the different languages from which it was translated."[11] It then goes on to share a few of the passages from Esdras that have parallels in LDS theology. These passages include prophecies related to the Second Coming such as the resurrection, the exaltation of the just, and the return of the Lost Ten Tribes to receive their rewards. It also quotes the efforts of Esdras to restore lost Old Testament texts that were destroyed or hidden due to all the conflict of his day. The article ends with the invitation to read the book of Esdras: "We advise all to read it, and then judge its merits."

The book of Esdras shows up in another episode of Church history, when it became so influential that it led to a break-off group who eventually moved to New Mexico.[12] A member of the church named James Brewster read about additional books produced by Esdras in 2 Esdras 14, yet these texts were later lost to history. Brewster, however, claimed revelatory gifts to restore some of these lost texts. In the end, Brewster published three books that he claimed Esdras had meant to be guides for the people in the last days. The first, published in 1842 when Brewster was about fifteen years old, was called *The Words of Righteousness to All Men*. According to a journal entry by Joseph Smith on the last day of 1842, Joseph received a visit by John Darby, who wanted to follow Brewster's planned migration to California. In their conversation, Joseph Smith stated that James Brewster's father, Zephaniah, had approached him earlier to share his son's new revelatory product with him.[13] The Prophet said he saw the manuscripts and enquired of the Lord and "the Lord told me the book was not true—it was not of him if God ever called me or spoke by my mouth or gave me a revelation he never gave revelations to that Brewster Boy or any of the Brewster race."[14]

A notice was also published in *Times and Seasons* about Brewster and some members of the Church who chose to follow him. "We have lately seen a pamphlet, written, and published by James C. Brewster; purporting to be one of the lost books of Esdras; and to be written by the gift and power of God. We consider it a perfect humbug, and should not have noticed it, had it not been assiduously circulated, in several branches of the church."[15] The notice goes on to say that some members had been suspended for their involvement with Brewster and would have been cut off had they not "promised to desist from their ridiculous and pernicious ways." Despite the Prophet's disapproval, Brewster gained some initial followers and organized the Church of Christ in 1848 centered on the Bible, the Book of Mormon, and the revelations of Esdras. In 1850, those willing to follow their new prophetic spokesman organized a journey to the promised land of "Bashan" (California), but this immigrant group fractured and soon fizzled out. Yet throughout the existence of the movement, the authority of Esdras was frequently invoked not only in the published manuscripts but in sermons and commands.

Beyond these cases of Apocrypha use during the time of Joseph Smith, we can search in vain for instances of Joseph Smith preaching from the Apocrypha; they don't seem to exist. In Joseph Smith's sermons and writings, he did not refer to specific stories, teachings, or figures from the Apocrypha. According to the writings of early Christian fathers, such as Irenaeus,[16] one of the criteria for including a text into the ancient Christian canon was whether it was being used by congregations, that is, quoted in sermons or copied to be shared among members (see also the entry on "Canon" in the LDS Bible Dictionary). This may be a reason the Apocrypha was not included in the LDS canon: it was simply not a major source for sermons or writings. Occasionally the Apocrypha's prophecies were interpreted as applying to the Last Days, so the early Saints saw possible allusions to their situation in these writings, as will be explored later in this book when discussing specific texts from the Apocrypha. Yet despite the good early Saints sometimes found in the Apocrypha and the sense they may have felt that the Apocrypha helped make the Bible complete, they believed the man-made interpolations in it made it unfit to be considered scripture and be included in the Standard Works.

After the time of Joseph Smith, a few Church leaders have quoted small passages from the Apocrypha in General Conference talks or in their writings, mostly to provide historical context for the period right before the New Testament. In these cases, the two most cited sources are Esdras—for his restoration of lost Old Testament scriptures—and the Wisdom of Jesus ben Sira (also known as Ecclesiasticus) for its wisdom sayings. One example that seems to take the Apocrypha more seriously than others comes from a discourse by Elder Orson Pratt delivered in the Salt Lake

Tabernacle on January 2, 1859, wherein Pratt referred to Esdras's efforts to restore lost scriptures to the Jews after they had been destroyed by the Assyrians.[17] Pratt continued with some rhetorical questions: "But how are this generation to know whether Esdras was a true Prophet or not? How are they to know that he was actually inspired of God to perform so great a work? It seems that the learned have no confidence in him, or they would not have placed his books among the Apocryphal writings as being doubtful." He also reviewed the various opinions early Christians held as to which texts should be included in the canon and which ones should be rejected.

Erastus Snow also quoted from Esdras to explain what happened to the Lost Ten Tribes. According to Snow's review of Esdras's account:

> After they were led into captivity, planted in the far east of the Assyrian Empire, took counsel among themselves and began to repent, and they said among themselves in council: Let us call upon the Lord and see if he will not lead us into a country where we may dwell together, and keep the commandments and judgments which he gave unto our fathers, which we never kept in our own land. And God heard their prayers, and the Lord led them and they journeyed, a year and a-half's journey to what he called the north country, and God divided the waters before them, and he planted them in a land by themselves; and the Book of Mormon clearly shows, in that notable parable about the olive tree, that God has planted branches of the house of Israel not only on the American continent, but on other distant portions of the globe, where he nourishes them.[18]

James E. Talmage, in the sixth chapter of his influential work *Jesus the Christ*, refers to passages from 2 Maccabees while giving the historical background during the period before the Roman Empire. Elder Talmage also gave a brief description of the Apocrypha in his *Articles of Faith*: "The Apocrypha comprise a number of books of doubtful authenticity, though such have been at times highly esteemed. Thus, they were added to the Septuagint, and for a time were accorded recognition among the Alexandrine Jews. However, they have never been generally admitted, being of uncertain origin. They are not quoted in the New Testament. The designation apocryphal (meaning hidden, or secret) was first applied to the books by Jerome" (249). Twice in the 1950s, a member of the Seventy, Levi Young, quoted from the Apocrypha the words of Ecclesiasticus chapter 17. In both talks he quoted from these verses in his introductory comments to show the endowment of power given to man from God. In his 1953 address, he followed the quotation with the words: "So many words in holy writ will create within us the Spirit of the Lord as we hear them today, for it is the Easter time."[19] In 1956, he ironically quoted from Ecclesiasticus in his introduction to the importance and value of the Standard Works. The words of chapter 17 led him to think about the Creation account in the Holy Bible in Genesis 1. The inherent goodness of those words leads a reader to "think of the Holy Bible and the other holy books, the Book of Mormon, the Doctrine and Covenants, and the Pearl of Great Price. This being the anniversary of the founding of the Church of Jesus Christ of Latter-day Saints by the Prophet Joseph Smith, it is good to think of them, for they give us the teachings of God, our Father."[20]

Joseph Fielding Smith's introduction to a quotation from Ecclesiasticus is telling. He used the quotation to show the interest later Jews had in Elijah, but he was careful to point out: "He was not one of the inspired writers, and this book is one of the books of the Apocrypha."[21] In a more recent General Conference address, Elder Holland used a passage from Ecclesiasticus to express his sentiment: "There is a line from the Apocrypha which puts the seriousness of this issue better than I can. It reads, 'The stroke of the whip maketh marks in the flesh: but the stroke of the tongue breaketh the bones' (28:17)."[22] It is interesting that some General Authorities demonstrate familiarity with the Apocrypha by pulling out small quotations, but they do not grant the Apocrypha as a whole authoritative status.

In 1983, Brigham Young University held a symposium to discuss the merits of the Apocrypha and other non-canonical writings. Robert J. Matthews had wise counsel for how to approach the Apocrypha. He stated, "There is much interesting and useful reading in the apocryphal literature and one can often decide what is correct by the Spirit. But if we try to make those decisions without the Spirit, we may make colossal errors. Much apocryphal literature is obviously spurious," he warned. However, "the presence of ideas and names in latter-day revelation that are not found in the Bible but are found in apocryphal writings should quicken our interest in these ancient things."[23] With a more cautious approach, Stephen Robinson warned, "It has been my experience that Latter-day Saints are usually much too anxious to accept ancient documents at face value and seldom bother to ask themselves whether the apocrypha they so readily employ to support their modern arguments might not have been forgeries even when they were first written. Of course, not all the apocryphal books involved the possibility of deceit. Some of the documents were written anonymously merely for edification and entertainment and were circulated in antiquity merely as good and useful books. They were never intended to be taken as inspired or authoritative."[24] Robinson rightly points out that we should avoid the temptation to pull out a passage that seems to agree with our beliefs without examining its context to determine if the original author was really teaching the same principle.

Another concern, as we will see as we proceed through a discussion of the Apocrypha, is what to do about passages that do not agree with our beliefs, especially ones that border on the fanciful or are obviously historically inaccurate. It may be that some books from the Apocrypha were meant to be read as fictional stories teaching valuable lessons. For example, Jesus frequently taught in parables, which were stories using objects that would be familiar to listeners. As far as we can tell, there never was an actual man beaten on the road to Jericho that was rescued by a

benevolent Samaritan, yet that story is one of the most enduring from the New Testament. Maybe figures like Judith were not
historical people in real historical moments, but the story of her
courage and piety can be used to encourage strength in others.
The Doctrine and Covenants 91:1–2 also points out that some
errors could be due to tampering of the texts: "There are many
things contained therein that are true, and it is mostly translated
correctly; There are many things contained therein that are not
true, which are interpolations by the hands of men." This passage
explains why the Apocrypha was not included in the LDS canon:
it includes things that are not true and are interpolations of men.
But there are also great truths in it that can be discerned through
the Spirit. The rest of this book will introduce the various books
of the Apocrypha in hopes that, by becoming familiar with its
content, you will be interested enough to read the Apocrypha for
yourself to find what might be of value to you.[25]

Notes

1. Portions of this chapter were first presented at the BYU Church History
    Symposium: Joseph Smith and the Ancient World, March 7, 2013.
2. Joseph Smith's Bible was full of marks for revision throughout the Old
    and New Testaments, but the Apocrypha had no such marks.
3. I do not know of any formal discussion by the early Church as to whether
    to include the Apocrypha in the Standard Works or not. It may simply
    be that a consequence of section 91 was the exclusion of the Apocrypha
    from any further consideration for the LDS canon.
4. A collection of essays by LDS scholars related to apocryphal writings
    was published in 1986. Although the Apocrypha was brought up in
    some of these essays, they were mostly looking at the broader category
    of apocryphal writings including the Dead Sea Scrolls, Nag Hammadi
    manuscripts, and early Christian apocryphal stories. See *Apocryphal*

Writings and the Latter-day Saints, ed. C. Wilfred Griggs (Provo, UT: Religious Studies Center, Brigham Young University, 1986).

5. "Letter to Brethren in Zion," 25 June 1833, accessed at http://josephsmithpapers.org/paperDetails/letter-to-brethren-in-zion-25-june-1833?p=1.

6. Autobiography of Edward Stevenson, LDS Church Archives, in *They Knew the Prophet*, comp. Hyrum L. Andrus and Helen Mae Andrus. Found in *Encyclopedia of Joseph Smith's Teachings*, ed. Larry E. Dahl and Donald Q. Cannon, 40.

7. "Recollections of the Prophet Joseph Smith," *Juvenile Instructor* 27 (1892); accessed at http://www.boap.org/LDS/Early-Saints/REC-JS.html.

8. "Hosea Chapter III," *The Evening and the Morning Star*, Vol. 1, No. 2 (July 1832): 14.

9. "The Beauty of the Writings of the Prophet Esdras," *Times and Seasons*, Vol. 2, No. 17 (July 1, 1841).

10. "The Beauty of the Writings of the Prophet Esdras," 464.

11. "The Beauty of the Writings of the Prophet Esdras," 464.

12. California had been their original goal.

13. Apparently twice Zephaniah Brewster went to visit Joseph Smith, the second time in June 1841. See *The Joseph Smith Papers. Journals. Vol. 2*, ed. Dean C. Jessee, Mark Ashurst-McGee, and Richard L. Jensen (SLC: Deseret Book, 2011), 206, n. 93.

14. *The Joseph Smith Papers. Journals. Vol. 2*, 205–206. Joseph Smith also told John Darby that James Brewster may set out for California, but he would not get there unless someone picked him up and fed him along the way.

15. "Notice," *Times and Seasons*, Vol. 4 (1 Dec. 1842), 32.

16. As explained by Bruce M. Metzger in *The Canon of the New Testament: Its Origin, Development, and Significance* (Oxford and New York: Clarendon Press and Oxford University Press, 1987), chapter XI, section I.

17. Orson Pratt, "Evidences of the Bible and Book of Mormon Compared," *Journal of Discourses* 7 (1859): 24.

18. Erastus Snow, "The 'Twin Relics,' Slavery and Polygamy, Etc.," *Journal of Discourses* Vol 23, No. 34 (1882): 299. For more discussion on these teachings from Esdras, see the chapter on 2 Esdras.

19. Levi Edgar Young, "He is Risen: And He Will Come Again," *Conference Report* (April 1953): 30.

20. Levi Edgar Young, "The Standard Works," *Conference Report* (April 1956): 32.

21. Joseph Fielding Smith, *Doctrines of Salvation*, 2:107.

22. Jeffrey R. Holland, "The Tongue of Angels," *Ensign* (May 2007).

23. From "Symposium Examines Apocryphal Literature," *Ensign* (Dec. 1983).
24. From "Symposium Examines Apocryphal Literature."
25. There are many different versions of the Apocrypha to choose from. Many study Bibles, either online or in paper form, will include the Apocrypha. My personal preference is the New Revised Standard Version (NRSV).

3

ADDITIONS TO THE BOOK OF ESTHER

THE BASIC STORY OF ESTHER IS FAMILIAR TO MOST BIBLE READERS. The Jewish people living in exile under Persian rulers face near annihilation after a wicked official, Haman, promotes his personal vendetta against the Jews. The Jews barely escape thanks to the efforts of a Jewish court official, Mordecai, and his niece, Esther. Because Esther has become part of the Persian ruler's harem, she is able to gain admittance into the king's presence and plead for her people's deliverance. This miraculous turn of events was thereafter celebrated at the Jewish festival of Purim by recounting (and even reenacting) the events associated with this story. But later interpreters and translators felt uncomfortable about aspects of the Hebrew Bible's book of Esther.

The single biggest theological issue with the Hebrew book of Esther is the absence of God in the story: he is not mentioned once.[1] Although God's guidance of Mordecai and Esther can be implied from the account, his intervention is never explicitly stated, and instead the heroes Mordecai and Esther are credited with the fortuitous outcome. Another religious issue is trying to make sense of why a good Jewish girl is in the harem of a foreign, Gentile king without any hint of the inappropriateness of this relationship, or of living and eating like a Gentile. Unlike many other biblical stories that go to great lengths to condemn marriage outside of the covenant or to live separately from the Gentiles, the book of Esther seems to commend it (after all, Mordecai encouraged Esther's efforts to beautify herself so she would be selected by the king). It may be because of these issues that no fragment from the book of Esther was found among the Dead Sea Scrolls, while portions of every other book of the Hebrew Bible were found among the scrolls.

The Greek translators of the Septuagint seemed to have similar uneasiness with the Hebrew version of Esther. As was mentioned in chapter 1, the Septuagint translation of the Hebrew Bible was likely done in Alexandria, a city in Egypt with a large Jewish population, during the intertestamental period. These Alexandrian Jews, along with the many other Jews living outside of the land of Israel (often called Diaspora Jews), faced many challenges living as an ethnic and religious minority in a pagan society. One of the greatest threats facing these communities was the lure of assimilation: the temptation to modify or discard their adherence to Mosaic law in order to better fit in among Gentile neighbors.[2] The Septuagint translators in Alexandra may have felt that Esther, despite her heroism on behalf of her people, did not set a sterling example of fealty to God and the law of Moses. Thus, in order to make Esther a better role model for Diaspora Jews, the existing story was changed dramatically.[3] Most notably, six additions (amounting to 107 verses) were inserted into the story, and various smaller emendations were made in the existing text.[4] These additions and changes are what make the version of Esther in the Apocrypha significantly different from the Hebrew version. No longer are God's role (the words "Lord" or "God" appear more than fifty times in the Greek additions) nor Esther's true feelings about being married to a Gentile obscure (she seems to loathe it and the royal trappings that go along with her status). The basic storyline remains the same, but the disclosure of these features makes it a very different religious narrative.

Addition A (chapters 11 and 12)[5] comes at the beginning of the story and relates a dream Mordecai has one night when two dragons fight amidst great earthquakes and tumult over the earth. A righteous nation—the Jews—petition God for deliverance, and from a small spring comes a great river—Esther's assistance. The fight between the dragons foreshadows the contest between Mordecai and Haman; thus, through his dream, Mordecai learns what God intends to do.[6] The second part of *Addition A* tells how Mordecai learns about a plot against the king. Mordecai tells the king about the plot and is subsequently rewarded with a position in the king's court. Further foreshadowing occurs at the end of *Addition A* when Haman is determined to injure Mordecai and his people because of what happened to the plotters against the king. *Addition A* makes it clear why Mordecai is in a privileged position in the king's court and foreshadows some of the future clashes that will occur for Mordecai and the Jews, but through which God will deliver them.

Addition B (13:1–7) comes after Esther 3:13 and records the royal edict issued by Haman against the Jews.[7] Under the name of King Artaxerxes, the decree targets the Jews as hostile to the kingdom because of their unique lifestyle and law code. Haman determines they must be destroyed—women and children included—because they allegedly disregard the ordinances of the kings.[8] A date is set for the extermination, probably so that those who want to leave the kingdom can do so beforehand, but many Jews react with horror and immediately turn to God for assistance. This deadline is similar to the situation some Nephites face at the beginning of 3 Nephi, when they are told they will be put to death if the sign prophesied by Samuel the Lamanite does not appear before a pre-appointed day. Like the Israelites later in this story, the Nephites are spared and the day becomes a day of rejoicing instead of destruction.

Addition C (13:8–18; 14:1–19) follows Esther's request through Mordecai in 4:17 that all the Jews fast for her before she attempts to enter the king's presence unsummoned. It includes two prayers, one by Mordecai and one by Esther. In Mordecai's prayer, he acknowledges that he did not bow down to Haman because he did not want to set human glory above the glory of God (13:14). Now he petitions God to deliver them as he had the children of Israel from Egypt (13:16).[9] Queen Esther is seized with deadly anxiety and flees to the Lord (14:1). Taking off her beautiful clothing, she covers her head with ashes and dung. She recognizes God as the only true king and asks for his help. She confesses the sins of the people that have led to their exile, but does not want God to forsake his inheritance and surrender his scepter "to what has no being" (14:11). She pleads for courage and eloquent speech for her presentation before the king, and asks that the king's heart might be changed. Significantly, she then reveals her personal feelings of being married to a gentile king:

> I hate the splendor of the wicked and abhor the bed of the uncircumcised and of any alien. You know my necessity—that I abhor the sign of my proud position, which is upon my head on days when I appear in public. I abhor it like a filthy rag,[10] and I do not wear it on the days when I am at leisure. And your servant [Esther referring to herself] has not eaten at Haman's table, and I have not honored the king's feast or drunk the wine of libations.[11] Your servant has had no joy since the day that I was brought here until now, except in you, O Lord God of Abraham (14:15–18).[12]

Esther closes her prayer with the plea to "save us from the hands of evildoers. And save me from my fear!" (14:19). *Addition C* brings the involvement of God to the forefront as prayers are addressed to him for deliverance, rather than Mordecai and Esther simply making their own plans for how to approach the king. It also reveals Esther's true feelings about many issues that Jewish interpreters probably had concerns about in the Hebrew version of Esther. She abhors being married to a Gentile, does not like the lofty status of queen, avoids Gentile food, does not participate in the king's feast, and her only joy is in God.

Addition D immediately follows *Addition C* and describes Esther's preparation to enter the presence of the king adorned to petition him for help for her people. The emphasis is on her invoking the aid of God and her fear for this perilous act. When the king first looks up at Esther "in fierce anger," she falters and faints. "Then God changed the spirit of the king to gentleness, and in alarm he sprang from his throne and took her in his arms until she came to herself. He comforted her with soothing words" (15:8). With a touch of the golden scepter, Esther is forgiven for her unsummoned entrance and she begins to praise the king, but faints again.[13] *Addition D* ends here and the story continues, as in the Hebrew version, with Esther asking the king to prepare a banquet for Haman, where she will be able to unveil his plot against her people. In this most dramatic moment of the story, with Esther entering the king's presence at peril to her life, God's role is clearly added: he changed the spirit of the king so the subsequent events could unfold in the Jews' favor.

Addition E (16) comes after Haman's plot against the Jews is foiled and he is hanged in punishment (after Esther 8:12). A decree is made allowing the Jews to observe their own laws[14] and defend themselves against their enemies on a designated day. *Addition E* is a copy of this royal edict sent to all the provinces. It outlines how some people want to hurt subjects within the empire (the Jews) and are jealous of their prosperity. It promises changes to protect the peace of the kingdom. The decree describes Mordecai as "our savior and perpetual benefactor" and Esther as "the blameless partner of our kingdom" (16:13). The Jews are found not to be evildoers, but "are governed by most righteous laws and are children of the living God, most high, most mighty, who has directed the kingdom both for us and for our ancestors in the most excellent order" (16:15–16). The edict revokes Haman's earlier decrees and must be posted publicly for all to see. A day is set aside (the thirteenth day of the twelfth month, Adar) for the Jews to defend themselves against oppressors: "For God, who rules over all things, has made this day to be a joy for his chosen people instead of a day of destruction for them. Therefore you shall observe this with all good cheer as a notable day among your commemorative festivals, so that both now and hereafter it may represent deliverance for you and the loyal Persians, but that it may be a reminder of destruction for those who plot against us" (16:21–23). The festival seems to be a hint at the Jewish festival of Purim, which is established in the subsequent chapters of the Hebrew version.[15]

Addition F (10:4–11:1) gives the interpretation of Mordecai's dream from the beginning of the story (*Addition A*) and provides a colophon (a brief inscription describing the writing of a manuscript) for the text.[16] The images in Mordecai's dream are explained. Esther is the little spring that became a river. The two dragons are Mordecai and Haman. The nations are those who sought to destroy the Jews, while the nation that was saved is Israel. God is praised for his signs and wonders. God "made two lots [the translation of Purim], one for the people of God and one for all the nations, and these two lots came to the hour and moment and day of decision before God and among all the nations. And God remembered his people and vindicated his inheritance" (10:11–12). The dream's interpretation ends with an exhortation to observe the festival of Purim annually to celebrate God's great act of deliverance.

The colophon at the end of the manuscript testifies to the authenticity of the book of Esther: "In the fourth year of the reign of Ptolemy and Cleopatra, Dositheus, who said that he was a priest and a Levite, and his son Ptolemy brought to Egypt the preceding Letter about Purim, which they said was authentic[17] and had been translated by Lysimachus son of Ptolemy, one of the residents of Jerusalem" (11:1). This colophon dates this version of Esther with its additions to around 114–113 BC.[18]

CONCLUSION

The Greek version of the book of Esther includes significant additions to the story that highlight the central role of God throughout the unfolding events. Beyond the lengthy additions inserted into the text, words and phrases are altered within the text to reveal God and create a religious tone not found in the Hebrew version. Mordecai and Esther are still heroic and instrumental in bringing forth the deliverance of Jews from the possible edict of destruction set forth by Haman, but they are clearly instruments in God's hands. They petition, rely on, and acknowledge God throughout. Through the additions in the Apocrypha, a clearer picture of Esther's faithfulness to the law and her discomfort with her current situation emerges. The text clearly comes from a diaspora setting (away from the land of Israel) where Jews are constantly under threat. As such, the book of Esther inspires Jews to believe that God will deliver them, even if it is in the last moment, because they are his inheritance.

LDS readers are familiar with the story of Esther from the Old Testament and likely focus on the text's primary message of Esther being in the right place at the right time to help her people: "who knoweth whether thou art come to the kingdom for such a time as this?" (Esther 4:14). This message resonates with LDS beliefs in being sent to earth to fulfill particular missions and accomplish errands as part of God's great plan. But the Greek version in the Apocrypha expands upon this mission by emphasizing *God's* role in saving Esther and the Jewish people. While LDS readers may not focus as much on some of the "problems" early Jewish readers saw in the Hebrew version (as found in the Old Testament) related to whether Esther did or did not observe the law of Moses, or the problematic close interactions between Jew and Gentile, they probably feel more comfortable with the Greek version's highlighting of God's role, Esther's commitment to and observance of her faith, and the heightened role of prayer and fasting in bringing about

God's purposes. While in both versions Esther is an instrument to save her people, the Greek version emphasizes she is *God's* instrument, and it reveals her faith in him and how she received spiritual strength from her own and others' prayers. That is the type of instrument that many LDS disciples aspire to be—to be used by God to bless the lives of others—and they often accomplish that role through fasting and prayer. Like Alma and the sons of Mosiah in the Book of Mormon, who gloried in being instruments in God's hands, some worried that it could be taken too far in glorying in their own successes and abilities (see Alma 26:10–16, 35–37; 29:9–10, 14–16). But as long as they remained humble and gave the glory to God, they could receive God's power and fulfill their desires to be God's instruments in delivering his children from sin and spiritual captivity.

NOTES

1. "Although the Persian king is mentioned 190 times in 167 verses of Esther, the Lord God of Israel is not mentioned once, nor are such basic OT themes as Law or Covenant. Also missing from the [original text] are such key Jewish concepts as prayer, election, salvation, Jerusalem, temple, [dietary laws], and the like. In fact, fasting is the only religious practice mentioned." Carey A. Moore, *Daniel, Esther, and Jeremiah: The Additions* (Anchor Bible 44; Garden City: Doubleday, 1977), 157.

2. Referring to Jewish literature from this time, Larry Helyer states that "the ever-present danger lurking just beneath the surface of the text is assimilation into the pagan culture. Assimilation refers to the process whereby a minority group gradually adopts the values and characteristics of the majority culture. For Jews this would have involved a turning away from the distinctive lifestyle called for by the Mosaic covenant and, most importantly, from the basic creed of Israel: 'Hear, O Israel: The Lord is our God, the Lord alone' (Deut 6:4)." Helyer, *Jewish Literature*, 55.

3. This and other related literature was "designed to reinforce Jewish identity in the midst of pagan culture. The intention of the authors, therefore, was to instill hope in the God of Israel and pride in their heritage as his chosen people . . . [T]hey must never forget this lesson: if Jews are faithful to the covenant, God will at last reward and restore them." Helyer, *Jewish Literature*, 55.

4. Some scholars feel that some of the additions were originally composed in Hebrew or Aramaic and in this way became part of the Greek translation of the Septuagint. Michael Fox argues, "Additions B and E were undoubtedly composed in Greek, while F probably was; C and D were probably composed in Hebrew or Aramaic, while A is uncertain." Michael V. Fox, *Character and Ideology in the Book of Esther* (Columbia, SC: University of South Carolina, 1991), 265–66. Regardless of the original language or dating of each addition, it is clear that none of them were part of the 'original' version of Esther. "The most important indicator in this regard is the secondary character of the Additions: without them, the story is a coherent whole; with them, contradictions are unnecessarily introduced into a formerly consistent narrative." David A. deSilva, *Introducing the Apocrypha: Message, Context, and Significance* (Grand Rapids, MI: Baker Academic, 2002), 115.

5. The chapter and verse numbering of the additions follows Jerome's placement of these sections at the end of the Book of Esther though they are interspersed chronologically throughout the narrative.

6. Addition A (and its later interpretation in Addition F) serves an important narrative function in the Septuagint version of Esther. "Additions A and F provide a framing narrative for the whole story, setting the court intrigue between Haman and Mordecai and then the pogroms between Jews and Gentiles in the interpretive framework of an apocalyptic vision and its interpretation. The interpretative power of this framework is not to be underestimated. The reader of Greek Esther knows from the beginning that God has determined the outcome of this story and will be at work to bring about the end that God has chosen." deSilva, *Introducing the Apocrypha*, 112.

7. The edicts recorded in Addition B and Addition E "enhance the impression of historiography as the major genre of the book through the reproduction of the full texts of official edicts, a common feature of that genre." deSilva, *Introducing the Apocrypha*, 111.

8. Such a decree would have been unusual in Persia, which (at least for an ancient empire) was remarkably respectful of religious diversity. This dramatic conflict between the Jews and powerful oppressors likely reflects Jewish anxieties at the time the additions were written. "The absolute conflict between the nations and Israel in the LXX [Septuagint]

is far more severe than the sporadic and occasional hostility between Gentile and Jew, interspersed with episodes of goodwill, found in the MT [Hebrew Bible]. This is a product of the historical period of the LXX, during which the Hellenistic empires were, in their later period, far less tolerant of Jewish monotheism and ethnic solidarity than the Persians had been." Sidnie White Crawford, *The Additions to Esther* (NIB III; Nashville: Abingdon Press, 1999), 949.

9. "Some readers might feel an emptiness at the heart of MT Esther as a biblical book: where is the faith that should direct Mordecai's actions? The answer is given here: Mordecai's faith is based on the covenant between God and Israel, represented by Abraham and the exodus. Mordecai recalls the scriptural tradition of Israel and concludes that God will not abandon the Jews, even though the circumstances look very bleak." Crawford, *Additions to Esther*, 957.

10. "The description of her crown as a 'filthy rag' is particularly sharp; the Greek term ῥάσκος καταμηνίων (*rakos katamenion*) is better translated as 'menstruous rag.' In Jewish tradition, menstrual blood is ritually unclean and should not be touched (Lev 15:19–24). Esther's whole life as queen is, in fact, miserable to her." Crawford, *Additions to Esther*, 959.

11. Esther's comment that she did not drink the "wine of libations" (offerings of alcohol to pagan deities) shows that she avoids even the appearance of idolatry. Comments such as these serve as messages to the intended audience of Diaspora Jews that any participation in pagan idolatry should be shunned. See deSilva, *Introducing the Apocrypha*, 111.

12. Quotations from the Apocrypha are from the New Revised Standard Version as found in *The New Oxford Annotated Apocrypha. The Apocryphal/ Deuterocanonical Books of the Old Testament*, ed. Bruce M. Metzger and Roland E. Murphy (New York: Oxford University Press, 1991).

13. Both Esther's melodramatic swooning and the king's heroic 'rescue' of her are similar to elements of popular Hellenistic romances from the period in which Esther was translated and amended. "[Esther] is made to conform to an ideal favored in the popular romantic and melodramatic novels of the late Hellenistic period . . . The Additions introduce a number of elements known from the Hellenistic romances, including explicit and extensive explorations of thought and feelings, the heroine's piety, female frailty, overwhelming emotions and fainting—by males as well as females." Michael V. Fox, "Three Esthers," in *The Book of Esther in Modern Research* (ed. Sidnie White Crawford and Leonard J. Greenspoon; New York: T&T Clark international, 2003), 59.

14. "These verses contain commands that would bring joy to the Jewish reader. The Jews are to be allowed to live under their own laws, a major issue in the Hellenistic period. Under the Persians, each ethnic group

was allowed to be self-governing, provided they obeyed their Persian overlords. At the beginning of the Hellenistic period, under the Ptolemies until 198 BCE [BC] and then under the Seleucids until 175 BCE [BC], the Jews were allowed to govern themselves by the Torah. However, during the reign of Antiochus IV Epiphanes in 175 [BC], that privilege was revoked, and from then on the Jews were constantly engaged in a struggle to follow both the law of the land and their own law. The inclusion of this provision in v. 19 points to a date after 175 BCE [BC]." Crawford, *Additions to Esther,* 967.

15. Esther's association with the festival of Purim is likely one of the reasons that the original text does not include the name of God or other explicit religious elements. The Jewish festival of Purim has always been associated with a lighthearted, carnivalesque atmosphere; Carey Moore notes that "according to the Mishnah, while celebrating Purim Jews were to drink wine until they were unable to distinguish between 'Blessed be Mordecai' and 'Cursed be Haman' (*Megillah 7b*). Such a ruling is undoubtedly the reason for no mention of the Deity, especially since several passages in the MT either contain surrogates for the Deity . . . or presuppose the power or providence of God." Moore, *The Additions,* 157.

16. Some of the interpretations given for the dream are problematic. For example, it is understandable for the detestable Haman to be depicted as a dragon (a traditional ancient symbol for destruction and evil), but it makes little sense for the righteous Mordecai to be depicted as one as well. To complicate matters, some of the interpretations given for the vision here are different than those supplied by an alternative Greek text of Esther (referred to in academic literature as the A-Text). Casey Moore suggests an explanation for these problems: "Since some features of the dream's interpretation are confusing, if not incompatible with the broadest features of the Esther story, and since the dream in its theme, imagery, and literary style does seem to resemble the dreams and visions found in such a second-century B.C. Palestinian book as Daniel, it is more likely that the dream was originally a separate Hebrew (Aramaic?) entity circulating quite independently of the Esther story and was later adopted and adapted into it . . . however, although some features of the dream were less appropriate than others (for instance, Mordecai as a dragon-figure), the original features were nonetheless retained." Moore, *The Additions,* 248–49.

17. The comment that this work is "authentic" presupposes that someone might have considered this version of Esther as *inauthentic;* perhaps Dositheus and Ptolemy were defending the authenticity of the additions that this copy of the text included. The names cited in this colophon are

apparently given to lend this claim some weight, but these characters are not known to us from other sources.

18. This dating assumes that the "Ptolemy and Cleopatra" referred to in the colophon are Ptolemy XIII Soter II and his wife Cleopatra. Unfortunately, every Hellenistic king of Egypt took the name of Ptolemy (the name of Alexander the Great's general who took control of Egypt following Alexander's death), and many of them had wives named Cleopatra. Other possible candidates include Ptolemy XII Auletes and Cleopatra V (which would date the book to 78–77 BC), or Ptolemy XIII and Cleopatra (lover of Julius Caesar and Marc Antony).

4

DANIEL STORIES: SONG OF THE THREE YOUNG MEN, SUSANNA, BEL AND THE DRAGON

"DANIEL IN THE LIONS' DEN" IS ONE OF THE MOST RECOGNIZABLE biblical stories and has been retold countless times by adults and children. Besides the well-known stories about Daniel in the Old Testament, the Apocrypha contains additional stories about this remarkable young man. Three additional Greek passages shed more light on why Daniel was so trusted among the people and how God guided the actions of his life. They also provide an important glimpse into the culture and concerns of Diaspora Jews wrestling with issues of living as a religious minority among pagan neighbors.[1]

Although the order and placement of these stories within the Hebrew version of Daniel varies among ancient manuscripts, all three are included in later Greek and Latin (the Vulgate) versions of Daniel.[2] In other words, these additions became integral to the book of Daniel from the second century BC on.[3] All ancient manuscripts place the "Prayer of Azarias and the Song of the Three Jews" in Daniel 3 at the moment when the three young men were in the burning furnace. Some place "Susanna" at the beginning of the book, while others place it at the end or as the penultimate chapter. "Bel and the Dragon" is also commonly placed at the end of Daniel, but sometimes after Daniel 6 (after the account of Daniel in the lions' den). Although no Hebrew or Aramaic versions of these additions have been found, and despite some evidence suggesting Greek as the original language,[4] most researchers believe that these tales were initially written in Hebrew or Aramaic and then later translated into Greek.[5]

Song of the Three Young Men

Ever wondered what Shadrach, Meshach, and Abed-Nego thought or said while stuck in the fiery furnace? The Septuagint version of Daniel answers this question with a report from the midst of the furnace. This addition to Daniel is placed at the moment when the three young men are thrown into the furnace in the Hebrew version of Daniel. It consists of three parts: the prayer of Azariah, a description of the state of the three young men in the furnace, and a long hymn sung by the three while they were enveloped by flames. Sometimes the prayer and the song are included in the fifteen "Odes" appended to the book of Psalms in Septuagint manuscripts. Both of these works of poetry bear signs of having been translated into Greek from Hebrew, making it likely that they were written by a Jew living in the Holy Land.[6]

Even though the names of the three men can vary depending upon which language is emphasized, they all are talking about the same three young men. The traditional book of Daniel in the Old Testament uses their Babylonian names given them by the chief eunuch of King Nebuchadnezzar: Shadrach, Meshach, and Abed-Nego. Their Hebrew names are Hananiah, Mishael, and Azariah, respectively. The Greek pronunciation of their Hebrew names is commonly used in the Septuagint: Ananias, Misael, and Azarias.

This first addition (v. 1–22) opens with the three young men walking around in the midst of the fiery furnace "singing hymns to God and blessing the Lord" (v. 1). Azariah[7] then begins a prayer praising God and asking for assistance in this difficult predicament.[8] His prayer fits the pattern of a specific ancient form of prayer, known as penitential prayer, and includes the following elements:

- Confession of sins acknowledging that the exile is just punishment for past sins—"You have executed true judgments in all you have brought upon us and upon Jerusalem, the holy city of our ancestors; by a true judgment you have brought all this upon us because of our sins. For we have sinned and broken your law in turning away from you; in all matters we have sinned grievously" (v. 5–6).

- Reminder of covenant promises—"For your name's sake do not give us up forever, and do not annul your covenant.[9] Do not withdraw your mercy from us, for the sake of Abraham your beloved and for the sake of your servant Isaac and Israel your holy one, to whom you promised to multiply their descendants like the stars of heaven and like the sand on the shore of the sea" (v. 11–13).

- Plea for divine assistance—"And now with all our heart we follow you; we fear you and seek your presence. Do not put us to shame, but deal with us in your patience and in your abundant mercy. Deliver us in accordance with your marvelous works,[10] and bring glory to your name, O Lord. Let all who do harm to your servants be put to shame; let them be disgraced and deprived of all power, and let their strength be broken" (v. 18–21).

Azariah mentioned that the prayer was given with a contrite heart and a humble spirit because that was all they could offer,[11] since they did not have a place to bring sacrifices or burnt offerings (not to mention their current predicament in the midst of a furnace).

The next section of the addition (v. 23–27) is a narrative description of the furnace experience. The Babylonians continue to stoke the furnace, resulting in flames over forty-nine cubits high, or seven times seven—seven being a sacred number in Daniel (4:25; 9:2, 25; 10:2, 13) and elsewhere—and hot enough to burn

Babylonians standing too near (v. 24). "But the angel of the Lord came down into the furnace to be with Azariah and his companions, and drove the fiery flame out of the furnace, and made the inside of the furnace as though a moist wind were whistling through it." Dew is often equated with God's grace and blessings in scripture: Hosea 14:5—"I will be as the dew unto Israel"; in Micah 5:7 the remnant of Jacob shall be "as a dew from the Lord"; Zechariah 8:12 promises that "the heavens shall give their dew"; and in a scripture about future resurrection, the dead will arise from the dust "for thy dew is as the dew of herbs, and the earth shall cast out the dead" (Isaiah 26:19). In restoration scripture, the doctrine of the priesthood is promised to distil upon one's soul "as the dews from heaven" (D&C 121:45) and the knowledge of God shall descend "as the dews of Carmel" (D&C 128:19). For Daniel's three friends, "the fire did not touch them at all and caused them no pain or distress" (v. 26–27). This brief description identifies the fourth person in the Hebrew version as an angel of the Lord, and it explains how he was able to protect the three young men from the effects of the flames.

The last section of the addition (v. 28–58) is a lengthy psalm or song of the three young men sung from the midst of the furnace. It may have originally been an independent text, an ode or psalm, which was later attached to the three young men here. It includes rhythmic praises of God in the form of an antiphonal liturgy where a congregation repeats the second refrain ("sing praise to him and highly exalt him forever").[12] The psalm praises God's power and glory, and then exhorts practically *all* of God's creations to bless him, even the dews and falling snow, lightning and clouds, and so on.[13] It ends by describing the situation of these young men: "Bless the Lord Hananiah, Azariah, and Mishael; sing praise to him and highly exalt him forever. For he has rescued us from Hades and saved us from the power of death, and delivered us from the midst of the burning fiery furnace; from the midst of the fire he has delivered us. Give thanks to the Lord, for he is good, for his mercy endures forever. All who worship the Lord, bless the God of gods, sing praise to him and give thanks to him, for his mercy endures forever" (v. 66–68).[14]

Susanna

The story of Susanna[15] is a suspenseful courtroom drama that presents the case of a virtuous woman who has become the target of lust by perverted elders of the community.[16] There are different versions of Susanna found among ancient Greek witnesses that change some of the setting or details, but the basic story is consistent.[17] Although the main characters of the story are Jews, the story appeals to a universal audience because of the triumph of virtue and the innocence of youth. It was probably written in the second century BC in Greek.[18]

The story begins by giving background about the main characters and the setting. It takes place in Babylonian exile with a man, Joakim, married to Susanna, "a very beautiful woman and one who feared the Lord" (v. 2). Susanna has been raised obedient to the Law of Moses by righteous parents. Joakim is rich and has a fine garden adjoining his house.[19] Two other main characters are elders of the people appointed as judges. According to the Lord's description concerning them, "wickedness came forth from Babylon, from elders who were judges, who were supposed to govern the people" (v. 5).[20] These two elders frequently visit Joakim's house, where they often decide cases brought to them there.

During the noon hour, when the people leave Joakim's house for lunch, Susanna frequently walks about her husband's garden. The two elders begin to watch her and "they began to lust for her. They suppressed their consciences and turned away their eyes from looking to Heaven or remembering their duty to administer justice. Both were overwhelmed with passion for her, but they did not tell each other of their distress, for they were ashamed to disclose their lustful desire to seduce her" (v. 8–12). Daily they continue to eagerly watch for her and each feign to depart from the other for lunch, but then they both turn back to catch a glimpse of Susanna. Upon encountering each other, each ask for what purpose the other is there. They confess to each other their lust for Susanna and begin plotting together how they can catch her alone.

One hot day Susanna enters the garden to take a bath. "No one was there except the two elders, who had hidden themselves and were watching her" (v. 16). After Susanna dismisses her maids, the two elders get up from their hiding places and run to her. They proclaim their burning desire for her and give her an ultimatum: lie with us[21] or "we will testify against you that a young man was with you, and this was why you sent your maids away" (v. 21). Susanna reluctantly realizes her trap: "For if I do this, it will mean death for me; if I do not, I cannot escape your hands. I choose not to do it; I will fall into your hands, rather than sin in the sight of the Lord" (v. 22–23). Susanna and the elders begin shouting and soon a crowd gathers to see what is the matter.[22] When the elders tell their story, "the servants felt very much ashamed, for nothing like this had ever been said about Susanna" (v. 27).

A trial ensues the next day as the elders continue their plot to put Susanna to death for having resisted their wicked advances.[23] Susanna arrives to the trial veiled, but "the scoundrels ordered her to be unveiled, so that they might feast their eyes on her beauty" (v. 32). Susanna and those with her weep, and "through her tears she looked up toward Heaven, for her heart trusted in the Lord" (v. 35). The elders bear their false testimony about finding Susanna alone in the garden with a young man. When they tried to seize the young man, he got away. The narrator interjects an important point here: "because they were elders of the people and judges, the assembly believed them and condemned her to death" (v. 41).

At this dire moment, Susanna cries out and petitions God for assistance. "O eternal God, you know what is secret and are aware of all things before they come to be; you know that these men have given false evidence against me. And now I am to die, though I have done none of the wicked things that they have charged against me!" (v. 42–43). The Lord's response is immediate[24] and brings Daniel into the fray: "Just as she was being led off to execution, God stirred up the holy spirit of a young lad named Daniel, and he shouted with a loud voice, 'I want no part in shedding this woman's blood!'" (v. 44–46). Daniel takes the stand and rebukes the people for condemning a daughter of Israel "without examination and without learning the facts" (v. 48). The crowd heeds Daniel because of his status as an elder, and the trial resumes.

Daniel orders the two elders be separated and then he interrogates each one separately. His key question for each one is to identify under which tree in the garden they had seen Susanna with the young man. When each identifies a different tree in their response, their lies are exposed and Daniel forewarns them of God's swift judgment in a Greek wordplay with the trees they had mentioned.[25] "Then the whole assembly raised a great shout and blessed God, who saves those who hope in him" (v. 60).[26] The elders receive the punishment they had intended for Susanna, while Susanna's innocent blood is spared. The story ends with its likely purpose for being included in the Daniel corpus: "from that day onward Daniel had a great reputation among the people" (v. 64).[27] This story demonstrates Daniel's wisdom and obedience to the Lord's promptings. It also highlights the corrupt nature of some of the elders of the community and the virtuous strength of the Israelite women. In addition, "The tale reinforces, in the person and ruminations of Susanna, the importance of remaining loyal to God and God's commandments despite the temporal dangers one might incur in the process, a lesson taught also by [2 Maccabees]."[28] It is one of the earliest courtroom dramas and has become a gem among short stories in world literature.[29]

Bel and the Dragon

Bel and the Dragon is actually three episodes tied together, each contrasting the ridiculousness of idolatry with the worship of the true God. As with other attacks on idolatry in the Old Testament (especially Isaiah), Bel and the Dragon satirizes the notion of worshipping images that have no life while ignoring the living God. Repeatedly, Daniel shows the folly of Babylonian religion as he remains faithful to God despite living in exile away from God's covenant land and temple.[30] Interestingly enough, each of these narratives also centers around food, and eating is either the means by which Daniel shows the power of the true God, or Daniel needs food while in the lions' den. Although these tales are set in Babylon, it is likely that these stories were written either in Egypt (where the worship of idols and animal-figured gods was common) or Palestine.[31]

The first episode centers on the large image of the Babylonian god, Bel, in a series of exchanges between the king and Daniel. Every day, large amounts of flour, sheep, and wine are offered to Bel.[32] "The king revered it and went every day to worship it. But Daniel worshipped his own God" (v. 4). When the king asks Daniel why he does not worship Bel, he responds that he does not worship idols made with hands, but rather "the living God, who created heaven and earth and has dominion over all living creatures" (v. 5). The king asks Daniel if he does not think that Bel is a living god. "Do you not see how much he eats and drinks every day?" (v. 6). Daniel laughs[33] and tells the king that Bel does not eat anything because he is only made of clay inside and bronze outside.

The king becomes angry and summons his priests to see who is eating all these provisions offered to Bel. He promises them that if they can prove that Bel is eating them, then Daniel will die "because he has spoken blasphemy against Bel" (v. 9). Daniel accepts the challenge, not unlike Elijah and his willingness to compete with the priests of Baal in 1 Kings 18. Daniel, the king, and the seventy priests of Bel and their families enter the temple of Bel. The priests excuse themselves so the king can set out the food and wine and then seal the door shut with his signet. They tell the king, "When you return in the morning, if you do not find that Bel has eaten it all, we will die; otherwise Daniel will, who is telling lies about us" (v. 12). The narrator ruins the suspense and reveals to the reader why the priests are unconcerned, "for beneath the table they had made a hidden entrance, through which they used to go in regularly and consume the provisions" (v. 13).[34]

After the priests depart, the king sets out the food for Bel, but before the door is sealed shut, Daniel orders his servants to bring ashes and scatter them around the floor. Then everyone exits and the door is sealed with the king's signet. "During the night the priests came as usual, with their wives and children, and they ate and drank everything" (v. 15).

The next morning everyone returns to the temple and, after the seals are checked to ensure they are still intact, enter in. "As soon as the doors were opened, the king looked at the table, and shouted in a loud voice, 'You are great, O Bel, and in you there is no deceit at all!' But Daniel laughed and restrained the king from going in. 'Look at the floor,' he said, 'and notice whose footprints these are.' The king said, 'I see the footprints of men and women and children'" (v. 18–20). The king is furious and has the priests and their families arrested. They show the king the secret entrances that they used to access the chamber and consume the offerings to Bel. The end result? "The king put them to death, and gave Bel over to Daniel, who destroyed it and its temple" (v. 22).

The second episode revolves around another supposed god, a great dragon (serpent) that the Babylonians revered.[35] This god was not an image made of hands, but apparently a living serpent that was believed to be immortal.[36] The king again confronts Daniel about why he does not worship this god, especially seeing it was a "living god" (v. 24). "Daniel said, 'I worship the Lord my God, for he is the living God. But give me permission, O king, and I will kill the dragon without sword or club.' The king said, 'I give you permission'" (v. 25–26).

"Then Daniel took pitch, fat, and hair, and boiled them together and made cakes, which he fed to the dragon. The dragon ate them, and burst open.[37] Then Daniel said, 'See what you have been worshiping!'" (v. 27). When the people hear what happened, they begin to conspire against the king, saying he has become a Jew because now Bel, the dragon, and the priests are all killed. They demand the king deliver Daniel to them "or else we will kill you and your household" (v. 29). Feeling the pressure, the king hands Daniel over to them and they promptly throw Daniel into the lions' den, similar to the account in Daniel 6, but this time it will be for six days. The den is occupied by seven lions who are accustomed to daily consuming two human bodies and two sheep, "but now they were given nothing, so that they would devour Daniel" (v. 32).

While Daniel is stuck in the lions' den, the story takes a slight diversion to Judea where the prophet Habakkuk is preparing stew for the reapers in the field.[38] "But the angel of the Lord said to Habakkuk, 'Take the food that you have to Babylon, to Daniel, in the lions' den.' Habakkuk said, 'Sir, I have never seen Babylon, and I know nothing about the den.' Then the angel of the Lord took him by the crown of his head and carried him by his hair; with the speed of the wind he set him down in Babylon, right over the den" (v. 34–36). Habakkuk delivers the food to Daniel and Daniel expresses appreciation that God has not forgotten him. Daniel eats while the angel returns Habakkuk to his own place.[39] When the king returns on the seventh day to mourn for Daniel, he surprisingly finds Daniel alive! "The king shouted with a loud voice, 'You are great, O Lord, the God of Daniel, and there is no other besides you!' Then he pulled Daniel out, and threw into the den those who had attempted his destruction, and they were instantly eaten before his eyes" (v. 41–42).

Conclusion

Like the other apocryphal works discussed in this book, the additions to Daniel were likely excluded from the Jewish canon for several reasons. They were composed far later than other uncontested canonical works, giving them less prestige in the eyes of their Jewish audience. It is also probable that Jewish readers recognized these stories as inauthentic add-ons to the original stories of Daniel.[40] While the Jewish rejection of these stories made some Christian writers hesitant to fully embrace them, many of the Church Fathers referred to these stories in their writings.[41] Christians adapted these books (as they did with other apocryphal books) in creative ways: writers like Hippolytus of Rome saw Susanna as an allegory for the Church[42] and the Song of the Three Young Men was used in Christian liturgies for centuries.[43] (Bel and the Dragon stories, however, were not as popular.)

The additional stories of Daniel from the Apocrypha fit in the same style and thematic concerns as the stories in the Hebrew book of Daniel found in the Old Testament, so it is not surprising that all Greek and Latin versions of Daniel included them after the second century BC. Within these stories, Daniel refuses to submit to the surrounding idolatry, but stands as a witness to the true God even at the risk of his own life. Daniel is wise and cunning and uses those characteristics to point out the absurdity of the false worship of the Babylonians. In the end, the false priests and corrupt elders are defeated, and the king can only acknowledge the greatness of the Israelite God. The victorious results of these stories must have given strength and courage to Israelites living in diaspora away from the land of Israel. They continue to provide positive role models for covenant people today.

Like the story of Esther, the story of Daniel is familiar and frequently recited among LDS readers. The additional stories of Daniel in the Apocrypha do not add much new information about Daniel and his three friends but are further examples of their obedience and faithfulness to God in the midst of a pagan, idolatrous environment. The three friends can be seen as examples of offering up a broken heart and a contrite spirit rather than sacrifices, just as Latter-day Saints are asked to do today. In return for their offering, God blesses them and delivers them from their fiery trial. The story of Susanna provides a strong, positive role model of a virtuous woman who is willing to stick to her beliefs even while those who should be righteous leaders fail. She demonstrated integrity as she lived up to her honorable reputation. The additional stories of Daniel reiterate the positive application of wisdom or reason in conjunction with faith in God as Daniel was blessed with superior knowledge to save Susanna and himself from religious opponents. As Latter-day Saints believe, the glory of God is intelligence (D&C 93:36), and knowledge and wisdom is sought after. As Jacob taught, "to be learned is good if [we] hearken unto the counsels of God" (2 Nephi 9:29).

NOTES

1. "At the time the editor [of Daniel] was working, the diaspora from Egypt to Persia and from Greece to Arabia was exposed daily to the attraction of foreign deities immediately at hand, while the Lord of Jerusalem had his abode far away in his sanctuary on Zion, in the Promised Land . . . The Jewish minority, lost in the immense spaces of pagan empires and living for generations on foreign soil, wanted and needed to be reassured that the Lord of Jerusalem, although far distant, could offer His help anywhere." Bickerman, *The Jews*, 64.

2. "The longer version of Daniel is known primarily from the Greek, surviving in two rather different editions. The older edition, the 'Septuagint' proper, survives in its entirety only in a single manuscript, Codex Chisianus from the ninth century, and in the Syriac translation of Origen's edition of the Septuagint. The more recent edition, called 'Theodotion,' displaced the older 'Septuagint' edition in the usage of the

Christian church by the late third century, so that all the major codices of what we call the Septuagint actually contain the Theodotion edition of Daniel." deSilva, *Introducing the Apocrypha*, 222–23.

3. "The stories about Daniel and his friends were part of a living body of tradition. Although they may have been of diverse origin, they crystallized as a collection in what we call Daniel 1–6. Between 167 and 164 B.C.E. [BC] this collection was supplemented by a cycle of visions ascribed to Daniel (chaps. 7–12), and together they were issued as a single book . . . Less than a century after its compilation, Daniel 1–12 was itself expanded. The ancient Greek translations of the book—one known as the Old Greek and the other ascribed to a Jewish proselyte of the second century C.E. [AD] named Theodotion—included three lengthy additions that served to enrich and enhance the cycle of stories about Daniel and the three young men." Nickelsburg, *Jewish Literature*, 22–23.

4. James VanderKam points out that a key piece of evidence in the language debate comes from the book of Susanna. "Since antiquity there has been a debate about the original language of the story—Greek or Hebrew/Aramaic. The point around which the argument has turned is the set of puns in [Susanna] vv. 54–55 and 58–59. They involve the name of the tree and the punishment on the judge who specified that tree: *schinon—schisei* and *prinon—kataprise* (Old Greek; they are virtually the same in Theodotion). Note that these are not only puns, but the two tree names rhyme as do the verbs related to them. Julius Africanus (third century CE [AD]) argued that these word plays worked in Greek and that this fact pointed to Greek as the original language. An objection to his argument has been that the Greek translator could have fashioned the puns, while different word plays may have existed in the Semitic original. Though this is possible, no likely candidates for Semitic puns have emerged." VanderKam, *Introduction to Early Judaism*, 77–78.

5. "Despite the fact that no Hebrew-Aramaic manuscript of Daniel has been found containing these additions (even among the Dead Sea scrolls), scholars nevertheless favor a Hebrew original for the liturgical compositions and a Hebrew or Aramaic original for the additional legends. This is based on the presence of Semitisms in the Greek, but this must be weighted carefully because it could be explained by three different causes: (1) a Greek author is composing in conscious imitation of the Septuagint; (2) an author whose basic linguistic framework is Hebrew or Aramaic is composing a text in Greek; (3) a Greek translator is translating rather woodenly a Semitic original. It is not the mere fact of Semitisms but rather their disproportionately high number that argues most strongly in favor of Hebrew or Aramaic originals for these additions." deSilva, *Introducing the Apocrypha*, 223–24.

6. "The probability of a Hebrew original for the Prayer of Azariah and the Song of the Three Young Men, if not the connecting narrative (Pr. Azar. 23–27), points to a Palestinian provenance." deSilva, *Introducing the Apocrypha*, 227.

7. "That Azariah offered the prayer rather than Hananiah is curious . . . Azariah, it seems, was not the most important of the three young men; for in the MT regardless of whether they are listed by their Hebrew or Aramaic names, Azariah was *always* mentioned last. The fact that even in the Addition itself he is never mentioned first when the others are also named (v. 66, and vs. 1 of the LXX) has prompted some scholars to think that the Prayer of Azariah (vss. 3–22) may originally have referred to an Azariah other than Meshack, and that the identity of names explains why this rather inappropriate prayer was inserted here. Certainly the name was quite common, there being at least twenty-five Azariah's mentioned in the Bible." Moore, *The Additions*, 56.

8. While Azariah's prayer has been somewhat adapted to the circumstances of his story, it is likely that that the prayer previously existed independent of the story. George Nickelsburg explains: "Azariah's prayer appears to have been a previously existent composition reused for its present purpose. Its insertion here conforms to a typical Jewish literary pattern: deliverance comes in response to prayer. However, the contents of this prayer hardly fit the young men's present predicament. They are more appropriate to the general circumstances of the Babylonian exile or to the time of Antiochus Epiphanes' persecution of the Jews, that is, the supposed or the real setting of the book of Daniel (see below, chap. 3). Reference to the cessation of the cult and lack of leadership (v 15) and to the unjust and wicked king (v 9) may indicate that the prayer was actually composed during the persecution." Nickelsburg, *Jewish Literature*, 26.

9. "[The] sense of being in the midst of foreigners who are watching is also clear in the deuteronomic phrase in v. 11: 'for your name's sake.' The danger is that the people's circumstances will be such that the covenant with God will appear to be annulled (v. 11b; cf. the deuteronomic fear of abrogating the covenant in Deut 31:16, 20; Judg 2:1; 1 Kgs 15:19; and in the prophetic literature in Isa 24:5; Jer 11:10; 14:21; Zech 11:10, 14)." Daniel L. Smith-Christopher, *The Additions to Daniel* (NIB VII; Nashville: Abingdon Press, 1994), 161–62.

10. The Greek for this phrase is *ta thaumasia sou*: "Literally 'your wonderful things' (cf. Ps 9:1); the plagues against Pharaoh in Moses' day were called *thaumasia* (cf. Exod 3:20 of LXX). As it turned out, the survival of the three young men in the fiery furnace could only be termed 'miraculous.' This verse, incidentally, is one of the few in the prayer which seems especially appropriate to its context." Moore, *The Additions*, 59–60.

11. "The inability to offer sacrifice sets up an important mention of a 'humble spirit and a contrite heart' (v. 16), which is deemed superior to temple sacrifice. Indeed, references to humbleness of spirit and contrition of heart are often seen in contexts of severe doubt about the efficacy of the sacrificial system: [Psalms 51:16–17; Isaiah 57:15; Isaiah 66:2.]" Smith-Christopher, *The Additions to Daniel*, 162.

12. Some view Psalms 136 and 148 as examples of antiphonal liturgy with repeated phrases. "The hymn (The Song of the Three Jews) is a litany showing much indebtedness to Psalms 136 and 148, in terms of both content and liturgical refrains. Though a single composition, the hymn actually comprises two separate parts: an ode, identified by the introductory phrase 'Blessed are you . . . ' (Song of Thr 29–34), and a psalm in which each exhortation begins with the words 'Bless the Lord . . . ' (Song of Thr 35–68). The ode in particular has strong links to Second Temple liturgical language." Helyer, *Exploring Jewish Literature*, 51.

13. "It is not difficult to see in this list a reference to the ancient comparisons between the God of the Bible, Yahweh, and the ascendant God of the Canaanites, Baal. The Canaanite storm god and thus the 'rider of the clouds,' Baal ruled over meteorological phenomena such as this list represents, particularly those that begin and end the list, wind and lightening." Smith-Christopher, *The Additions to Daniel*, 168.

14. "Finally, as a climax, v 66 refers to the three young men and the reason for singing the hymn. The brevity of this reference in the context of such a long hymn suggests once again that the author of the addition has employed an extant liturgical work, inserting this verse to make the hymn relevant to its new context." Nickelsburg, *Jewish Literature*, 27.

15. "Occurring as a feminine personal name in the New Testament but not in the Old (cf. Luke 8:3; I Chron 2:31–35 has the masculine personal name), this name is derived from the plant world, Heb. *sosanna*, 'lily' (cf. II Chron 4:5; Song of Songs 2:2; Hosea 14:5)." Moore, *The Additions*, 95.

16. One LDS study of this story and its high literary quality is by Steven C. Walker, "'Whoso is Enlightened . . . Shall Obtain Benefit': The Literary Art of the Apocrypha," *Apocryphal Writings and the Latter-day Saints*, ed. C. Wilfred Griggs (Provo, UT: Religious Studies Center, Brigham Young University, 1986), 109–124.

17. An excellent summary of the differences between the Old Greek and the later Theodotian version of the story (which came to be the preferred text) can be found in deSilva, *Introducing the Apocrypha*, 231–32.

18. "The common dating of the Old Greek translation of Daniel to 100 B.C.E. [BC] indicates this as the terminus ad quem for the composition of Susanna; however, the fact that it was not included in the original

book of Daniel does not necessarily indicate a mid- or late-second-century date of composition. It could have been written at any time in the Hellenistic or late Persian period." Nickelsburg, *Jewish Literature*, 24.

19. "Such a high standard of living was evidently quite possible for Jewish exiles in Babylon; consider, for example, Jer 29:5, where Jeremiah advises the Jewish exiles in Babylon, 'Build houses and live in them; plant gardens and eat their produce.'" Moore, *The Additions*, 95. "The Greek term used for Joakim's garden (*paradeisos*) is a Persian loan word from which we also get the English word 'paradise' (see 2 Chr 33:20; Neh 2:8). There is another term that generally refers to a small garden (a vegetable garden? See Neh 3:16, 26). When this term is used together with the Greek term for a 'paradise' (Eccl 2:5; Sir 34:30–31), it gives the reader the impression that the 'paradise,' in contrast to the smaller garden, is a large area kept in a somewhat natural state of beauty. Note that the Garden of Eden is called a 'paradise.'" Smith-Christopher, *The Additions to Daniel*, 177.

20. "It is thought that this motif arose from Jeremiah's reference to Ahab and Zedekiah, two false prophets in Babylon who 'have perpetrated outrage in Israel and have committed adultery with their neighbors' wives, and have spoken in my name lying words that I did not command them; I am the one who knows and bears witness, says the Lord' (Jer 29:23)." VanderKam, *Introduction to Early Judaism*, 76.

21. "Literally 'So assent to us [cf Exod 23:1], and be with us [cf. Gen 39:10 and Tobit 3:8 of the LXX].' . . . [This] indelicate Greek expression for sexual intercourse occurs only here and in vs. 21, where the elders are propositioning Susanna. Elsewhere in 'Susanna' when the narrator is speaking of the sex act or the elders are testifying, less colorful and more neutral language is used (*suggenesthai*, 'to have intercourse with,' vss. 11,39; *anepesemeth*, 'lay down with,' vs. 37; *omilountas*, 'making love,' vs. 54). To the general public these dignified elders may have seemed like distinguished gentlemen. But their blunt ultimatum showed Susanna what they really were. They wanted her body—or her life!" Moore, *The Additions*, 98.

22. "When faced with such overwhelming power over her, Susanna responds with the cry of the oppressed, 'with a loud voice' (v. 24; see also vv.42 and 60). Susanna thereby also fulfills Deut 22:24, which states that if a woman is threatened with rape within the city (that is, where she could be heard) she must call out; otherwise, she is suspected of complicity. The same Greek term used here is used of the Jews crying out from the oppression of Pharaoh (Exod 2:23; 14:10 LXX), and it is the same 'weapon' used by Hagar in the wilderness, when she cries out to God

(Gen 21:16), who delivers her." Smith-Christopher, *The Additions to Daniel*, 179.

23. The details of the 'courtroom' proceedings here furnish "some information about the life of Babylonian Jewry in the early Hellenistic age. We learn that the Jewish community had jurisdiction over even capital cases, at least for offenses in the field of family law, and that the 'whole assembly' judged the cases that came before it—under the direction of the elders—according to the Law of Moses. As in the Torah, the concordant testimony of two witnesses was necessary as well as sufficient proof of guilt, and false witnesses were forced to suffer the same punishment they had attempted to have inflicted upon the accused." Bickerman, *The Jews*, 96.

24. "The critical point in the story becomes the turning point: 'The Lord heard her cry' (Sus 44). This line recalls the ancient story of bondage in Egypt: 'God heard their groaning, and God remembered his covenant with Abraham, Isaac, and Jacob. God looked upon the Israelites, and God took notice of them' (Ex 2:24–25). The point of the story is clear: the God of the patriarchs is still there; he will be the mainstay of Jews in exile." Helyer, *Exploring Jewish Literature*, 47.

25. σχίνον, *schinon* (mastic tree) vs. σχίσει, *schisei* (angel of God will *cut* you) and πρίνον, *prinon* (evergreen oak) vs. πρίσαι, *prisai* (angel of God will *split* you). "To represent in English these instances of ironic word-play one would perhaps paraphrase in some fashion as, 'Under a *clove* tree . . . the Lord will *cleave* you,' and 'Under a *yew* tree . . . the Lord will *hew* you.'" Metzger, *Introduction to the Apocrypha*, 111.

26. This verse captures one of the likely purposes of the story of Susanna: to lead its audience to trust and glorify God. "God is mentioned or alluded to fifteen times in 'Susanna's' sixty-four verses. In fact, with the exception of the two villains, *everybody in the story* mentions God: the narrator of the tale (cf. vss. 5, 9, 44, 45; and vs. 62 of the LXX), Daniel (vss. 53, 55, 59), the righteous presiding elders (vs. 50), Susanna's parents and relatives (vs. 63), the congregation (vs. 60), and, of course, Susanna herself who, though she feared God (vss. 2, 23), trusted in him (vs. 35), prayed to him (vs. 42), an so was delivered. It is no coincidence that it was only the wicked elders who did not mention God. *That*, after all, had been their problem all along: they themselves were not at all concerned about him (cf. vs. 9)." Moore, *The Additions*, 89.

27. While one version (the Theodotion redaction) ends with praise for Susanna and a note of Daniel's rising fame, the other ancient version of this tale (the Old Greek redaction) ends on quite a different note. The last verse of the older text reads, "For this reason the young are the beloved of Jacob in their simplicity, and we are to be on guard that the

young become mighty sons. Then the young will be pious and the spirit of knowledge and understanding will be in them forever." "From the endings it appears that the Old Greek is a story about the danger that corrupt leaders posed for the Jewish community which was saved from a terrible miscarriage of justice by Daniel (to whom an angel, at God's command, had given a spirit of understanding, v. 45). It concludes with a plea for training the young properly." VanderKam, *Introduction to Early Judaism*, 77.

28. deSilva, *Introducing the Apocrypha*, 234.

29. "From a literary point of view, this story is a model of artistic fiction. In a natural and very effective manner, Susanna's destiny is made to hang in the balance. Plot, surprise, struggle, unfolding of character, are present here in just the right proportions; and the whole is told succinctly and pungently. If it is a part of art to conceal art, this story qualifies as great literature." Metzger, *Introduction to the Apocrypha*, 110.

30. "The fact that the authors return repeatedly to the theme of the folly of idolatry suggests the importance of this topic for Jews, particularly in the Diaspora. In Palestine, the question was usually more of an intellectual one: idolatry was taken as a sign of the Gentile's ignorance in the matters of true piety. The more closely Jews interacted with Gentiles and the more involved they became in Gentile circles, the more they would be exposed to idolatry and the invitation—and perhaps expectation— to perform those rites that expressed piety and solidarity with their Gentile comrades . . . Beyond these specific instances, there remained the important work of 'world maintenance'—legitimizing the Jewish worldview and thus the ongoing existence of a distinctive Jewish culture by delegitimizing prominently visible aspects of the major alternative worldview." deSilva, *Introducing the Apocrypha*, 239.

31. "The attack on both idolatry and zoolatry makes Egypt the place where the stories would be most on target with regard to the religious alternatives encountered by God-fearing Jews, who could profit from some reinforcement of the unique truth of their own religious heritage despite the lavish expenditures and apparent devotion of their neighbors towards the gods." deSilva, *Introducing the Apocrypha*, 240.

32. The actual Babylonian name for this deity was Marduk. "Bel is the Babylonian pronunciation of the word Baal, meaning 'lord,' familiar from Canaanite religion." Vanderkam, *Introduction to Judaism*, 136.

"Bel, whose proper name was Marduk, was perhaps the most popular god in the Babylonian pantheon, and in about 2250 B.C. became the patron deity of Babylon. One of the seven wonders of the ancient world was the temple of Bel, a colossal structure of magnificent proportions. Cuneiform tablets have been discovered telling how Nebuchadnezzar lavished upon it elaborate decorations of gold, silver, costly woods, and lapis lazuli. Several sources of evidence testify to the quantities of various animals, fish, and fowl, as well as honey, milk, fine oil, and various kinds of wine which were presented as offerings to Marduk as part of the daily ritual. After generations of worshipers had come to this magnificent temple, in 479 B.C., so Herodotus tells us, it was plundered and destroyed by Xerxes I on his return from Greece." Metzger, *Introduction to the Apocrypha*, 116.

33. "It is important to note that laughter in the Hebrew Bible is usually an act of derision and mockery (only a few exceptions to this can be noted, such as Gen 21:6; Eccl 2:2; 3:4). Abraham and Sarah laugh from incredulity bordering on irony (Gen 17:17; 18:12–13, 15). In Job, laughter is a sign of scorn or mockery, particularly as the reversal of fortune (Job 8:21; 17:6; 22:19; cf. Ps 80:6; Jer 20:8; 48:26, 39; Lam 1:7; 3:14; Ezek 23:32; Amos 7:9)." Smith-Christopher, *The Additions to Daniel*, 188.

34. "Literally 'they used it up.' Some of the food they may have eaten then and there, but obviously some of it was taken back home (cf. vs. 21 of LXX). Whether the Bel story is true or not, such shenanigans did go on in some pagan temples (so Chrysostom *Homily on Peter and Helicon*). For a similar incident in the Temple of Asclepius at Epidaurus, see Aristophanes *Plutus* iii 2." Moore, *The Additions*, 137.

35. "In international folklore, the dragon or serpentine monster has had a long history. In the ancient Near East the serpent was frequently regarded as a religious symbol, and the Bible contains traces of serpent worship among the ancient Hebrews (Num. 21:8f and II Kings 18:4). On Babylonian seals and cylinders men are depicted worshiping gods apparently serpentine in form. It must be admitted, however, that though the Addition to Daniel gives the impression that the dragon was a live snake (as distinct from an image) worshipped as a god, there is no evidence outside this narrative that such was the custom in Babylon." Metzger, *Introduction to the Apocrypha*, 119–120.

36. "The story of Bel and the Dragon must be of Babylonian origin. There were sacred snakes everywhere, even in Greece, but no one, not even the Babylonians, ever pretended that sacred animals were immortal; the Egyptians even mummified them. Nor could the story have been invented in Syria-Phoenicia, where Bel was not worshipped before the first century C.E. [AD]. But the Babylonians took the international motif of the invincible monster seriously: hundreds of reliefs of a horned serpent with the feet of a lion and the wings of an eagle protected the walls of Nebuchadnezzar's Babylon. No wonder that Jeremiah (51:34) compared the all devouring king of Babylon to the Babylonian monster

(*tannim*), the attribute of the supreme deity, Bel (Marduk) of Babylon." Bickerman, *The Jews*, 97.

37. "Inasmuch as many modern scholars have regarded the Snake narrative as a Judaized 'version,' or faint echo, of the famous Babylonian story of Marduk killing the primordial goddess Tiamat, it should not surprise us that a few scholars have seen some ingredient in Daniel's concoction as a mistranslation of an element in the Marduk-Tiamat tale. The relevant passage in *Enuma Elish* describes the titanic battle beteween Marduk and Tiamat.

> *The Evil Wind,* which followed behind, he [Marduk] let loose in her face.
> When Tiamat opened her mouth to consume him,
> *He drove in the Evil Wind that she close not her lips.*
> *As the fierce winds charged her belly,*
> Her body was distended and her mouth was wide open.
> He released the arrow, it tore her belly,
> It cut her insides, splitting the heart.
> Having thus subdued her, he extinguished her life." Moore, *The Additions*, 143.

38. "Why has our author selected this relatively obscure prophet to assist Daniel? There is a thematic connection: Habakkuk's prophecy deals with the problem of why the Lord allowed pagan Babylon to destroy Judah and prophesies judgment for her violent crimes (cf. Hab 1:12–13; 2:2–17). The insertion of Habakkuk into our story thus subtly alludes to the demise of this empire with all its pretensions to grandeur. But even more relevant to our story is the denunciation of idol worship in Habakkuk 2:18–19, with its triumphant conclusion: 'See, it is gold and silver plated, and there is no breath in it at all.' Jewish readers of Bel and the Dragon doubtless made these connections." Helyer, *Exploring Jewish Literature*, 48.

39. Some legends of the Jews include the account of Habakkuk bringing food to Daniel, but it is usually associated with Daniel's first stay in the lions' den and Habakkuk's concern is not how to find the location, but how to transport the meal such a great distance. They also shared the meal together amidst the lions before Habakkuk was returned to Judea.

40. "Why, then, were these Additions rejected by the rabbis? The most probable answer is that the ancient Jewish leaders recognized, even as we do today, the intrusive or secondary character of the Additions. Interesting though the story of Susanna may be in its own right, as 'Susanna' stands in the Septuagint text of Daniel, it is decidedly out of place—in a variety of ways; and so is 'The Prayer of Azariah'. As for 'Bel and the Snake,' the rabbis may have known for an incontestable

fact that this Addition, which was probably added after the first two Additions, was not part of the 'original' book of Daniel . . . In sum, by the time of the Council of Jamnia, if not earlier, Jews had come to prefer an older and more authentic text of Daniel, one 'uncontaminated' by the Additions." Moore, *The Additions*, 30.

41. "Since there is usually nothing in the manuscripts of the early versions of the Book of Daniel to indicate that these sections are interpolations, most of the Church Fathers quoted from them as parts of the canonical Daniel. Those few, however, who knew and adhered to the Hebrew canon rejected them. Jerome in particular called attention (in his Preface to Daniel) to their absence from the Hebrew Bible, and instead of making comments of his own added a brief resume of Origen's remarks 'on the fables of Bel and Susanna.'" Metzger, *Introduction to the Apocrypha*, 100.

42. "Early in the third century Hippolytus, bishop of Rome, wrote, 'Susanna is a type prefiguring the Church; Joakim her husband prefigures the Messiah. The garden is the election of the saints, who, like trees that bear fruit, are planted in the Church. Babylon is the world; and the two elders are set forth as a figure of the two peoples that plot against the Church— the one, namely, of the circumcision, and the other of the Gentiles.' This allegorical interpretation no doubt accounts for the frequent occurrence of pictorial representations of Susanna in early Christian art." Metzger, *Introduction to the Apocrypha*, 112.

43. "The Song of the Three Young Men also came to be used in the litany of the early and medieval Church, from which it has passed into modern liturgies. In the Roman office it occurs in the private thanksgiving of the priest after the Mass, as well as at Lauds on Sunday and festivals. Because the passage opens with the words, 'Benedictite, omnia opera Domini,' the canticle is commonly called 'The Benedicite.' In the Morning Service in the Anglican or Episcopal Prayer Book, the Benedicite stands as an alternate to the Te Deum and begins with the familiar words, 'O all ye works of the Lord, bless ye the Lord.' One must acknowledge that this ancient song of praise is an altogether worthy link between Jewish and Christian forms of piety and worship." Metzger, *Introduction to the Apocrypha*, 104–5.

5

First Book of Esdras

The First Book of Esdras (Greek for Ezra) is one of many scriptural and apocryphal books associated with Ezra, a pivotal figure from the end of the Old Testament. In many ways, Ezra is viewed as a second Moses because he reconstituted the religious community returning from exile and brought forth the law to the people. Because of this, it is not surprising to see later texts attached to the name and figure of Ezra. Since different titles are given for the canonical books of Ezra and Nehemiah in different Bibles, and because there are additional texts in the Septuagint, it can get confusing which Ezra text is which. There are primarily four different Ezra texts found in the King James Version and the Apocrypha. Ezra and Nehemiah are the Old Testament books by those names as found in our current canon. 1 Esdras is a paraphrase of 2 Chronicles 35–36, the book of Ezra, Nehemiah 7:38–8:12, and a tale about Darius's bodyguards. 2 Esdras is a Latin Apocalypse that has Ezra as the primary character, but spends most of its time discussing events associated with the end of times. (1 and 2 Esdras are completely separate books and thus 2 Esdras is not a continuation of 1 Esdras like 2 Kings is of 1 Kings.)

1 Esdras is considered deuterocanonical by the Greek and Orthodox Churches, but it is placed in an appendix of the Roman Catholic Bible. It is the Apocrypha book most closely associated

with the Old Testament because it reproduces much of the same material found in Ezra and Nehemiah.[1] This close relationship has raised questions as to whether

1. this text is an earlier or alternative form of the biblical book of Ezra[2]
2. it is a later text in which the compiler carefully selected material about the temple and Torah from an earlier form of Ezra
3. both the biblical book of Ezra and the Apocrypha book of Esdras go back to an independent original.[3]

In any case, the oldest version of this text is in Greek and probably dates to the second century BC, and 1 Esdras was used by the Jewish historian Josephus in his *Antiquities of the Jews* (see books 10 and 11).[4]

Since most of the material from this book parallels sections of the Old Testament (from King Josiah in the late seventh century until the return of the exiles and the rebuilding of the Temple under the faithful leadership of Zerubbabel, Sheshbazzar, and Ezra in the mid-fifth century BC), I will forgo a lengthy summary of this book and instead point out some of the major differences. 1 Esdras begins with King Josiah celebrating the Passover in Jerusalem around 621 BC, shortly before his death at the hands of the Egyptians in Megiddo. The first two chapters parallel 2 Chronicles 35:1–36:23 (the end of 2 Chronicles) with some changes here and there. One change is that some of the words of God that Josiah refused to heed (resulting in his death) came from Jeremiah the prophet rather than the Egyptian pharaoh. This shift helps explain why God allowed a usually righteous king to be killed. The rest of the first chapter describes the successive kings of Judah whose rebellious actions culminated in the Babylonian attack on Jerusalem, the temple's destruction, the removal of the holy vessels, and the exile of the people (1:54–56).

Chapter 2 begins the retelling of the story found in the Old Testament book of Ezra. It opens with Cyrus, the Persian ruler who conquered the Babylonians, commissioning the rebuilding of the Jerusalem Temple. However, under the next Persian ruler, Artaxerxes, there was opposition by the local population living in Samaria and other places to the rebuilding of Jerusalem's walls and temple. After corresponding with the Persian ruler, it was determined that because of Jerusalem's past rebellious history, all reconstruction should stop. The text then leaves the status of Jerusalem hanging for a little while as it switches its focus to Persia.

Chapters 3 and 4 contain the additional story of Darius's bodyguards, which is not found in the Old Testament and probably existed as a popular court tale independent of Ezra.[5] One night King Darius throws a grand banquet with much eating and drinking. After Darius retires to his bedroom, his three guards begin a conversation about what is the strongest thing in the world. They decide to each write down their choice and put it under his pillow. They hope when Darius awakes and reads them, he will reward the wisest one with great riches. (According to the Jewish historian Josephus, it is the king who proposes this contest; see *Antiquities* XI.3.2.) After the king awakes, the writings are presented to him, and he summons the three young men to his court to explain their statements.

The first one, who had selected "wine" as the strongest thing in the world, explains among other things how wine "leads astray the minds of all who drink it" and can make "equal the mind of the king and the orphan, of the slave and the free, of the poor and the rich" (3:18–19). Since wine is able to force people to do many things they normally would not, he considers it the strongest.

The second speaks of how the "king" is the strongest because he can rule over the men who dominate the land and sea. Whatever he commands is obeyed. "They kill and are killed, and do not disobey the king's command; if they win the victory, they bring everything to the king" (4:5). Farmers pay taxes to support the king. Since the king is obeyed in so many different ways, he is the strongest.

The third, identified as Zerubbabel, acknowledges the strength of the other two, but argues that one thing rules over even wine and kings: women. "Women gave birth to the king and to every people that rules over sea and land" (4:15) and even kings will do silly things in the presence of women (4:29–31). "If men gather gold and silver or any other beautiful thing, and then see a woman lovely in appearance and beauty, they let all those things go, and gape at her, and with open mouths stare at her, and all prefer her to gold or silver or any other beautiful thing. A man leaves his own father, who brought him up, and his own country, and clings to his wife" (4:18–20). "Many men have lost their minds because of women, and have become slaves because of them" (4:26). In sum, "men cannot exist without women" (4:17).

At this point Zerubbabel trumps his discussion of women as the strongest thing by explaining how "truth" is actually the strongest of all. (This section is possibly an addition to the original popular tale to give an ethical or religious emphasis and rationale for Zerubbabel rebuilding the temple).[6] Wine, kings, and women all have unrighteousness in them, but "the whole earth calls upon truth, and heaven blesses it" (4:36). "Truth endures and is strong forever . . . it does what is righteous instead of anything that is unrighteous or wicked. Everyone approves its deeds" (4:38–39). "To it belongs the strength and the kingship and the power and the majesty of all the ages. Blessed be the God of truth!" (4:40). When Zerubbabel stops, everyone shouts, "Great is truth, and strongest of all!" (4:41)—the most quoted line from 1 Esdras in later Christian texts. Darius then asks Zerubbabel to ask for whatever he wishes because he is the wisest and will thereafter sit next to the king as a "Kinsman." Zerubbabel uses this opportunity to ask for permission and royal support to restart the rebuilding of the Jerusalem temple, which had been put on hold by the previous ruler. Darius promptly writes letters to various officials that include orders to give safe conduct to those going to Jerusalem, requests for building supplies, and approval for royal funds to be used to support the Jerusalem temple. Zerubbabel and the Jews praise God for this positive turn of fortunes.

Chapter 5 details the lists of returnees to Jerusalem going there under royal protection and in a merry procession replete with music. These lists parallel those in Ezra 2 and include Judeans, tribes and clans with their leaders, priests, Levites, temple singers, gatekeepers, temple servants, and descendants of Solomon's servants. Some who claimed to be priests were put on "probation" because they could not prove their genealogy so they could not "share in the holy things until a high priest should appear wearing Urim and Thummim" (5:40). The rest of Chapters 5 and 6 discuss the renewal of work on the temple, although this work is again halted because of local opposition. This may be an error in the compilation of this text; it seems to conflate two different time periods, that of the reign of King Cyrus and that of the reign of King Darius.

Most historians propose a chronology for the rebuilding of the temple resembling something like this:

- An initial return during the time of Cyrus (538 BC) was led by Sheshbazzar and resulted in the dedication of a sacrificial altar, the observance of festivals and sacrifices, and the laying of the foundation of the temple.
- The work on the temple was halted until further exiles could return to help.
- A new group of exiles returning under Zerubbabel and Jeshua around 521 BC resumed construction on the temple.
- Samarians opposed the reconstruction, but royal support overturned the opposition.
- The prophets Haggai and Zechariah encouraged the people to rebuild the temple and assisted in its construction.
- The temple was dedicated in 516 BC.

The reaction of the Jerusalem community to the new temple is mixed. Those "old men who had seen the former house, came to the building of this one with outcries and loud weeping, while many came with trumpets and a joyful noise, so that the people could not hear the trumpets because of the weeping of the people" (5:63–65). The presumption here is that some of the old-timers were weeping because the new temple was not as glorious as the old one—Solomon's Temple.[7]

Chapter 7 recounts the completion of the temple and the subsequent offerings presented at the dedication of the temple. A Passover officiated by purified priests and Levites was also held.

Chapters 8 and 9 tell the story of Ezra and his efforts to reconstitute the religious community in Jerusalem after he leads a group of exiles back from Babylon. The chronology of Ezra and Nehemiah is notoriously difficult, and these chapters are no different. (It is noteworthy that 1 Esdras does not mention Nehemiah, perhaps because "his mission was quite separate from that of Ezra, but it may also be due to the fact that the traditions relating to Ezra and Nehemiah developed quite distinctly within Judaism."[8]) Artaxerxes is mentioned as the ruler of Ezra's return, but it is uncertain whether Artaxerxes I or Artaxerxes II is meant. If the first, he returned around 458 BC and came before Nehemiah. If Artaxerxes II is meant, then Ezra returned around 398 BC. In either case, he returns as a scribe of the law to restore the Mosaic law and its practices to the people of Jerusalem. In fact, that may be part of the purpose of 1 Esdras: to acknowledge Ezra's role in establishing the law as the basis for true Judaism, especially among Jews living in diaspora. After fasting and prayer, Ezra set apart priestly leaders and restored the vessels of the temple.

The last issue that Ezra has to resolve is that of mixed marriages between Israelites and their neighbors, which violated the Law of Moses. When Ezra hears about these sins, he tears his garments and his holy mantle, pulls out hair from his head and beard, and sits down in anxiety and grief (8:71). Ezra commences to pray to God, asking for forgiveness for the Israelites' sins. His actions draw a large crowd of people in front of the temple and they begin weeping as well. A spokesperson from the multitude cries out that they have sinned but that they will make an oath to put away all the foreign wives with their children. Ezra then makes the leaders of the priests and Levites take this oath.

A proclamation is sent out for every returnee from exile throughout Judea and Jerusalem to gather at Jerusalem or else they will forfeit livestock for sacrifices and will be expelled from the multitude. A large crowd gathers at the temple under bad weather. Ezra chastises the people for their wickedness in marrying foreign women and commands them to separate "from the peoples of the land and from your foreign wives" (9:9). They agree to do so, but ask to do it in their own scheduled time in their own regions because it will take too much time for such a large crowd in Jerusalem to appear before religious judges to sort through the matter (and the weather was too cold to keep standing in the open air). This plan is agreed upon, and it takes about three months for all the people to present themselves to the priests and resolve this matter. A lengthy list is included in the text of those who were found guilty of having foreign wives.

1 Esdras ends with another gathering of people in the open square before the east gate of the temple in Jerusalem, this time to hear Ezra reading the law to the congregation. A temporary wooden platform is set up and Ezra begins reading aloud the law— most likely the first five books of Moses or selections from them. The people rejoice and worship the Lord, designating the day holy to the Lord. Some men continue to read and explain the law to the people, perhaps doing some translating into Aramaic for those who are not as fluent in Hebrew, until all go their way to eat and drink and enjoy themselves "because they were inspired by the words which they had been taught" (9:55).

Thus, 1 Esdras places great emphasis on the reconstruction of the temple and the reconstitution of the religious community in Jerusalem after the exile based on Ezra's and others' ministries. However, there are many historical issues with this text—the reigns of the Persian kings, the return of the temple vessels with three separate groups, the relationships among community leaders and neighboring opponents, and so on—that indicate the text's composite character from different sources by someone either unaware of or ignoring the historical inaccuracies. In any case, it is a text that places great emphasis on rededication: first with the focus on rebuilding the *temple* and resuming the worship there, and second on helping the *people* purify and recommit themselves to obeying the law and marrying within the covenant.

CONCLUSION

Since much of 1 Esdras overlaps with the Old Testament stories of Ezra and the return of the Babylonian exiles, there is not much substantive new information. The first chapter of 1 Esdras reviews the history of prophets preaching in Jerusalem during the time of Zedekiah. It states that God sent messengers to call them back so that he could spare them and his temple. "But they mocked his messengers, and whenever the Lord spoke, they scoffed at his prophets, until in his anger against his people because of their ungodly acts he gave command to bring against them the kings of the Chaldeans" (1:51–52). It is within this same climate that the Book of Mormon opens in 1 Nephi, leading eventually to Lehi's rejection and departure from Jerusalem.

LDS readers may see in 1 Esdras the challenge of creating a society of faithful believers in the midst of a wider society. Early Church leaders struggled to create Zion amidst those not of their faith, and often those who were very antagonistic toward it. While Ezra's "policies" no doubt caused much consternation among the Jews, their purpose was to create a stronger, more unified community in the end, centered on the temple (and many LDS readers may see a parallel between Ezra's wooden platform at the temple where he instructed the people from the Law and King Benjamin's address to his people from a wooden platform at their temple site, as in Mosiah 2–5). And just as many of the Jews had to leave their intermarriages and figure out how to accommodate the changes to their families that resulted from that policy, so early LDS polygamous families faced daunting changes to their family situations after the Manifesto and cessation of plural marriages.

The story of the bodyguards, unique to the Apocrypha and not found in the Old Testament, emphasizes the power of truth, certainly a tenet shared by Latter-day Saints. Truth should always be the aim of teaching and is confirmed by the power of the Holy Ghost. Doctrine and Covenants 93:24 gives the definition of truth as "knowledge of things as they are, and as they were, and as they are to come" (see also Jacob 4:13). Doctrine and Covenants 84:45 teaches "the word of the Lord is truth, and whatsoever is truth is light, and whatsoever is light is Spirit, even the Spirit of Jesus Christ." Finally, Doctrine and Covenants 91, the revelation telling Joseph Smith he did not need to translate the Apocrypha as part of the JST, teaches that whoever reads the Apocrypha, "let him understand, for the Spirit manifesteth truth; and whoso is enlightened by the Spirit shall obtain benefit therefrom" (91:4–5).

NOTES

1. Its major differences with the canonical books are "(i) in its outer limits, (ii) in the relationships among the books of Chr-Ezr-Neh, (iii) in the order of the chapters, and (iv) above all in the Story of the Youths [bodyguards]." From Zipora Talshir, *I Esdras. From Origin to Translation* (Atlanta: Society of Biblical Literature, 1999), 5. For a helpful table laying out the major sections of 1 Esdras in comparison with the canonical books, see page 4.

2. Scholars like Lester Grabbe and Dieter Böhler feel that 1 Esdras predates the canonical Ezra–Nehemiah account and thus was used as a source for these books. See Lester Grabbe, *Ezra-Nehemiah* (London and New York: Routledge, 1998), 109–115 and Dieter Böhler, *Die heilige Stadt*

in Esdras α und Esra-Nehemia: Zwei Konzeptionen der Wiederherstellung Israels, OBO 158 (Freiburg, Schweiz: Universitätsverlag; Göttingen: Vandenhoeck & Ruprecht, 1997).

3. For a stimulating collection of essays that argue all sides of this issue (as well as other connections between 1 Esdras and the canonical books), see *Was 1 Esdras First? An Investigation into the Priority and Nature of 1 Esdras*, ed. Lisbeth S. Fried (Atlanta: Society of Biblical Literature, 2011).

4. 1 Esdras provides a great case study for textual criticism between the Hebrew Bible and the Septuagint. "Both the text crystallized in the MT [Masoretic Text] and the text preserved in 1 Esd underwent a massive amount of changes after the texts took their different courses. Nevertheless, the variance between the texts seems to be due to the natural course of their transmission." From Talshir, *1 Esdras. From Origin to Translation*, 269.

5. Zipora Talshir presented a thesis that the story of Darius's bodyguards forms the core, in fact the *raison d'être*, of 1 Esdras, to which was added the canonical material from 2 Chronicles, Ezra, and Nehemiah as a framework for this story. See *1 Esdras. From Origin to Translation*, 6, 58–59. Other popular court tales, a genre of wisdom literature, include Ahiqar, Judith, Daniel, and Esther.

6. For a discussion of the relationship between these items and whether "truth" might have been added to the first three, see Talshir, *1 Esdras. From Origin to Translation*, 64–76.

7. See Josephus, *Antiquities of the Jews*, 11.5.81–83.

8. R. J. Coggins, *The First and Second Book of Esdras* (Cambridge: Cambridge University Press, 1979), 5. For examples of this separation, Coggins notes that 2 Maccabees 1:18–2:13 and Ecclesiasticus 49:13 mention Nehemiah without reference to Ezra, while in the chronicles of the Samaritan community and here in 1 Esdras, Ezra is the focus of the attention without mention of Nehemiah.

6

SECOND BOOK OF ESDRAS

2 ESDRAS (GREEK FORM OF EZRA) FOLLOWS IN A STRONG TRADITION of texts associated with the biblical figure of Ezra who helped re-found the religious community in Jerusalem after the Babylonian Exile. However, there are some chronological issues with this text: Ezra is supposedly writing about thirty years after the temple was destroyed in 586 BC, but he was not born until about a century later. Additionally, the destruction of the temple that this text refers to is probably the one at the hands of the Romans in 70 AD, many centuries after Ezra's ministry. These chronological issues may be an example of what Joseph Smith referred to about the Apocrypha generally: "There are many things contained therein that are not true, which are interpolations by the hands of men" (D&C 91:2). Or, the Ezra being mentioned is not the Ezra during the Persian Period discussed in the canonical books of Ezra and Nehemiah and thus presents its own independent tradition; however, the pseudepigraphic connection with the biblical Ezra makes this view unlikely. Interestingly, this text is one of the few that were discussed in early LDS Church periodicals and which members were invited to read.

An article referring to some of the prophecies from 2 Esdras was published twice, first in the *Gospel Reflector*, a publication by the presiding elder in Philadelphia, B. Winchester, in 1841, and then later that year republished in *Times and Seasons*.[1] The first part of the article sets forth the value of Esdras's writings: "Perhaps there are none of the writings of the ancient prophets that are more accurate, and distinct in pointing out future events."[2] It addresses the concern of whether his writings were inspired since they were written in Greek, rather than Hebrew like the other prophets, but the author felt that this was the same figure as Ezra of the Old Testament, so his writings were worth reading. It then goes on to share a few of the passages from Esdras that have parallels in LDS theology. These passages include prophecies related to the Second Coming, such as the resurrection and exaltation of the just and the return of the Lost Ten Tribes to receive their rewards. It also quotes the efforts of Esdras to restore lost Old Testament texts that were destroyed or hidden due to the conflicts of his day. The article ends with the invitation to read the book of Esdras: "we advise all to read it, and then judge its merits."

2 Esdras, the Latin apocalypse, was not included in the Greek Septuagint, where the books of Ezra and Nehemiah are titled 2 Esdras. The Latin Vulgate included the apocalypse, but called it 4 Esdras.[3] It gets even more complicated in other versions of the Bible, but suffice it to say that we will call the Latin pocalypse 2 Esdras. But what is an apocalypse?

An apocalypse is a specific type of text popular in early Jewish and Christian texts and can refer to an entire book or just a section of a text. The equivalent Greek word literally means "revelation." Apocalypses share information that can only be *revealed* by heavenly sources, often in two forms: a heavenly journey, or a dream or vision. In either case, there are typically angelic intermediaries interpreting what is being seen and it is the dialogue or instruction between the mortal figure and the angels that gets recorded in these texts for others to read. Two of the most common topics of apocalypses are *predictions of the future* divided into sequential periods and *descriptions of heavenly settings* such as God's throne, the heavenly temple, and judgment scenes. Some examples of apocalypses within the Bible include the last part of Daniel (chapters 7–12), which incorporates four different apocalypses, and the last book of the New Testament—the Book of Revelation or the Apocalypse of John.

Throughout the text of 2 Esdras (chapters 3–14) are seven different revelations or apocalypses that form the core of the book, probably originally written in Hebrew (or Aramaic) around the end of the first century AD. Later, an introductory section in Greek was added (chapters 1–2; sometimes called 5 Ezra), then even later the last two chapters (15–16; sometimes called 6 Ezra) were added by another author in Greek. The Hebrew was translated into Greek because a portion of it is quoted in Greek by Clement of Alexandria in *Stromata* (late second century AD).[4] Practically all the original Greek manuscripts were lost, but not before various translations were made in other languages. Latin and Syriac versions seem to derive from one independent Greek translation, while a second independent Greek translation "is reflected in the Ethiopic and Armenian versions, two independent Arabic versions, a partial Georgian version, and a fragment in Coptic."[5] The Latin versions were passed down in the Catholic tradition and a version of 2 Esdras is printed in an appendix to the New Testament in Catholic Bibles under the title 4 Esdras.

There has been considerable scholarly debate over whether each of the seven visions was an independent account brought together in this text, or whether the author composed them together to show the transformation from a "despairing skeptic to a believer in the imminent redemption of Israel."[6] Each vision, or episode, is preceded by a period of time (for example, seven days) wherein Ezra is alone preparing to receive revelation.[7] In response, God or the angel Uriel appears to him and uncovers the events and teachings of the episode. The first four visions begin with a speech by Ezra before God, while the last three are revelations from the divine side through vision or theophany. The fourth vision seems to be an important, pivotal point in how 2 Esdras proceeds structurally.

Throughout all these visions, the dialogical format of the narrative is dominant, often with contrasting points of view that are left unresolved. Through this process, Ezra seems to change to a more humble and grateful figure rather than someone who is in distress or complaining against God.[8]

The introductory two chapters lay the framework for the apocalypse: Israel has sinned and become a rebellious people by forgetting God and worshipping strange gods (1:6). Despite God's deliverance of the Israelites from Egypt through his mercy and mighty works, they have forsaken him and he will turn to other nations and give them his name (1:24). Because they have killed the prophets, he will leave their house desolate as they are scattered (1:32–34; 2:7). The new inheritors of the land and the covenant are the Christians (although they are never explicitly named as such; 1:35; 2:10–11). Thus 2 Esdras blends the chronology of Ezra in the fifth century BC with the rise of Gentile Christians in the first and second centuries AD. In other words, the spokesperson to the later Christians is the earlier Ezra because when he came to the Israelites, they rejected him. At the end of the introduction, Ezra sees the Son of God crowning the faithful who had confessed his name in mortality and were now transitioning to immortality (2:42–47). In that glorious context, Ezra is invited to take the message of God's greatness to his people.

FIRST VISION (3:1–5:15)

Ezra's first vision comes in response to his concerns over the desolation of Zion and the wealth of those who lived in Babylon. Some have identified this text as belonging to the literary genre of "crisis of faith" literature because of the disasters that have befallen God's people.[9] He reflects on God's creation, the Fall, the Flood, Abraham, the Exodus, and King David and sees that since the beginning there was an evil heart, or evil nature, in mortals that kept causing them to sin against God. Yet God did not "hinder them" (3:8) in their sins or "take away their evil heart from them" (3:20); he maintained humankind's agency, preserving the law in mortals' hearts alongside the evil root (3:22). The evil seems to win out, and Ezra acknowledges the Israelites' wickedness, but he wonders if the non-Israelites were any better and thus questions why they succeeded in conquering God's chosen people, Israel, and God's chosen city, Jerusalem. (It is always a difficult theological proposition to maintain the belief in a God "who is characterized by power, love, and justice" in the midst of the "atrocities within history, over which the divine supposedly reigns." This leads to a "work of theodicy—that is, an attempt to understand and defend belief in the justice and sovereignty of God in view of the desperate condition of God's world."[10])

It is at this point that the angel Uriel, the other prominent character in this text who instructs Ezra as he answers his questions, comes to Ezra and tries explaining to him, despite Ezra's denial, that Ezra cannot comprehend the way of the Most High. To reinforce his lesson, Uriel asks Ezra to perform three "impossible" tasks with very familiar things: "weigh for me the weight of fire, or measure for me a blast of wind, or call back for me the day that is past" (4:5). When Ezra protests that no one can do such a thing, Uriel explains that it is impossible for humans to completely comprehend mortal things, so how could he ever expect to comprehend the way of the Most High? Ezra humbles himself and falls on his face, allowing Uriel to explain through a parable that those "who inhabit the earth can understand only what is on the earth, and he who is above the heavens can understand what is above the height of the heavens" (4:21).

The heavenly knowledge that can only come from heavenly sources forms the heart of an apocalypse and thus sets the stage here for the revelations Ezra is about to receive. Yet Ezra does not seem as interested in things from above as in the current situation he finds himself in with Israel: he wonders why they are in bondage to godless Gentiles and why the written covenants seem to be disappearing (4:23). Uriel's response is that it is the end of an age and the covenants will not yet be fulfilled because of the people's wickedness (4:26–27). Ezra wonders how long these things will be, to which Uriel replies that we cannot hurry the Most High, for even the righteous souls in their chambers wonder how much longer until they will be resurrected (4:33–35). But God has set a plan and has a predetermined number of souls who will come to earth, and until that number is completed they will continue to wait (4:36–37). Ezra presses on seeking to learn more. He wonders whether his moment in time is closer to the beginning of time or closer to the end of it. Again using a parable, Uriel explains that though the quantity of time that has passed is far greater that what is left, there is still some time remaining (4:50). However, Uriel is forbidden to answer Ezra's next question: whether he would still be alive to see the end. Uriel ends the first vision by describing various signs that will be given to show the end and then invites Ezra to pray and fast for knowledge of even greater things.

SECOND VISION (5:21–6:34)

The second vision of Ezra's apocalypse begins with Ezra's prayer questioning God about why, after choosing one people above all the others to give the law, he had now handed his chosen people over to others, dishonored them, and scattered them among the nations. "And those who opposed your promises have trampled on those who believed your covenants. If you really hate your people, they should be punished at your own hands" (5:29–30). Again, the angel Uriel arrives to respond to Ezra's query and begins to explain to him that he cannot understand God's ways and judgment by asking Ezra if he can fulfill a list of impossible tasks (like gathering scattered raindrops). When Ezra acknowledges that he cannot do those things, the angel replies that, likewise, he cannot discover God's judgment or the love he has promised to his people (5:40). Uriel further explains that not everyone could come to earth at the same time (the ideal time being at the beginning of the messianic age), so there are times and eras for every people.

Ezra then seeks for clarification on when the early age will end and the messianic (millennial) era will begin. A series of signs are explained to him from a mighty voice that shakes the earth. The list of signs of the last days includes infants speaking, storehouses being found empty, and fierce warfare even among former friends. Following this amazing and destructive period, the remnant will see God's salvation and the end of the world. The remnant will see formerly translated beings and the hearts of all will be "changed and converted to a different spirit. For evil shall be blotted out, and deceit shall be quenched; faithfulness shall flourish, and corruption shall be overcome, and the truth, which has been so long without fruit, shall be revealed" (6:26–28). At the end of this vision, Ezra receives a final exhortation: "Believe and do not be afraid! Do not be quick to think vain thoughts concerning the former times; then you will not act hastily in the last times" (6:34).

THIRD VISION (6:38–9:25)

The third vision is a lengthy overview of the postmortal state of the wicked and righteous, and a discussion of the final judgment. Ezra first reviews God's creative acts for each day of the creation of the world leading up to the creation of mortals. God created this world especially for his chosen people, chosen from among all human-kind, but during this difficult period God's elect are dominated by others. This dire situation leads Ezra to the poignant question, "If the world has indeed been created for us, why do we not possess our world as an inheritance? How long will this be so?" (6:59). The angel's response confirms that the world was made for them, but, as a result of the fall of Adam, they needed to pass through difficult experiences in order to lay hold on greater blessings and the fruit of immortality. So instead of worrying too much about his present situation, Ezra is encouraged to look forward to what is to come.

Ezra then turns his attention to future events including the coming of the Messiah, the Messiah's earthly reign (the length of which varies between different translations: many say four hundred years, but one Arabic translation has 1,000 years), resurrection, and judgment. One of the main points about the Day of Judgment is similar to Amulek's teaching in the Book of Mormon—a moment will arrive when the time for repentance has passed, when the night of darkness takes over wherein there is no more repentance (see Alma 34:32–35). At this point, according to 2 Esdras, even the prayers of the righteous can do nothing for the wicked because just as one person cannot sleep for or be ill for another person, "so no one shall ever pray for another on that day, neither shall anyone lay a burden on another, for then all shall bear their own righteousness and unrighteousness" (7:105).[11] Thus the responsibility for one's final reward or punishment falls on oneself. Each faces a "contest" here on earth and must choose "life" and avoid the common lack of eternal perspective spelled out by Ezra: "For while we lived and committed iniquity we did not consider what we should suffer after death" (7:56).

As part of this vision, Ezra also sees the seven torments that the wicked will experience after their death, culminating in "fear at seeing the glory of the Most High in whose presence they sinned while they were alive, and in whose presence they are to be judged in the last times" (7:87). Ezra also views the seven orders of the righteous of which the seventh culminates in their faces shining like the sun and their pressing "forward to see the face of him whom they served in life and from whom they are to receive their reward when glorified" (7:98).

Another common concern from Ezra that comes out in this vision is that the number of righteous saved in the end will be far less than the wicked that will be punished. The angel's response acknowledges this dilemma, but reiterates the responsibility each individual has to choose righteousness over evil. Just as a farmer sows many seeds in the ground and not all bear fruit, so it is with

God's children. After hearing Ezra's repeated concern, the angel wearies a little about this topic and exhorts Ezra: "Do not ask any more questions about the great number of those who perish. For when they had opportunity to choose, they despised the Most High, and were contemptuous of his law, and abandoned his ways. Moreover, they have even trampled on his righteous ones, and said in their hearts that there is no God—though they knew well that they must die" (8:55–58). Instead, the angel wants Ezra to think of himself among the righteous and realize what great preparations God has made for them: "because it is for you that paradise is opened, the tree of life is planted, the age to come is prepared, plenty is provided, a city is built, rest is appointed, goodness is established and wisdom perfected beforehand. The root of evil is sealed up from you, illness is banished from you, and death is hidden; Hades has fled and corruption has been forgotten; sorrows have passed away, and in the end the treasure of immortality is made manifest" (8:52–54).

The vision ends by describing the signs that would indicate when these last events would occur including "world earthquakes, tumult of peoples, intrigues of nations, wavering of leaders, [and] confusion of princes" (9:3). The righteous will be able to escape the calamities through their good works and faith, while the wicked will be awestruck and live in torments.

FOURTH VISION (9:28–10:59)

The fourth vision is a brief view of Jerusalem (Zion), her current desolation but her true glory. It begins with Ezra speaking to God about how God gave Israel the law, but they did not keep it and were destroyed, "yet the fruit of the law did not perish" (9:32). This situation runs counter to nature where usually something that is put into something else, like food or drink into a dish or cup, is "destroyed" but the receptacle remains. In this case, Israel is the receptacle of the law, but they perish while the law remains. Ezra then sees a woman weeping, which leads him to ask her why she is crying. She describes being barren for thirty years and then finally, after many prayers, she conceived and bore a son. After the woman raised her son and prepared for his wedding, her son died as he entered his wedding chamber. She could not be consoled, so she fled from her family and relatives to the field, where Ezra finds her mourning and fasting.

Ezra responds without empathy to the disconsolate woman, explaining to her that the more serious tragedy is the distressful situation of Zion. "For Zion, the mother of us all, is in deep grief and great distress. . . . you are sorrowing for one son, but we, the whole world, for our mother" (10:7–8). "Who then ought to mourn the more, she who lost so great a multitude, or you who are grieving for one alone?" (10:11). "For you see how our sanctuary has been laid waste, our altar thrown down, our temple destroyed; our harp has been laid low, our song has been silenced, and our rejoicing has been ended; the light of our lampstand has been put out, the ark of our covenant has been plundered, our holy things have been polluted," and many other tragedies (10:21–23).

Suddenly the woman's face begins to shine and her "countenance flashed like lightning" (10:25). Ezra becomes terrified. The woman lets out a loud, fearful cry and disappears. In her place, a city is built (10:27). This turn of events leads Ezra to cry out for the angel, Uriel, to remove him from this bewildering experience. Uriel arrives at Ezra's side to strengthen him and explain what he had seen.

The interpretation of Ezra's vision takes the rest of the passage as he learns that the woman represented Zion. Her barren years represent the 3,000 years the earth stood before Solomon's temple was built. Jerusalem and its temple are the son who was raised up for many years until it fell to Babylonian destruction—the son's death. The mother was actually mourning the same thing Ezra had been. God unveiled the mother's (Zion's) true glory and beauty to comfort and bless Ezra for his faithfulness. Again the message is reiterated: Zion and Jerusalem have been punished, but Zion is not forgotten and will return to her former self.

FIFTH VISION (11:1–12:39)

The fifth vision is full of bizarre animal imagery representative of different eras of Roman history. A strange eagle with three heads and twelve wings represents the different reigns of Roman rulers who frequently vied with each other for power. It is compared to the fourth kingdom of Daniel's vision of various beasts representing different world empires (see Daniel 7:7; in Daniel the fourth beast seems to represent the Greek empires, but here the beast is reinterpreted to be the Roman Empire).

A lion appears in the middle of the vision to signal the end of the eagle's existence. Later the lion is interpreted as the Messiah who comes from the offspring of David and pronounces the end of times. As part of his mission, the Messiah will display the wickedness of the ungodly before their face and bring them before the judgment seat to then destroy them. Some of their sins are delineated in the vision: "You have judged the earth, but not with truth, for you have oppressed the meek and injured the peaceable; you have hated those who tell the truth, and have loved liars; you have destroyed the homes of those who brought forth fruit, and have laid low the walls of those who did you no harm" (11:41–42). The Messiah will free a remnant of the righteous and make them joyful in the Day of Judgment.

At the end of the fifth vision, Ezra is commanded to write the things he has seen and hide place them in a hidden place (12:37). It is only to be shared with those who are wise and "whose hearts you know are able to comprehend and keep these secrets" (12:38). This esoteric treatment of the text reflects the literal meaning and positive sense of the word *apocrypha*—things that need to be "hidden" from the world at large and reserved for the elect.

SIXTH VISION (13:1–58)

Between the fifth and sixth vision, an interlude describes the people's concern at Ezra's lengthy absence from the city while he was beholding these visions. They worry that, in addition to the disasters that have fallen upon them, Ezra will also abandon them. Ezra reassures them that he, and the Most High, have not forgotten them in their struggle, but he had withdrawn to pray for them and Zion. He admonishes them to return to their homes as he continues to prepare for his next vision seven days later.

The sixth vision primarily portrays the activities of the Messiah. It begins with a great wind stirring up the waves of the sea. From the midst of the sea arises the figure of a man who flies with the clouds of heaven. Wherever he looks, everything trembles; and whenever he speaks, all who hear melt (13:3–4). A multitude gathers to fight against the figure (the Messiah), but they are burned up by a stream of fire coming forth from the figure's mouth. After the tremendous scene of destruction, the Messiah gathers together the righteous to him.

In the interpretation of the vision, the Messiah is identified as the Son of God (13:32) who has been reserved for the last days to deliver God's creation (13:26). While standing on Mount Zion, he shall meet an innumerable multitude gathered together to conquer him (13:34–35). The heavenly Jerusalem will be made manifest to the people and the Messiah will reprove the assembled nations, torture them with their own evil thoughts (represented by the flames), and destroy them by means of the law (the fire). The gathering of the righteous will include the tribes taken away by the Assyrians who had separated themselves into a more distant region (called Arzareth, Hebrew for "another land") by crossing the Euphrates River which God miraculously will stop. Thus, a remnant of those within Israel and a returning remnant of these earlier exiles will be preserved and gathered under the leadership of the Messiah.

Seventh Vision (14:1–48)

The seventh vision begins with Ezra hearing his name being called out from a bush, similar to Moses's experience with the burning bush. The focus on Moses continues with a discussion of Moses's time on Mount Sinai, where God revealed many wondrous things to him including the "secrets of the times" and "the end of the times" (14:5). Moses was commanded to share some things publically with the people, but keep secret other parts of his Sinai experience. Similarly, Ezra is told to publish some of his visionary experiences openly, but others he is told to keep secret. Ezra is also told that he is going to be taken up from among humankind (like Enoch) and "live with my Son and with those who are like you, until the times are ended" (14:9). The end times are approaching, he is told, because nine and a half of the twelve parts of the earth's history had already passed, so Ezra needs to set his house in order and renounce any evil or burdens of mortality.

Ezra's imminent departure raises a question in his mind: once he has left, who will warn those who continue to live upon the earth? To complicate this situation, Ezra points out that the law has been burned (an allusion to the destruction of the sacred records by the Babylonians), so the people have been left in darkness and "no one knows the things which have been done or will be done by you" (14:21). Ezra suggests a solution to this dilemma: grant him the Holy Spirit and he will (re)write "everything that has happened in the world from the beginning, the things that were written in your law, so that people may be able to find the path, and that those who want to live in the last days may do so" (14:22). Ezra's request is granted and he is told to tell the people he will be away from them for forty days, during which time he will be given the lamp of understanding which will not go out until he finishes writing everything. He is supposed to take with him only writing tablets and five scribes "trained to write rapidly" (14:24).

After admonishing the people to live righteously and not bother him for forty days, Ezra proceeds out to a field to begin his revelatory experience. A voice commands him to drink from a substance offered him: "something like water, but its color was like fire" (14:39). Upon drinking it, "my heart poured forth understanding, and wisdom increased in my breast, for my spirit retained its memory, and my mouth was opened and was no longer closed" (14:40–41). The five scribes feverishly take turns writing down what is dictated "using characters that they did not know" (14:42), a probable reference to the new square Hebrew script that became popular during this time. By the end of the forty days, ninety-four books have been written, twenty-four of which are meant for public consumption, while seventy are reserved for the wise among the people "for in them is the spring of understanding, the fountain of wisdom, and the river of knowledge" (14:47). The twenty-four books comprise the canon of the Hebrew Bible as accepted today: Torah—five books of Moses; Prophets—eight books, some of which were combined into one book (like 1 and 2 Samuel, 1 and 2 Kings, and the twelve minor prophets); Writings—eleven books such as Proverbs, Psalms, and some books combined (Ezra–Nehemiah, and 1 and 2 Chronicles). The seventy books are esoteric writings for only the wise.

These additional books of scripture ended up playing an interesting role in early LDS Church history and became so influential that they led to the formation of a break-off group discussed previously in chapter 2. James Brewster and his followers were convinced that he was restoring books that Esdras had meant to be guides for the people in the last days. The Church, through a notice in *Times and Seasons*, warned members against following Brewster and that the purported lost books of Esdras were "a perfect humbug."[12] Brewster's success was short-lived despite gaining some initial followers and organizing the Church of Christ in 1848 centered on the Bible, the Book of Mormon, and the revelations of Esdras. Throughout the existence of the movement, the authority of Esdras was frequently invoked, not only in the published manuscripts but also in sermons and commands.

An Appendix (15:1–16:78)

2 Esdras ends with a lengthy appendix written approximately two centuries after the accounts of the visions in the central section of the text. It warns of the confusion and destruction about to come upon the world because the people's wickedness has reached its limit. The Lord will avenge the persecution of the righteous and deliver the innocent as he did previously with the Exodus from Egypt. In the meantime, warfare will fill the land and many people will suffer. Then finally, "In a very short time iniquity will be removed from the earth, and righteousness will reign over us" (16:52).

Conclusion

The book of 2 Esdras is a sweeping, often confusing apocalypse covering many different topics and doctrines. It is reminiscent of the book of Revelation as it points toward many end time events. Many of these events are familiar to Latter-day Saints, including the arrival of the Messiah to deliver his people in Jerusalem, the descent of a heavenly Jerusalem to the earth, the millennium, resurrection, and judgment. Indeed, it describes many times and eras which parallel LDS belief in dispensations and God's plan eventually coming to fulfillment, including the belief that God has souls or spirits prepared to come to earth, and until they all arrive, human history with all its ills and joys continues.

Latter-day Saints strongly believe in the principle of agency, and 2 Esdras highlights how God allows mortal agency even when it causes mortals to sin against God and others. While this raises many theological questions about God's involvement or non-involvement in human tragedy, 2 Esdras as a theodicy tries to remind the reader that God's ways are not our ways and we will likely not be able to comprehend all his actions and reasons for allowing things to be as they are. While it may seem that God has at times forgotten his covenant people, 2 Esdras reconfirms that he never does, a major purpose of the Book of Mormon as well (see the title page). 2 Esdras 2:30 uses the memorable imagery of a hen gathering her chicks as a symbol for God's protection and deliverance of his people just like the New Testament (Matthew 23:37), Book of Mormon (3 Nephi 10:4–6), and Doctrine and Covenants (10:65). There may be times of scattering, but these will be followed by gatherings until all his covenant promises are fulfilled. Thus, this earth life truly becomes a time of probation and mortals are left free to choose. The teachings of Amulek and Lehi share some of these same sentiments: "Do not procrastinate the day of your repentance until the end; for after this day of life, which is given us to prepare for eternity, behold, if we do not improve our time while in this life, then cometh the night of darkness wherein there can be no labor performed" (Alma 34:33). "Men are free according to the flesh; and all things are given them which are expedient unto man. And they are free to choose liberty and eternal life, through the great Mediator of all men, or to choose captivity and death, according to the captivity and power of the devil" (2 Nephi 2:27).

NOTES

1. "The Beauty of the Writings of the Prophet Esdras," *Times and Seasons*, Vol. 2, No. 17 (July 1, 1841).
2. "The Beauty of the Writings of the Prophet Esdras," 464.
3. Ezra=1 Esdras, Nehemiah=2 Esdras, Paraphrase of Ezra/Nehemiah=3 Esdras—the equivalent of 1 Esdras discussed in the previous chapter.

Chapters 3–14 of 2 Esdras are also listed in the major collections of the Pseudepigrapha as 4 Ezra.

4. For example in Book 1, chapters XXI-XXII.

5. Karina Martin Hogan, "Ezra, Fourth Book of," in *The Eerdmans Dictionary of Early Judaism*, 624.

6. Hogan, "Ezra, Fourth Book of," 624.

7. For further discussion on how the structure of each vision seems to point to literary unity and one author wherein "meaning is conveyed by changes in context and framework as well as by explicit statements" see Michael E. Stone, *Fourth Ezra. A Commentary on the Book of Fourth Ezra*. Hermeneia—A Critical and Historical Commentary on the Bible (Minneapolis: Fortress Press, 1990), 21 (and throughout the commentary).

8. See Bruce W. Longenecker, *2 Esdras* (Sheffield: Sheffield Academic Press, 1995), 20–21. For the case that the fourth vision is the pivotal point in the text where Ezra changes or is "converted," see 59–69.

9. See Bruce W. Longenecker, *2 Esdras* (Sheffield: Sheffield Academic Press, 1995), 11–13.

10. Longenecker, *2 Esdras*, 11–12.

11. This section of 2 Esdras includes a lengthy passage that is not included in the Latin Vulgate or the King James Version, but is found in other versions. It may be that this section was omitted from some versions because of its emphasis on the denial of praying for the dead. As a result, some verses in chapter 7 have two numbers depending on whether this lengthy passage is accepted or not.

12. "Notice," *Times and Seasons*, Vol. 4 (1 Dec. 1842), 32.

7

THE PRAYER OF MANASSEH

IF ONE WERE SEARCHING FOR A PRIME EXAMPLE OF HOW GOD could show forgiveness and mercy to a horrible sinner, then Manasseh, one of the most wicked kings in the Old Testament, fits the bill. The Prayer of Manasseh is an extremely brief text (15 verses) in which the wicked king petitions the Lord for forgiveness of the many sins that weigh him down. Although only accepted as part of the later canon by Eastern Orthodox Christians, it has also been included in an appendix to the Roman Catholic Latin Vulgate. The prayer is found in Syriac in the *Didascalia Apostolorum* (third century AD), in Greek in the *Apostolic Constitutions* (fourth century AD) and "three manuscripts of the Septuagint, of which the oldest and most important is Codex Alexandrinus (fifth century [AD])."[1] In the Greek texts, it is usually placed with other odes or canticles immediately after Psalms. It was written in a style of Greek that sounds like a translation from Hebrew or Aramaic (semitizing Greek). Scholars have debated whether it had a Jewish origin as early as the first century BC, or whether it is a Christian text from later (at the earliest, around the late second century AD).[2]

Background

In 2 Kings 21, Manasseh, son of the righteous king Hezekiah, is introduced as a king who did evil in the sight of God and undid many of the religious reforms his father had carried out. Manasseh's most grievous sins are laid out—of which there are many. He rebuilt the apostate high places of worship his father had destroyed. He both condoned and participated in the worship of false, foreign gods—even within the sacred precincts of the Jerusalem temple. He burned his son in a pagan ritual, practiced soothsaying, and dealt with mediums and wizards. According to some Jewish traditions, Manasseh killed the prophet Isaiah by having him sawn in half in a hollow log. What added to Manasseh's personal sins was that he led his people into greater wickedness than even the nonbelieving nations around the Israelites. Consequently, dire prophecies of Judah's destruction were given and Manasseh is blamed for the later Babylonian conquest of Judah and Jerusalem.

2 Chronicles repeats many of the events and descriptions of royalty found in 2 Kings; however, sometimes it makes significant changes. In the case of Manasseh, 2 Chronicles 33 opens up the possibility that Manasseh wasn't always as evil as he is made out to be in 2 Kings. He did commit many of the sins outlined in the earlier text, but in the end he was captured by the Assyrians and hauled off with hooks and fetters (2 Chronicles 33:10–11). In his distress, Manasseh humbled himself and called upon the Lord. "[He] prayed unto him: and he [God] was entreated of him, and heard his supplication, and brought him again to Jerusalem into his kingdom. Then Manasseh knew that the Lord he was God" (33:13). When Manasseh returned to his land, he fortified the cities and, more importantly, reformed some of the false worship he had instigated, particularly taking away the foreign gods from the temple complex (33:14–16). However, the reform was not a complete religious overhaul as people continued to sacrifice in the high places, but now only to the Lord their God (33:17).

There is no mention in 2 Kings about Manasseh's captivity,[3] repentance, prayer, or reforms, but 2 Chronicles includes all this as it provides a redeeming end to Manasseh's reign and even points to other accounts of his prayer and life changes. "His prayer also, and how God was entreated of him, and all his sin, and his trespass, and the places wherein he built high places, and set up groves and graven images, before he was humbled: behold, they are written among the sayings of the seers" (33:19). Yet the words of his repentant prayer are not found in 2 Chronicles and it is unclear what the source "the sayings of the seers" is, so there seems to be a gap that later readers would want to fill. Perhaps it was precisely this gap that The Prayer of Manasseh from the Apocrypha seeks to fill, either by copying from an earlier source or creating a new text for a Greek-speaking audience.

PENITENTIAL PRAYER, PSALM, OR LAMENT

The prayer can be organized into three sections:[4]

1. *Invocation*: praise to the Lord for his works of creation (v. 1–4) and acknowledgment of the Lord's fury against sinners and of his multitudinous mercies (v. 5–7)
2. *Confession*: a personal lament and confession (v. 8–10)
3. *Entreaty*: a supplication for pardon (v. 11–13) and an expression of trust in God's grace and a concluding doxology [praise of God] (v. 14–15)

The Prayer of Manasseh begins with an acknowledgment of God's power as Creator, manifested in both his glorious splendor and his fearsome wrath (v. 1–5). Yet the key quality Manasseh focuses on in his own dire situation is God's mercy: "Yet immeasurable and unsearchable is your promised mercy, for you are the Lord Most High, of great compassion, long-suffering, and very merciful" (v. 6–7). With such qualities, God has promised repentance and forgiveness to sinners "so that they may be saved" (v. 7).[5]

Manasseh continues by acknowledging his many sins, more than the sand of the sea (v. 9). He feels unworthy even to look up to heaven, and is weighed down and rejected because of all his sins (v. 10). But now he humbles himself and implores God for kindness and forgiveness including the memorable phrase: "I bend the knee of my heart, imploring you for your kindness" (v. 11–12).

> I earnestly implore you, forgive me, O Lord, forgive me! Do not destroy me with my transgressions! Do not be angry with me forever or store up evil for me; do not condemn me to the depths of the earth. For you, O Lord, are the God of those who repent, and in me you will manifest your goodness; for, unworthy as I am, you will save me according to your great mercy. (v. 13–14)

Manasseh ends his prayer with a commitment to praise God continually the rest of his days just as the host of heaven sings his praise, "Yours is the glory forever" (v. 15).

CONCLUSION

The Prayer of Manasseh is a great example of how a sinner can humble himself and receive God's mercy and forgiveness. In some ways, Manasseh would be the prime example for Latter-day Saints that even the most despicable sinners can still repent and receive God's mercy because traditionally Manasseh is held responsible for brutally putting the prophet Isaiah to death and the prophet Isaiah is very important to Latter-day Saints. If even he can be forgiven, then certainly others can as well. The text also reminds the reader of the importance of avoiding false worship practices and ideas of others and the value of trying to make reforms when realizing one's mistakes.

Notes

1. Rodney A. Werline, "Manasseh, Prayer of," in *The Eerdmans Dictionary of Early Judaism*, 912.
2. For a strong argument for a Jewish origin, see J.H. Charlesworth, "Prayer of Manasseh," in *The Old Testament Pseudepigrapha. Vol. 2* (New York: Doubleday, 1985), 628.
3. Although Manasseh is mentioned as a vassal to the Assyrians in some Assyrian inscriptions, it never says he was captured and taken there.
4. From Charlesworth, "Prayer of Manasseh," 625.
5. The Prayer of Manasseh seems to make the point that repentance is only for sinners, not the righteous, so individuals like Abraham, Isaac, and Jacob, who did not sin, did not need repentance (unlike Manasseh, who certainly needed repentance) (v. 8). Some translations solve this apparent theological problem by emphasizing that God has not appointed repentance *only* to the righteous, but *especially* to the sinners. Perhaps one way to reconcile this verse is to see it analogous to Jesus's statements in the New Testament that he was not sent to the "whole" but to the sick: "I came not to call the righteous, but sinners to repentance" (Mark 2:17; see also Luke 5:32). In this interpretation, the statement is more for emphasis, not exclusion.

8

BARUCH AND THE LETTER OF JEREMIAH

THE BRIEF BOOK OF BARUCH (FIVE CHAPTERS) IS SET IN THE SIXTH century BC, during the time of the Babylonian Exile and the promised return to the covenant land of Israel. The book is named after Baruch, the close companion and scribe of the prophet Jeremiah. Baruch is mentioned in the book of Jeremiah (e.g., 36:27–32; 45:1–5), and archaeological finds may confirm his existence. In the mid-1970s, small bullae (clay impressions of a seal or stamp; a kind of ancient signature) were found with the name *Baruch, son of Neriah* (as well as other prominent administrative officials from this period). It may be more than a coincidence that in Jeremiah 32:10–15 Baruch is connected with these types of seals or bullae, given that Jeremiah instructs him to take a deed that had been signed and sealed and place it in an earthen jar as a witness that houses, fields, and vineyards would again be purchased in the land (after the Exile). Perhaps one of these bullae was used to seal this jar (similar to what the Dead Sea Scrolls were stored in) with Baruch's own seal. In any case, Jeremiah and Baruch witnessed the increasing wickedness of the people, their failure to heed the warnings of the prophets, and the subsequent conquest of Jerusalem.

The figure of Baruch was prominent in early Jewish and Christian writings, as at least three major texts associated with him have been collected in the group of writings called the Pseudepigrapha. 2 Baruch is also placed in the period of the Babylonian destruction of Jerusalem in 587 BC, but scholars view it as commenting on the Roman destruction of the temple in AD 70 through the prism of the earlier Babylonian invasion. This lengthy text (eighty-seven chapters!) includes a variety of material: visions, lamentations, prayers, expositions on the temple, and letters to the people of Israel. The setting for 3 Baruch is Baruch weeping for the destruction of Jerusalem by the Babylonians. As he weeps, an angel sent by the Lord comforts Baruch and takes him on a tour of five heavens. 4 Baruch also focuses on the Babylonian conquest of Jerusalem and purportedly includes material omitted from the book of Jeremiah. This story expands the role of Jeremiah and Baruch in the events surrounding the Babylonian conquest and even has them aiding the return of the exiles to Jerusalem (contradicting the biblical record).

The book of Baruch in the Apocrypha was probably originally written in Hebrew (at least the first part—1:1–3:8—is most likely), but there are no existing Hebrew manuscripts. Besides the Greek versions in the Septuagint, there are ancient translations in Latin, Coptic, Ethiopic, Arabic, and Armenian. The book of Baruch is a letter by Baruch living in exile writing back to those remaining in Jerusalem and begins with a prose introduction to the text that places Baruch in Babylon by the river Sud reading this book to the exiles (1:1–14). It then goes on to explain why God exiled the Israelites from their covenant land and the people's acceptance of this punishment because of their sins (1:15–3:8), a section likely based on or having much in common with Daniel 9:4–19. The second part of the book switches to poetry as it personifies wisdom and Jerusalem. First, wisdom is praised and presented as the solution to the Israelites' current problems (3:9–4:4). "Like Ben Sira 24, wisdom is equated with the Torah (4:1), though much of the poem seems to draw on (or be parallel to) Job 28:12–28 about the inaccessibility of wisdom."[1] Next, Jerusalem speaks to the people of Israel to encourage them to return to the God who has not forgotten them (4:5–29). Lastly, an unknown voice speaks to Jerusalem in preparation for the return of her inhabitants (4:30–5:9). Overall the focus of the text seems to view the return from exile as a second exodus.[2]

The Israelites' wickedness resulted in many tragedies. The temple was destroyed (2:26). Some starving Jews ate the flesh of their children (2:3). They became subject to the peoples around them and were scattered from their covenant land, specifically Jerusalem. In fact, the concept of the scattering of Israel is repeated many times (2:4, 13, 29; 3:8; 4:6). But the Israelites were not meant to be entirely destroyed, so the text highlights the exile as a learning environment where repentance could take place. God pledges that "in the land of their exile they will come to themselves and know that I am the Lord their God. I will give them a heart that obeys and ears that hear; they will praise me in the land of their exile, and will remember my name and turn from their stubbornness and their wicked deeds" (2:30–33). The people acknowledge, "You have put the fear of you in our hearts so that we would call upon your name; and we will praise you in our exile, for we have put away from our hearts all the iniquity of our ancestors who sinned against you. See, we are today in our exile where you have scattered us, to be reproached and cursed and punished for all the iniquities of our ancestors, who forsook the Lord our God" (3:6–8).

As the scattering was a reality for the Israelites, so the promised gathering would occur so that God could maintain his covenant people and the respect of his name throughout the entire world. If they repent and return to God, God promises that he will again bring the people of Israel into the land promised to their forefathers, Abraham, Isaac, and Jacob. "I will make an everlasting covenant with them to be their God and they shall be my people; and I will never again remove my people Israel from the land that I have given them" (2:35). Jerusalem was told to prepare the Israelites' return and look toward the east to "see the joy that is coming to you from God. Look, your children are coming, whom you sent away; they are coming, gathered from east and west, at the word of the Holy One, rejoicing in the glory of God" (4:36–37). "For God will lead Israel with joy, in the light of his glory, with the mercy and righteousness that come from him" (5:9).

Consequently, the text of Baruch focuses on pleas for deliverance and the obtaining of wisdom to bring God's promised blessings upon this formerly wicked people. "Hear, O Lord, our prayer and our supplication, and for your own sake deliver us, and grant us favor in the sight of those who have carried us into exile; so that all the earth may know that you are the Lord our God, for Israel and his descendants are called by your name" (2:14–15).

In Baruch's great poem in praise of wisdom, specifically the wisdom found in the law of God (4:1), Israel is reminded that they have forsaken God, the fountain of wisdom, and are exhorted to turn to wisdom so their end is not the same as the wicked and foolish: vanished and forgotten. Wisdom laments, "With joy I nurtured them, but I sent them away with weeping and sorrow. Let no one rejoice over me, a widow and bereaved of many; I was left desolate because of the sins of my children, because they turned away from the law of God" (4:11–12). Yet she holds out hope that if they cry to God, he will deliver them. "For I have put my hope in the Everlasting to save you, and joy has come to me from the Holy One, because of the mercy that will soon come to you from your everlasting savior. For I sent you out with sorrow and weeping, but God will give you back to me with joy and gladness forever" (4:22–23). Wisdom's final exhortation holds out God's everlasting kindness to Israel: "Just as you were disposed to go astray from God, return with tenfold zeal to seek him. For the one who brought these calamities upon you will bring you everlasting joy with your salvation" (4:28–29). There is always hope for repentant Israel because the covenants are eternal.

Conclusion

At first glance, the book of Baruch in the Apocrypha seems to have little to offer to an LDS reader besides reminders of the covenant relationship between God and his people and the warnings of punishments awaiting those unfaithful to their covenants. But these reminders are precisely the major messages of both the Old Testament *and* the Book of Mormon: both books recount multiple examples of peoples who forgot the Lord and were forsaken by God for a period, but never forgotten. Baruch repeatedly acknowledges the justice of God in what has happened to his people because they have sinned and rejected the warning voices of the prophets. "We did not listen to the voice of the Lord our God in all the words of the prophets whom he sent to us, but all of us followed the intent of our own wicked hearts by serving other gods and doing what is evil in the sight of the Lord our God" (1:21). "You have sent your anger and your wrath upon us, as you declared by your servants the prophets. . . . You have carried out your threats, which you spoke by your servants the prophets" (2:20, 24). Thus Baruch provides additional examples and exhortations to remain faithful to the covenants because God will always remain faithful to them. As part of God's salvation history here on earth, his people at times will be scattered and exiled due to their wickedness, but he always holds out the promise of future gathering in order to fulfill his covenantal promises. Covenants are eternal.

The Letter of Jeremiah

The Letter of Jeremiah is another text treating the period of the Babylonian conquest of Jerusalem and the subsequent exile (587 BC). In some versions of the Bible it is printed as the sixth chapter of Baruch, so I will combine it here with my discussion of Baruch. It is a short, seventy-three verse diatribe or passionate homily against idolatry. Its purpose was to prepare the Israelites for the polytheistic environment they would encounter in Babylon. As evidenced by its title, it is purported to be a letter from Jeremiah for those going into exile, yet it would be found useful for any Jews living among Gentiles in Diaspora. It bears strong connections to sections in the biblical book of Jeremiah, such as Jeremiah's letter to the exiles in Jeremiah 29:1–23, where he encouraged them to build up their communities in Babylon, as they would be there for seventy years—not a shorter period, as some false prophets and diviners were saying. It also relates to Jeremiah's sermon against idolatry in Jeremiah 10, using many of the same phrases.

A Hebrew original for Jeremiah's letter is likely, although only Greek manuscripts have been discovered. A small Greek fragment was found among the Dead Sea Scrolls (7QLXXEpJer) dated to the first century BC. Because of the letter's many references to Babylonian religious practices (see vv. 4, 11, 30–32, 41, 43), some scholars suggest a relatively early date of composition, perhaps as early as the sixth century BC.[3] Despite its close affinity to the Book of Jeremiah, most consider it pseudonymous.

The message of The Letter of Jeremiah is not hard to miss because it is repeated over and over again: because idols are made by human hands and have no life in them, they are not true gods and should not be worshipped.[4] Several refrains at the end of sections repeat this message: "they are not gods; so do not fear them" (16, 23, 29). "Why then must anyone think that they are gods, or call them gods?" (40, 44).[5] Besides these repeated admonitions, Jeremiah describes over and over again the lifeless nature of these idols and their inability to protect themselves from war, fire, and theft. How can they do anything for anyone else if they can't take care of themselves? They are made, clothed, and adorned by mortals and placed in temples that must be guarded and locked up lest something happen to them. They gather dust, decay, break, and are discarded and replaced by other handmade figures. Gifts, meals, and sacrifices are brought to them, but these offerings are simply enjoyed by the priests and attendants, such as was related in the story of Bel and the Dragon, one of the additions to the Book of Daniel. It is particularly troubling that they can do nothing for those in real need who seek their aid. "They cannot save anyone from death or rescue the weak from the strong. They cannot restore sight to the blind; they cannot rescue one who is in distress. They cannot take pity on a widow or do good to an orphan" (36–38).

Jeremiah warns his people that even though they'll see many people worshipping these images and carrying them in processions, they should only worship the living God, who is watching over their lives (5–7). In fact, this letter strongly defends the absolute monotheism of Judaism. Even the natural phenomena like the sun, moon, stars, lightning, fire, and clouds are obedient to the commands of God, but these idols are deaf, mute, and lifeless and are unable "to do good to anyone" (64). The letter concludes with the commendation: "better, therefore, is someone upright who has no idols; such a person will be far above reproach" (73).

CONCLUSION

This brief text has a few messages that could be applied to a Latter-day Saint perspective. Just as Jeremiah repeatedly urged his people to avoid the trappings and influence of their pagan neighbors, so we have been repeatedly taught to be *in* the world, but not *of* the world. We do not need to live in isolation from others, but we need to avoid allowing worldly things into our lives, especially when those things start changing our own beliefs and practices. While Latter-day Saints may not typically have issues with direct idolatry of graven images like ancient peoples often did, we can be swayed to trust in the arm of flesh rather than in God. In a strongly worded First Presidency Message, President Spencer W. Kimball cautioned members of the Church against putting the affections of their hearts on worldly things and trusting in man-made things rather than in God.[6] We often consider ourselves modern and sophisticated, and yet we can show the same lack of faith toward God because of "gods of stone and steel" as the ancient Israelites some-times did. We can maintain too firm a grasp on telestial things to the point that we lose out on celestial blessings. "Whatever thing a man sets his heart and his trust in most is his god; and if his god doesn't also happen to be the true and living God of Israel, that man is laboring in idolatry."[7]

Notes

1. Lester L. Grabbe, "Apocrypha," in *Dictionary of Biblical Criticism and Interpretation*, ed. Stanley E. Porter (London and New York: Routledge, 2007), 18.
2. Grabbe, "Apocrypha," 18.
3. See Daniel J. Harrington, "Jeremiah, Letter of," in *The Eerdmans Dictionary of Early Judaism*, 784. In support of a pre-200 BC dating, 2 Maccabees 2:1–3 seems to make an allusion to The Letter of Jeremiah.
4. Harrington made the point: "The fundamental criticism against the idols is that they cannot do what the God of Israel does (vv. 34–38, 66–69). The author never entertains the thought that the statues and images may have been regarded as representations of the various deities, not actual objects of worship. The author's main concern is keeping other Jews from foreign cults, not writing a treatise on comparative religion." From "Jeremiah, Letter of," 784.
5. Four other pronouncements repeat the same message, although they do not repeat each other word for word (52, 56, 65, 69).
6. Spencer W. Kimball, "The False Gods We Worship," *Ensign* (June 1976).
7. Kimball, "The False Gods We Worship," *Ensign* (June 1976).

9

TOBIT

BACKGROUND

LIKE MANY BOOKS OF THE APOCRYPHA, THE ORIGINS OF THE BOOK of Tobit are somewhat unclear. The book was believed to have originated as a Hebrew or Aramaic text. However, before the mid-twentieth century, scholars could only speculate on the original form of the story, since the earliest copies available were Greek or Latin translations. When fragments of Tobit in both Hebrew (4Q200) and Aramaic (4Q196–199) were discovered among the Dead Sea Scrolls, they confirmed that the book was initially a Semitic text that was later translated into various other tongues.[1] In fact, Jerome remarked "that he produced his Latin version from an Aramaic text that a Jew translated into Hebrew for him."[2]

Also unclear are the circumstances in which the book was written. The discovery of Tobit fragments among the Dead Sea Scrolls definitively confirms that the book was written before the first century BC, and since no mention is made of the Seleucid persecution of the Jews (detailed in 1–2 Maccabees), it suggests that it was written before 165 BC. Many scholars agree on a dating of roughly 200 BC.[3] However, there is far less consensus as to *where* the book was written. Various elements within the book serve to both suggest and contradict all potential candidates.[4] The concerns reflected in the story are those of a Jew striving to follow God in the midst of difficulties and opposition to his faith, even if some of the emphases (like burying the dead) are not central to the Old Testament.

The book of Tobit is a delightful tale that weaves together romance, trials, and miracles. It is set in the Assyrian Empire where Jews were living in exile.[5] The main character, Tobit, is devout and, despite living in a foreign land, observes all the commandments and customs of his Jewish religion. His penchant for strict observance lands him in trouble and creates some of the crises that must be overcome in the story. Yet even with these challenges, it is always clear (especially with the narrator's overt foreshadowing) that Tobit will come out on top in the end. For this reason, many interpreters of Tobit see the story following the structure of comedy—not that it is necessarily laugh-out-loud humorous, but that its plot follows the typical comic plot outline, where characters face an initial problem but are gently and easily led through it by a series of fortunate events.[6] As such, the tale both entertains and encourages hope and faithfulness in an exilic setting: it teaches that God will still care for and watch over his children in foreign lands if they remain loyal to him.[7]

The book of Tobit opens with a description about Tobit's earlier faithfulness despite living in the northern Kingdom of Israel as a member of the tribe of Naphtali.[8] Other members of his tribe sacrificed to the golden calf erected by King Jeroboam,[9] but Tobit refused and instead went often to Jerusalem unaccompanied to observe the requisite festivals (1:5–6). He always brought his tithes and offerings to the temple in Jerusalem and distributed additional donations to the orphans, widows, and converts (1:8). Even after being carried away into exile and living in Nineveh, Tobit remained faithful and always followed the kosher food laws (1:10–12).[10] While in Nineveh, Tobit became fixated on ensuring the proper burial of the Jewish dead, of which there were apparently many due to Assyrian persecution and punishment.[11] This custom landed Tobit in trouble with the authorities, who felt these corpses did not deserve a proper burial. When Tobit realized the authorities knew he was responsible for secretly carrying away these bodies for proper burial and that they wanted to kill him, he ran away (1:19). All of Tobit's property was confiscated and the only thing left was his family: his wife, Anna, and his son, Tobias. When the ruler Sennacherib was killed shortly thereafter, and with the aid of his nephew, who served as a government official, Tobit returned home to his family (2:1).[12]

Despite Tobit's close call with death and separation from family, he could not abandon his practice of properly burying his dead brethren. When he heard about another Jewish corpse lying in the marketplace, Tobit retrieved the body and waited until after sunset to bury it (2:7). After ceremonially washing himself (because he had touched a corpse), Tobit went into his courtyard and slept by a wall[13] where, unbeknownst to him, sparrows roosted. Sometime during the night, fresh droppings from the sparrows fell into his eyes and blinded him (2:10): quite a comic way for someone to become blind! Tobit's blindness made work problematic and led to financial difficulties for his family, resulting in a heartfelt petition to God (3:1–6).[14] Tobit's prayer acknowledged his own sins and the sins of his ancestors that resulted in God's punishment: exile from the land of Israel. Tobit ended his prayer with an invitation to the Lord to take his spirit away so he could be released from the trials and insults of this life.

The narrative leaves Tobit in this precarious position and shifts perspective to a sub-tale about some of Tobit's distant relatives, whose story will become interwoven with Tobit's. Sarah, daughter of Raguel (Tobit's relative), prayed to God to help her in her dire situation. She had been married to seven husbands, but every wedding night before the consummation of her marriages, the wicked demon Asmodeus[15] killed each of her husbands. Some began blaming Sarah for her husbands' deaths,[16] so she retired to her room ready to hang herself and end her suffering; but after thinking about what effect that would have on her father,[17] she turned to God instead. Like in Tobit's prayer, she asked to be released from this life so she would not be tormented by further reproaches.

At this point of the story, the narrator interjects blatant fore-shadowing. He states that God has heard the prayers of both Sarah and Tobit and he will send an angel, Raphael,[18] to heal them both: Tobit from his blindness and Sarah from the demon Asmodeus.

The story then shifts back to Tobit as he remembers that he has left ten talents of silver, a considerable sum of money, with a relative where they used to live in Media (modern Iran).[19] He begins to give a final testament and blessing to his son Tobias and counsels him to seek wisdom (common in other wisdom texts in the Apocrypha, such as the Wisdom of Solomon and the sayings of Jesus ben Sirach), take care of the poor, and retrieve this stashed money that would serve as an inheritance. Tobit also commanded Tobias to not marry a foreign woman, but to find a wife from among the House of Israel (4:12).[20] Tobias shared his willingness to do what his father had asked, but he did not know how to proceed since he had never been to Media nor met these distant relatives. Tobit reassured him that his relative would give him the money, but perhaps he should seek out a man to accompany and guide him to Media.

Tobias began his search for someone to guide him to Media. Immediately he came into contact with Raphael, but he did not know he was an angel. Raphael initially introduced himself as Azariah (the same Hebrew name as one of Daniel's friends who was thrown in the furnace, known usually by his Babylonian name Abed-nego) and stated that he knew the way to Media, having been there many times. Tobias got excited and rushed in to tell his father that he had found an Israelite who knew the way to Media. Tobit requested that Raphael be brought in so he could meet him. As they talked, Tobit shared his woes and interviewed Raphael to find out more about his background. There is great situational irony in this part of the story because the reader knows exactly who Raphael is while the characters in the story do not. That irony increases when Tobit tells his son, "May God in heaven bring you safely there and return you in good health to me; and *may his angel*, my son, accompany you both for your safety" (5:17; emphasis added). Tobit also tells his wife, who is greatly concerned for her son's safety on the journey, "Do not fear for them, my sister. For a *good angel* will accompany him; his journey will be successful" (5:21–22; emphasis added).[21]

Tobias and Raphael begin their journey and arrive at their first campsite for the night. When Tobias goes into the Tigris River to wash his feet, a large fish leaps out to swallow his foot.[22] Tobias cries out and Raphael tells him to catch the fish.[23] Tobias catches the fish and Raphael instructs him to "cut open the fish and take out its gall, heart, and liver. Keep them with you, but throw away the intestines" (6:5). These fish parts prove important later in the story, and are explained to Tobias when they continue on their journey. "As for the fish's heart and liver, you must burn them to make a smoke in the presence of a man or woman afflicted by a demon or evil spirit, and every affliction will flee away and never remain with that person. And as for the gall, anoint a person's eyes where white films have appeared on them; blow upon them, upon the white films, and the eyes will be healed" (6:8–9).

When the pair approach Ecbatana, Raphael suggests they stay with Raguel, Tobias's relative. Raphael then explains Sarah's tragic marital situation and tells Tobias that he has a hereditary claim on her as a kinsman. "Moreover, the girl is sensible, brave, and very beautiful, and her father is a good man" (6:12). Raphael next states that they will arrange the marriage that night. Tobias had already heard about the fate of Sarah's first seven husbands, so naturally he expresses grave concern about Raphael's proposal. Here's where the fish liver and heart come in handy. Raphael explains, "When you enter the bridal chamber, take some of the fish's liver and heart, and put them on the embers of the incense. An odor will be given off; the demon will smell it and flee, and will never be seen near her any more" (6:17–18). Raphael also suggests that they implore the Lord of heaven for mercy and safety. He counsels, "Do not be afraid, for she was set apart for you before the world was made" (5:18): an interesting concept for those from an LDS perspective, who believe in a premortal life of the spirit and foreordination.[24] Upon hearing Raphael's words, Tobias "loved her [Sarah] very much, and his heart was drawn to her" (6:18).[25]

As soon as the travelers arrive in Ecbatana, Tobias wants to go to his relative's house. Immediately Raguel comments to his wife how much the young man (Tobias) looks like his kinsman Tobit. Upon questioning Tobias, Raguel and his wife learn of his identity and connection to Tobit and jump up and kiss him and weep. A banquet is prepared and soon discussion turns to marriage. Although Raguel wants to delay the marriage until at least the next day, Tobias insists and Sarah is given to Tobias in marriage. A marriage contract is even written up, and then they begin to eat and drink. Sarah's mother prepares the bridal chamber and encourages her daughter through tears, "Take courage, my daughter; the Lord of heaven grant you joy in place of your sorrow. Take courage, my daughter" (7:16).

When the couple arrives at the bridal chamber, Tobias remembers Raphael's words and burns the fish's liver and heart. "The odor of the fish so repelled the demon that he fled to the remotest parts of Egypt.[26] But Raphael followed him, and at once bound him there hand and foot" (8:3). Tobias and Sarah also pray to the Lord for mercy and safety. In his prayer, Tobias emphasizes God's statement that "it is not good that the man should be alone" and petitions, "I now am taking this kinswoman of mine, not because of lust, but with sincerity. Grant that she and I may find mercy and that we may grow old together" (8:7).[27]

Meanwhile, Raguel is understandably concerned whether Tobias will survive the night. He summons his servants and asks them to dig a grave[28] so that if necessary Tobias can be buried without anyone finding out, which would lead to more ridicule and derision. When the grave is finished, Raguel suggests his wife send in one of the maids to check and see if Tobias is still alive. When she discovers that Tobias is still alive, they praise God and fill in the grave before daybreak. They rejoice that God has showed compassion on these "two only children," both of whom have shown earlier concern that if they died they would leave their parents without anyone to care for them. A fourteen-day celebration ensues (double the usual length of a wedding feast)[29] and Raguel promises Tobias half his estate now and the other half when Raguel and his wife die.

While the wedding feast goes on, Tobias sends Raphael to retrieve the money from the relative so that they can return as soon as possible to Tobit, since he would be counting the days that Tobias was gone. Raphael travels the rest of the way, retrieves the money, and brings the relative back to the wedding feast. Back in Nineveh, Tobit has been counting the days and realizes that it is taking longer than it should. He begins to worry that his relative has died so Tobias will not be able to retrieve the money, while his wife fears something even worse: the death of her son.[30]

When the fourteen days of the wedding feast are completed, Tobias asks Raguel for permission to return with Sarah to his parents because he knows his parents are worried. At first Raguel tries to extend Tobias's stay with the promise of sending a messenger to inform Tobias's parents that everything is okay, but upon Tobias's insistence he relents and "gave Tobias his wife Sarah, as well as half of all his property" (10:10). After embracing Tobias, Raguel blesses them to have a safe journey, prosperity, and children. He also counsels his daughter to honor her in-laws, and Sarah's mother gives final counsel and admonition to Tobias.

Tobias, Sarah, and Raphael next make the return trip to Nineveh. Tobias's mother, who has been intently watching the road each day, immediately recognizes them and runs to her son and embraces him, saying, "Now that I have seen you, my child, I am ready to die" (11:9). Tobit also comes, stumbling out the courtyard door because of his blindness. Without delay, Tobias takes some of the fish gall and applies it to his father's eyes. Tobias then peels away the white films from his father's eyes and restores Tobit's vision.[31] Tobit rejoices and praises God. Tobias then recounts the successes of their journey and his parents meet their new daughter-in-law. A seven-day wedding feast follows.

After the wedding feast, Tobit and Tobias prepare to pay Raphael for his services in accompanying and guiding Tobias along his journey. Since Raphael has gone beyond the normal call of duty by helping heal Sarah and Tobit, they decide to give him half of what was brought back with them. When they make that offer to Raphael, he finally reveals his true identity and gives to them words of wisdom. "I am Raphael, one of the seven angels[32] who stand ready and enter before the glory of the Lord" (12:15). Raphael acknowledges that it was he who brought and read the prayers of Tobit and Sarah "before the glory of the Lord, and likewise whenever you would bury the dead" (12:12). He was sent to test them as well as to heal them.[33] He also discloses that as an angel he did not really eat or drink anything, but it only seemed that way (it was a vision or like a mirage).[34] He calms their fear they suddenly feel in the presence of an angel, exhorts them to write down the things that have happened to them, and then ascends to heaven.[35]

The last two chapters are lengthy monologues from Tobit.[36] Chapter 13 is a long psalm or hymn of praise to God for his greatness, for all that he has done in the past for the House of Israel, and for how he had specifically blessed Tobit and his family. Tobit testifies that he is a God of both justice and mercy, stating that "if you turn to him with all your heart and with all your soul, to do what is true before him, then he will turn to you and will no longer hide his face from you" (13:6). Tobit also lauds the holy city of Jerusalem, which has been afflicted because of its inhabitants' wickedness, but which will attract inhabitants from the remotest parts of the earth. "Generation after generation will give joyful praise in you; the name of the chosen city will endure forever" (13:11). It is also prophesied that Jerusalem will be built up with gold and precious stones and "the gates of Jerusalem will sing hymns of joy, and all her houses will cry, 'Hallelujah! Blessed be the God of Israel!'" (13:17).

Chapter 14 recounts Tobit's death at the age of 112, but before he dies he gives his final counsel to Tobias and Tobias's sons. He warns them to flee Nineveh because it is going to be destroyed (it was destroyed by an alliance of Babylonians and Medes in 612 BC). Tobit reiterates the truthfulness of the warnings and prophecies of the prophets, "For I know and believe that whatever God has said will be fulfilled and will come true; not a single word of the prophecies will fail" (14:4).[37] Among those prophecies are the warnings of the scattering of the House of Israel and the eventual gathering and restoration of the people. All the nations will be converted to worship the true God.[38] Tobit encourages his posterity to live good, faithful lives, and he especially emphasizes the blessings that come through almsgiving and the punishments that come through injustice. Tobit receives an honorable funeral and burial; then later his wife was buried next to him. The story ends with Tobias leaving Nineveh, returning to his in-laws in Ecbatana, treating them with great respect, burying them upon their deaths, and then dying himself at the age of 117. Before he dies, "he blessed the Lord God forever and ever" and hears about the destruction of Nineveh as had been prophesied (14:15).

LEGACY

Despite its charm and apparent popularity among ancient Jews, the book of Tobit was eventually excluded from the collection of authoritative Jewish texts. While many factors likely contributed to this exclusion, its late date of composition and its antiquated views on marriage contracts were likely rationales for Jewish rejection.[39] Thus, the transmission of Tobit through the ages was left to Christians, who received a Greek version of the text along with the other scriptures of the Septuagint. Although some theologians had reservations about the book, Tobit was largely popular among Christians throughout history. It is cited in many ancient Christian works[40] and was repeatedly affirmed as canonical in many (though not all) early Christian councils. The high esteem many Christians had for Tobit helps explain why Church leaders insisted that Jerome (who did not consider Tobit to be scripture) includes the book in his translation of the Latin Vulgate.[41] The story has inspired many works of art throughout Christian Europe, including a series of paintings done by Rembrandt. It has also been an influence on weddings and marriage in many Christian groups: Tobias and Sarah's marriage was often held up as an example of a godly union.[42]

While most Protestants do not consider the book of Tobit to be scripture, it was often included with other apocryphal books in Protestant bibles, and Protestants have often valued Tobit as edifying literature. Even Martin Luther, who could often be harsh in his condemnation of 'questionable' scripture, gave a glowing review of Tobit in his introduction to the work:

> What was said about the book of Judith may also be said about this book of Tobit. If the events really happened, then it is a fine and holy history. But if they are all made up, then it is indeed a very beautiful, wholesome, and useful fiction or drama by a gifted poet. It may even be assumed that beautiful compositions and plays like this were common among the Jews. On their festivals and Sabbaths they steeped themselves in them; and through them, especially in times of peace and good government, they liked to instill God's Word and work into their young people . . . Therefore this book is useful and good for us Christians to read. It is the work of a fine Hebrew author who deals not with trivial but important issues, and whose writing and concerns are extraordinarily Christian.[43]

Conclusion

The book of Tobit's delightful tale brought pleasure and hope to ancient Jewish readers in exilic settings. Although the main characters suffered many challenges, they were watched over by heaven and sent angelic aid. The ubiquitous presence of angels in later Jewish texts may be a reflection of a changing Jewish conception of God, whom they considered more distant because of the punishments inflicted upon them, most notably their expulsion from the covenant land. Thus, angels were sent as intermediaries to bless the lives of the righteous.

Besides the narrative value of a good story, the book of Tobit's wisdom and praise of God is applicable to any age. It demonstrates that one can and should follow God even, or especially, in the midst of difficulties and opposition to one's faith. Trials are not reserved for only the wicked but, as demonstrated in this story, come to the righteous as well. Yet, the enduring message is that one is not alone in facing those trials—God is watching out for us even when we might be unaware. One way God often helps his covenant people is through the ministration of angels. The LDS concept of angels shares some similarities with the book of Tobit in that there are chief angels who have responsibilities and stewardships over mortals here on earth. There is also the notion that "guardian angels" can assist us in our trials. Elder Jeffrey R. Holland gave a masterful address on this topic in the October 2008 General Conference.[44] He taught that God will send angels in times of need "to bless his children, reassure them that heaven was always very close and that His help was always very near. . . . Usually such beings are *not* seen. Sometimes they are. But seen or unseen they are *always* near. Sometimes their assignments are very grand and have significance for the whole world. Sometimes the messages are more private. . . . I testify that angels are *still* sent to help *us*, even as they were sent to help Adam and Eve, to help the prophets, and indeed to help the Savior of the world Himself."

For an LDS audience, the last two chapters are also interesting because they recount many similar prophecies and understandings of God's plan and work with the House of Israel throughout history. Although the House of Israel will be scattered and forced to live away from the covenant land, God will not forsake them but will eventually gather them and bring them back to his holy city of Jerusalem.

NOTES

1. While some scholars believe that the Hebrew version of the text is the original, most believe that the story originated in Aramaic. For a thorough discussion of the pertinent issues in the debate, see Joseph A Fitzmyer, *Tobit* (Berlin: Walter de Gruyter, 2003), 19–28. Arguments that the text originated in Greek are no longer considered persuasive by the vast majority of scholars.
2. From Alison Salvesen, "The Growth of the Apocrypha," in *The Oxford Handbook of Biblical Studies*, ed. J.W. Rogerson and Judith M. Lieu (Oxford: Oxford University Press, 2006), 495.
3. Fitzmeyer, *Tobit*, 51–52.
4. In surveying noted commentators on Tobit, David deSilva touches on many of the key issues: "Pfeiffer favors Palestine, having ruled out the eastern Diaspora on account of the book's gross geographical errors where that part of the world is concerned, having ruled out Egypt on account of the book having been written in Aramaic, and having underscored the fact that Tobit and Ben Sira share a common set of values. A more judicious opinion is ventured by Moore, who acknowledges that one cannot be certain even whether the work originates from the Diaspora as opposed to Palestine, although, if pressed, he would opt for an eastern Diaspora setting. The book's interest in exilic life, with only dim recollections of the land of Israel, could suggest an origin beyond Palestine; the fact that five copies of Tobit were found at Qumran suggests, however, that its message was equally appropriate in Israel and may well have originated there. Tobit reflects Jewish values so broadly and addresses the challenges of living as a Jew at such a basic level, that it

is indeed difficult to determine its geographical setting from hints in the narrative." deSilva, *Introducing the Apocrypha*, 68–69.

5. While some in the past have argued in favor of the historicity of Tobit, it is widely recognized today as a work of historical fiction. In addition to the folkloric tone of the story, "historical errors throughout the book also point away from the genre of 'history' . . . Tobit, being of the tribe of Naphtali, would more likely have been deported earlier, with the rest of his tribe, when Tiglath-pileser took that region (2 Kings 15:29); Tobit could not have been a young man when the northern tribes seceded from the kingdom in 922 BCE [BC] (see Tob 1:4) *and* alive when at the time of their deportation under Tiglath-pileser (sometime between 740 and 731 BCE [BC]); Sargon II, not Shalmaneser, was the father of Sennacherib." David A. deSilva, *The Jewish Teachers of Jesus, James, and Jude: What Earliest Christianity Learned from the Apocrypha and Pseudepigrapha* (New York: Oxford University Press, 2012), 277 n.11.

6. Some refer to comic plot lines as "U-shaped." The character begins at a certain level but then descends into a problem or trial, but then ascends back to the same level as the beginning when the problem is resolved. All along the assumption is they will not remain in their dire straits (unlike a tragedy that usually leaves a character with an unresolved problem or trial).

7. For a discussion of humor within Tobit, see Erich S. Gruen, *Diaspora. Jews amidst Greeks and Romans* (Cambridge and London: Harvard University Press, 2002), 148–158. Others have also seen in Tobit the elements of a biblical romance. "A common form of the romance is the successful quest, which falls into three main stages: the dangerous journey, the mortal struggle, and the exaltation of the hero. The hero may embark on the journey for several reasons—e.g., to rescue a bride from a dangerous situation or to obtain hidden treasure. Frequently the journey involves a dragon-killing theme . . . [The hero] is human, not divine, but extraordinary events happen in his favor . . . At the successful completion of the quest, a 'new society' may form around the hero and heroine. This new society is often inaugurated by a festive ritual, such as a wedding or banquet." Irene Nowell, *The Book of Tobit* (NIB III; Nashville: Abingdon Press, 1999), 1026. See also Carey A. Moore, *Tobit* (Anchor Bible 40a; Garden City: Doubleday, 1996), 18–21.

8. Interestingly, this initial description is given in the first person by Tobit himself. Such first-person narratives are uncommon among ancient texts, and Tobit's direct speech provides a brief parallel to the first-person portions of the Book of Mormon written by Nephi, Jacob, Mormon, and Moroni.

9.   "The apostasy of Jeroboam I is recounted in 1 Kgs 12:19–20, 25–33: Lest the people would turn to 'the house of David,' go to Jerusalem to offer their sacrifices, and give their allegiance to Rehoboam, king of Judah, Jeroboam, son of Nebat, king of Israel (the northern kingdom), made 'two calves of gold' and set them up, one in Bethel and one in Dan, and persuaded the people to sacrifice there instead of at Jerusalem. The calf was probably intended as a base for Yahweh's throne, but it soon came to be an object of worship in itself. In reality, however, it was a political move on Jeroboam's part to undercut the influence of Rehoboam." Fitzmyer, *Tobit*, 106.

10. It is evident from this description of Tobit's religious piety that he— and, we may assume, the author of the book—cares deeply about the mandates of Jewish law, particularly those found in Deuteronomy. "Tobit is a model of Deuteronomic piety. He rejected worship at Jeroboam's cult shrine of Bethel (see 1 Kings 12:25–33) in favor of continuing to worship at the Jerusalem Temple, the sole place designated by God for offering sacrifices (Tob 1:4–6; 14:5–7; Deut 12:1–14). He observes the laws for tithing meticulously (Tob 1:6–8) and scrupulously observes the dietary regulations of Torah (Tob 1:10–11)." deSilva, *The Jewish Teachers*, 92.

11. The topics of death and burial permeate every part of the book of Tobit, and for good reason: Jews living at the time that Tobit was written were extremely concerned with these concerns. "To bury someone is *the* most important 'charitable act' in Tobit (vv 18–20; 2:3–8; 4:3–4; 6:15; 14:10–13), as well as in later rabbinic Judaism. According to *Megillah* 3b, burying the dead took precedence over studying Torah, having one's son circumcised, or preparing the paschal lamb. This emphasis on it in Tobit is an excellent example of how well-known laws and customs of the first and second centuries C.E. [AD] were sometimes also practiced in the Second Temple period. . . . For an Israelite to remain unburied and so become food for animals and birds of prey was the ultimate insult to the deceased (cf. Deut 28:26; 1 Kgs 14:11; 21:24; Jer 7:33; Ezek 29:5). Even the condemned criminal (Deut 21:23) and the enemy killed in battle (Ezek 39:11–16) should be buried. Probably compassion and certainly hygienic concerns lay behind such charitable practices." Moore, *Tobit*, 120.

12. This well-placed nephew, named Ahikar, is known in other ancient literature (such as the Elephantine papyri) as a legendary Assyrian sage. Scholars offer different theories why Ahikar has been inserted into the Tobit story; one researcher points out that "the wisdom teaching in the book of Tobit has a certain affinity to the teaching of Ahikar, also as far as the two central themes (proper burial and almsgiving) are concerned. And the ups and downs of Tobit correspond to Ahikar's chequered

career. The Ahikar tradition was so well known among the Jews in the East that it was a natural thing for the author of the book of Tobit to allude to it, and he could be sure that his reader would understand it. Thus 'the Ahiqar tale served as a foil for both the Tobit narrative and its didactic purpose.'" Benedikt Otzen, *Tobit and Judith* (London: Sheffield Academic Press, 2002), 25.

13. Ever the observant Jew, Tobit follows ritual purity laws after touching the dead body of the fellow Jew: he ritually washes himself and then, to avoid contaminating his home during the period of his uncleanness, he sleeps in his courtyard. (See Numbers 19:11–22.)

14. Bruce Metzger notes that Tobit makes "frequent reference to heartfelt prayer to God, which hallows the whole conduct of life (4:19, 6:17, 8:5–8, etc.). Particularly instructive is the care which the author obviously took with the form and contents of Tobit's (3:1–6) and Sarah's (3:11–15) prayers. Each begins with an invocation and an act of adoration, followed by the specific supplication and a lengthy retrospective explanation. Since the same structural arrangement also characterizes Tobias's prayer (8:5–7), it is likely that such was the typical form in which Jewish prayers were cast in the author's day." Metzger, *The Apocrypha*, 39.

15. The name *Asmodeus* does not have easily identifiable Hebrew or Aramaic roots. "The name is usually explained as Old Persian or Avestan, equaling *aesma daeva*, "demon of wrath," an associate of Ahriman, the god of evil, known from Avestan literature." Fitzmyer, *Tobit*, 150.

16. Rumor against Sarah reaches the point that even a servant girl makes accusations to Sarah's face: "You are the one who kills [or strangles] your husbands! See, you have already been married to seven husbands and have not borne the name of a single one of them. Why do you beat us? Because your husbands are dead? Go with them! May we never see a son or daughter of yours!" (3:8–9).

17. In addition to the natural parental grief her father would feel at her death, Sarah feared the social scorn her father would encounter should she commit suicide. "[Others would say], in effect, 'With only one child to look after, you should have been able to have taken better care of her!' Then too, the death of an only child, especially a son, was doubly tragic (cf. Tob 5:18; Jer 6:26; Amos 8:10; Zech 12:10), for in such a child had rested 'the hope and continuation of the family.'" Moore, *Tobit*, 149.

18. The angel Raphael is not mentioned in the Hebrew Bible. "'Raphael' appeared earlier as the name of one of the ancestors of Tobit. Now it is used as the name of the angel whose mission bears out its meaning, "God has healed," and there is clearly a play on his name. He is sent as a superhuman being to cure Tobit's blindness and to offset the effect of the evil demon Asmodeus on Sarah . . . In *1 Enoch* 40:9 Raphael is listed

among four special angels and is the one 'in charge of all diseases and all the wounds of the sons of men.'" Fitzmyer, *Tobit*, 160–61.

19. It is noteworthy that Tobit remembers this hidden reserve of money immediately after he finishes his prayer to God: as George Nickelsburg puts it, it is as if "God has jogged his memory" and set in motion the events that will answer both of the righteous prayers he has just received. See Moore, *Tobit*, 163.

20. Compare this to Abraham, who was insistent that Isaac not marry a Canaanite and sent his servant to find a suitable wife among his kinsmen (Gen 24). "Endogamy is an important issue in the book of Tobit, and the reason is obvious: in the exilic situation it is urgent that marriages are arranged within Jewish families, lest the Jews by marrying foreigners should disappear into heathen society." Otzen, *Tobit and Judith*, 37.

21. One of the most valuable ways in which the book of Tobit sheds light on Hellenistic Judaism is in its contributions of modern understanding of Jewish angelology and demonology. "It is chiefly with reference to angels and demons that the book of Tobit takes its place as a valuable source of our knowledge of the development of this doctrine. As is well known, the Old Testament has relatively little to say about angels, and even less about demons. On the other hand, in the New Testament the presence and activity of both angels and demons are everywhere taken for granted. The contrast between the two Testaments is less sharp when one takes into account the intertestamental literature written during and just after the Exile in Babylonia and Persia, where the Old Testament rudiments of these beliefs were expanded in many directions. The book of Tobit reflects the legitimate development of this subject." Metzger, *Introduction to the Apocrypha*, 38.

22. In one version of the text, the fish attempts to eat Tobias whole—a large fish, indeed! Such an exaggeration makes the fish (and Tobias's triumph over it) a symbol of encountering and overcoming death: a theme which will repeat itself as Tobias faces potential death in Sarah's bridal chamber. See Nowell, *The Book of Tobit*, 1029.

23. "In medieval iconography, Tobiah's overcoming the fish foreshadows Christ's defeat of Satan." Moore, *Tobit*, 200.

24. Such a declaration of foreordained wedlock is rare for biblical scripture. "The idea of a marriage determined aforetime by heaven is expressed nowhere else in the OT so clearly as here. The marriage of Rebekah to Isaac is recounted in a less pronounced form of that idea in Gen 24:14, where the slave sent by Abraham to the city of Nahor to get a bride for his son Isaac prays that the Lord will 'appoint' the maiden who comes to draw water as the wife to be. The bond of marriage is understood as instituted by God (Gen 2:24). See also 24:44, 'let her

be the woman whom the Lord has appointed for my master's son.'" Fitzmyer, *Tobit*, 218.

25. "Having heard all of the angel's words, Tobiah immediately falls in love with Sarah—a strange concept to our modern ears. Tobiah loves her because she has been designated by God for him and because she is the means for his obedience to his father. Tobiah's love is an act of the will, not a movement of the emotions." Nowell, *The Book of Tobit*, 1031.

26. "Egypt was the traditional home of magic and witchcraft (see Exodus 7:11). The notion that foul odors would drive away demons was common in the ancient world. Josephus reports that a certain Jewish exorcist named Eleasar drove demons out of people by holding a ring in which an aromatic herb was embedded to the nose of the one afflicted. The practice, which comes from the tradition of folk medicine, is magical. In the book of Tobit, however, the magical nature is muted; it is recommended by an angel along with prayer as only one part of a complicated remedy." Nowell, *The Book of Tobit*, 1040.

27. The Latin rendition of this story gives a differing account of how events proceeded on Tobias's and Sarah's wedding night. Tobit 8:4–5 in the Vulgate read as follows: "Then Tobiah exhorted the maiden and said to her, 'Sarah, arise and let us pray to God today and tomorrow, and the next day because for these three nights we are joined to God. And when the third night is over, we shall be in our own wedlock. For we are the children of saints, and we must not be joined together like the heathen who do not know God.'" In other words, Tobias (at Raphael's direction) postpones the consummation of his wedding until after three days of fasting. This passage is unique to the Vulgate (and those translations which are based on it), and most scholars believe that it was an insertion made by Jerome during his rapid translation of the book. Regardless of its origins or authenticity, the passage inspired some Christians during the Middle Ages to delay marital intimacy for three days after their wedding. For an examination of the subject, see Moore, *Tobit*, 242–244.

28. "One of the frequently occurring Greek verbs in the book of Tobit is *thapto*, 'to bury': it is found 17 times. Correspondingly the noun *taphos*, 'grave', occurs six times. Moore has produced statistics: death and burial are referred to in 22 per cent of the verses of the book of Tobit—53 out of 244 verses. Thus it is not too much to say that burial is a central theme in the book." Otzen, *Tobit and Judith*, 42. This reference to burial is a turning point in the story: instead of Tobit's furtive burials of fellow Israelites which brought him such grief, this failed burial will lead to a positive end to Tobit's story.

29. "The 'fourteen days' stand in contrast to the 'seven days' mentioned by [a later textual variant] in 11:19, which was the normal length of an ancient

— 123 —

Jewish marriage celebration, as in Gen 29:27; Judg 14:12–18. The double of the seven days emphasizes the importance of this marriage. Part of the reason for the length of time is the desire of the parents to see to the joy of the daughter who will be departing from them. Compare the length of time ('at least ten days') that the relatives of Rebecca insist on keeping Abraham's servant with them in Gen 24:55–56." Fitzmyer, *Tobit*, 251.

30. Recall 1 Nephi 5:1–9, where Sariah complains against Lehi for sending her sons back to Jerusalem and mourns their supposed death. Anna, like Sariah, later gives thanks to God at the safe and successful return of her progeny.

31. "The verb [*apelepisen*], 'peeled off,' is related to the noun used in Acts 9:18 for the 'films' that fell from Paul's eyes, a primitive way of explaining the cause of blindness. See Tob 2:11 . . . Cf. Pliny the Elder, *Nat. hist.* 29.8.21, who also uses a similar mode of explaining eye afflictions: . . . 'that a film in the eyes should be moved away and not pulled off.'" Fitzmyer, *Tobit*, 279.

32. "When he finally reveals himself to the hero, [Raphael] describes himself as 'one of the seven angels' (Tobit 12:15). This same number crops up again in sections of *1 Enoch*. In the section known as the 'Book of the Watchers,' Enoch learns that there are seven chief angels, each with his own area of specialization (*1 Enoch* 10). The Jews typically considered seven to be the number of completion or perfection, and that notion probably inspired the idea of seven archangels. But it's also possible that the authors of *1 Enoch* and Tobit were both inspired by Ezekiel 9, where seven angels carry out the judgment of Jerusalem." Tomasino, *Judiasm Before Jesus*, 79.

33. "Raphael's statements concerning healing and testing provide a necessary caution concerning the theory of retribution [a Deuteronomic theme present throughout Tobit]. In this theory, the good are rewarded, and the wicked are punished. But Raphael says that he was sent to put Tobit to the test precisely because of his good deed of burying the dead. It seems that doing good results in suffering rather than in blessing. But 'at the same time', he is also sent to heal Tobit and Sarah. Suffering and healing come simultaneously from God. This ambiguity is a major part of the book's message. Only from God's perspective can blessing and suffering be understood." Nowell, *The Book of Tobit*, 1056.

34. "In the thinking of the day, angels neither ate nor drank (but see Gen 19:3, where Lot's angelic guests did!). For example, in the *Test. of Abraham* the archangel Michael reminds God: 'Lord all the heavenly spirits are incorporeal, and they neither eat nor drink. Now [Abraham] has set before me a table with abundance of all the good things which are earthly and perishable. And now, Lord, what shall I do? How shall I

escape his notice while I am sitting at one table with him?' The Lord said, 'Go down to him, and do not be concerned about this. For when you are seated with him I shall send upon you an all-devouring spirit, and, from your hands and through your mouth, it will consume everything which is on the table. Make merry with him in everything.'" Moore, *Tobit*, 273. Contrast this with the instances in which the resurrected Jesus ate with his disciples to show them that he was *not* a spirit (see Luke 24:36–43; John 21:12–14).

35. God and his angels frequently instruct mortals to write things down; numerous instances can be found throughout the Bible, the Book of Mormon, and Doctrine and Covenants. While some revelations mention these records as witnesses to be used against wrongdoers in the Day of Judgment (see 2 Nephi 22:10–15), they can also serve as reminders of God's grace and mercy towards men (see Moroni 10:3). The story of Tobit can stand as a reminder of God's watchful care over his people.

36. Chapters 13 and 14 are markedly different from the rest of the book—a shift often noted by commentators. "Critics have often thought that the two final chapters represent an addition to the book: Tobit and his family are nearly forgotten, and Israel and Jerusalem are brought into the foreground; the overall view of these chapters is eschatological, and they are totally dependent upon Old Testament texts . . . But if Tobit 13–14 is left out, the book of Tobit is deprived of an important theological dimension. The book is not just an innocent tale about the exciting experiences of the Tobit family, it is a book that on a high artistic and theological level takes up the existential problem of the exile, and in a most sophisticated way helps the Jews in the eastern Diaspora to survive and not give up the hope of return." Otzen, *Tobit and Judith*, 45.

37. "Tobit's final psalm and testament contain the book's eschatology. The first part of the testament's predictions (14:4–5a) is largely 'prediction after the fact,' since the author writes in the late third or early second century B.C.E. [BC]. The statement about the inevitability of the fall of Nineveh reveals a specific doctrine of prophecy: 'Everything that was spoken by the prophets of Israel, whom God sent, will occur. None of all their words will fail, but will come true at their appointed times' (14:4). Thus, Nahum's oracles (especially Nah. 1:1; 2:13–3:19) against Nineveh must become reality, and Tobias and Sarah plan for their future accordingly. This is a conviction shared by the early Christians, as they read their own past, present, and future history from those same oracles of God. Indeed, the claims of 14:4 and 8 are vindicated in the world of the narrative, which does not close with the death of

Tobit but with the fall of Nineveh in 14:15." deSilva, *Introducing the Apocrypha*, 81.

38. Some scholars have noted that Tobit's prophecies about the conversion of Gentiles to the Lord are similar to Jesus's proclamations in the New Testament that "many shall come from the east and west, and shall sit down with Abraham, and Isaac, and Jacob, in the kingdom of heaven" (Matt 8:11). Both also state that membership in the house of Israel is not a guarantee of safety: Tobit notes that "all the Israelites who are saved in those days and are truly mindful of God will be gathered together . . . but those who commit sin and injustice will vanish from all the earth" (Tob 14:6–7). "What is striking in regard to the relationship of Tobit to the Jesus saying is that, in both, there is a similar relativizing of Jewish ethnic privilege and prioritizing of obedient response to God as prerequisite to entering the kingdom of God, though Jesus, as is typical, presents this in a far more radical and confrontational manner." deSilva, *The Jewish Teachers*, 100.

39. "In the case of Tobit, Orlinksy has argued that the culprit was Tob 7:11–15, which has Raguel (i.e., the father of the bride) writing out the marriage agreement. This contradicted the later halakhic view of that great lay Pharisee of the first century B.C.E., Simon ben Shetah, who insisted that the marriage document (*ketubah*) be written by the *bridegroom* (*Shabb.* 14b)." Moore, *Tobit*, 51.

40. "Tobit is quoted in *Didache* 112 (ca.100) and was used by such apostolic fathers as Clement of Rome (30?–?99) in *2 Clement* 16.4 (cf. Tobit 12:8–9) and Polycarp (135) in his *Epistola* 10:2 (cf. Tobit 4:10; 12:29). Irenaeus of Lyons (170–235 [cf. 1:30, 11]) reports that the Ophites included Tobias among the prophets of the Old Testament. Clement of Alexandria (150?–?215) mentions the story of Tobit and his son in *Stromata*, i, 21, 123; ii, 23, 139; vi, 12, 102) as does Origen (185?–?254) in *Epistola ad Africanum* 13 and Cyprian of Carthage (d. 258) in *Testimonia* iii, 1, 6, 62." Moore, *Tobit*, 53.

41. "We know that Jerome only half-heartedly agreed to translate the Apocrypha. His Jewish friends had convinced him that the apocryphal books ought to be left out of his new Latin translation, as they were not found in the Hebrew Bible. But the Church Synods in North Africa in the 390s decided that the Apocrypha had obtained full biblical authority in the Septuagint, and this state of things should not be altered in the Vulgate. Jerome's words in the preface show his attitude to the assignment, and we can understand that his peculiar procedure of translating [which he finished in a single day] would result in a very free rendering of the contents of the Aramaic text used." Otzen, *Tobit and Judith*, 64.

42. Bruce Metzger notes that references to Tobit abound in Christian wedding liturgy, popping up in everything from tenth-century English rites to the wedding sermons of Old Order Amish. See Metzger, *An Introduction to the Apocrypha*, 40–41.
43. Quoted in Fitzmyer, *Tobit*, 31.
44. Jeffrey R. Holland, "The Ministry of Angels," *Ensign* (November 2008), 29–31.

10

JUDITH

INTRODUCTION

THE BOOK OF JUDITH IS A HEROIC, ALBEIT PERPLEXING, TALE.
While it is fantastic to have a scriptural story centered on a woman,
Judith's deceptive methods are sometimes called into question.
Partly for this reason, as well as its many historical and geographical
inaccuracies, its inclusion in the canon has vacillated. Regardless,
the story was passed down in several Greek versions, two Latin
ones, a Syriac one, and later Hebrew retellings (it may have been
originally written in Hebrew, but no Hebrew fragments have been
found).[1] The events of the story have also inspired many works
of art, so in the end the tale remained entrenched in Christian
culture.[2]

Right from the first verse, historical problems abound: "It
was the twelfth year of the reign of Nebuchadnezzar, who ruled
over the Assyrians in the great city of Nineveh" (1:1). Even most
casual Bible readers know the name Nebuchadnezzar as a great
Babylonian ruler who was responsible for the destruction of the
Jerusalem Temple. Yet here he is the leader of the Assyrians! In
addition, he is described as ruling from Nineveh, which in reality
was destroyed in 612 BC shortly before his reign. It would seem

that any ancient writer would know these basic facts, so some interpreters have pointed towards these inaccuracies as purposeful intent by the author. Since the entire story of Judith is filled with irony,[3] these historical mistakes signal playfulness by the author as the fictional storyline is set up.[4] Perhaps one of the "weapons" Jewish writers had living under dominant empires was to satirize their power and tell stories where Jews, and especially in this case a Jewish woman, gain the upper hand.

While the text suggests an author with satirical and ironic intentions, we know very little about the person (or people) responsible for composing the story of Judith. As was customary in most ancient literature, the author is left unstated.[5] While the descriptions of Judith's religious piety sound nearly Pharisaic,[6] there is no concrete evidence that the author was a Pharisee (or member of any particular Jewish group). Regardless, the author was clearly concerned about defending the Jews and Judaism against encroaching foreign threats. This overall theme has led many to propose that Judith was written during the Hasmonean era, following the events detailed in 1 Maccabees.[7] However, the use of some Persian names (like Holofernes) and terms may reflect an origin in the period when Persia ruled over Israel.[8] One thing is certain: regardless of who wrote it or when it was written, the author of Judith created a masterpiece of Jewish storytelling that was treasured by both Jews and Christians throughout the ages.[9]

THE STORY

The book of Judith begins with battles and military actions by Nebuchadnezzar against the Medes (Persia).[10] When Nebuchadnezzar's requests for military assistance from all the surrounding regions (Syria, Jerusalem, Egypt, and so on) are denied, he becomes very angry and vows revenge on the whole territory (1:7–12). True to his threat, once he defeats the Medes he begins preparations for a westward campaign (2:1–3). Holofernes, the chief general of Nebuchadnezzar's army, is chosen to lead a massive army of 120,000 foot soldiers and 12,000 cavalry (archers on horseback) and subdue the region for Nebuchadnezzar's arrival (2:4–18). The geographical route of the forces is dizzying: they weave back and forth throughout the region, finding success in all their battles (2:21–27).[11] Some regions hear about the Assyrian army's strength and brutality and sue for peace, basically offering complete submission (2:28–3:4). Holofernes accepts these surrenders, but demolishes all their shrines so they can only worship Nebuchadnezzar and call upon him as a god (3:8).

The Israelites in Judea become terrified and worry about the fate of Jerusalem and the temple, "for they had only recently returned from exile, and all the people of Judea had just now gathered together, and the sacred vessels and the altar and the temple had been consecrated after their profanation" (4:3). (This is another example of a gross anachronism; it was king Nebuchadnezzar himself who had sent the inhabitants of Judea into exile, and yet now they have supposedly recently returned from exile.)[12] Throughout Judea and Samaria, they begin fortifying their villages and storing up food (4:5). The High Priest, Joakim, leads the preparations and sees an opportunity to stop the Assyrians at a narrow mountain pass[13] near Bethulia (an unidentifiable village somewhere in Samaria).[14] A tremendous fasting and prayer campaign among the Israelites ensues with everyone dressing in sackcloth—including wives, children, hired laborers, slaves, and even the cattle (4:9–10).[15] The temple altar in Jerusalem is not spared from sackcloth as multitudes prostrate around it and put ashes on their heads (4:11–12). It must have worked, for the text states that "The Lord heard their prayers and had regard for their distress" (4:13).

Holofernes hears reports about the Israelite preparation and becomes angry. He seeks military intelligence from some of the local Moabite and Ammonite commanders, and an Ammonite named Achior gives information. After describing the historical background of the Israelites (a good summary of many Old

Testament events), Achior points out their chief weakness: "As long as they did not sin against their God they prospered, for the God who hates iniquity is with them. But when they departed from the way he had prescribed for them, they were utterly defeated in many battles and were led away captive to a foreign land" (5:17–18).[16] Achior resumes anachronistically reporting how the Jerusalem Temple was razed to the ground and only recently have the Israelites returned from exile to their former settlements (5:18–19). So, Achior suggests, if any sin can be found among the Israelites, then the Assyrians will be successful; but if not, their God will defend them "and we shall become the laughingstock of the whole world" (5:21)—a true foreshadowing of the future events of the story. Achior's counsel is promptly rejected by both Holofernes and the military officers, who are not afraid of the Israelites and believe that Nebuchadnezzar is the only true god.[17] As punishment for his presumptive words, Achior is harshly packed off to join the inhabitants of Bethulia to suffer the same fate they will (6:10).

The inhabitants of Bethulia bring the bound Achior into their town and begin to interrogate him about what had happened. Achior repeats the substance of his conference with Holofernes, leading the people to turn to the Lord to seek his assistance. Meanwhile, Holofernes moves his army and lays siege against the small village of Bethulia. "When the Israelites saw their vast numbers, they were greatly terrified and said to one another, 'They will now strip clean the whole land; neither the high mountains nor the valleys nor the hills will bear their weight'" (7:4). After Holofernes seizes the springs around Bethulia, the Israelites' situation worsens and "their courage failed" (7:19).[18] They hold out for thirty-four days until their water containers run dry and their cisterns are nearly depleted. "Their children were listless, and the women and young men fainted from thirst and were collapsing in the streets of the town and in the gateways; they no longer had any strength" (7:22).

All the inhabitants of the village gather around the chief elder of the town, Uzziah, and other leaders of the town and accuse them of leading them into this disaster by refusing to surrender to the Assyrians. "Now we have no one to help us; God has sold us into their hands, to be strewn before them in thirst and exhaustion. Now summon them and surrender the whole town as booty to the army of Holofernes and to all his forces. For it would be better for us to be captured by them. We shall indeed become slaves, but our lives will be spared, and we shall not witness our little ones dying before our eyes, and our wives and children drawing their last breath" (7:25–27). Uzziah exhorts them to take courage and hold out for five more days because "by that time the Lord our God will turn his mercy to us again, for he will not forsake us utterly. But if these days pass by, and no help comes for us, I will do as you say" (7:30–31).

At this critical juncture when the deadline is set, Judith (whose name means "Jewess")[19] enters the story and becomes the primary character for the second half of the tale. The narrative leaves no doubt about Judith's pious character and beauty. After a lengthy genealogy (with no parallels to Old Testament figures), it is explained that Judith has been a widow for over three years. During that time, she has lived in a tent on her roof with "sackcloth around her waist and dressed in widow's clothing" (8:5). She has fasted every day of that period except on Sabbaths and the days before Sabbaths, and on certain Jewish festival days of rejoicing (this is the first time among Jewish sources that habitual fasting is presented as an act of piety). She is described as "beautiful in appearance, and was very lovely to behold" (8:7), features which become important later in the story. Upon her husband's death, she was left with plenty of money, slaves, land, and livestock.[20] "No one spoke ill of her, for she feared God with great devotion" (8:8).

When Judith hears about the people's harsh words against Uzziah and the timetable he had set, Judith summons the elders of the town to her. She bluntly tells the elders that what they had said to the people is wrong. "Who are you to put God to the test today, and to set yourselves up in the place of God in human affairs? You are putting the Lord Almighty to the test, but you will never learn anything! You cannot plumb the depths of the human heart or understand the workings of the human mind; how do you expect to search out God, who made all these things, and find out his mind or comprehend his thought? (8:12–14). Some scholars have noted strong similarities between this passage and 1 Corinthians 2:10–11 and 16. "Both contrast the 'depths' (a word for 'inner designs, thoughts,' and the like) of a person with the 'depths' of God and reason by analogy (Paul) or by lesser to greater (Judith) that just as one cannot know another human being's depths, so one cannot (on one's own, at least) know the mind of God. Both also use peculiar terminology (*eraunao*, 'search out'; *bathos*, 'depth, deep things'). The case is indeed strong that Paul has been influenced in his thinking by Jdt. 8:14 (directly, or indirectly by someone who had read and meditated upon the verse)."[21]

Judith explains that God can choose to help at any time he pleases, or allow them to be destroyed. "Do not try to bind the purposes of the Lord our God; for God is not like a human being, to be threatened, or like a mere mortal, to be won over by pleading" (8:16). Instead, Judith suggests they simply pray and if it pleases him, God will hear their voice.[22] Judith acknowledges that their ancestors were punished for idolatry, but those in Bethulia have been faithful and are the last protection for the temple and its altar. Judith points out that they are being tested as their ancestors, such as Abraham and Jacob, had been. She also teaches the people that "the Lord scourges those who are close to him in order to admonish them" (8:27)—a principle similar to that taught in Helaman 12:3 ("in the days of their iniquities hath he chastened them because he loveth them").

Uzziah acknowledges the truth of Judith's words and then asks her to pray for them so that the Lord can send rain to fill their cisterns. Instead, Judith suggests a secretive mission, "something that will go down through all generations of our descendants" (8:32). Judith won't tell them her plan; she only asks them to let her out of the village at night, promising she will deliver Israel by her hand before the deadline for surrender.

Before beginning her mission, Judith prepares herself spiritually. She puts ashes on her head and cries out to the Lord. In her prayer, Judith recounts Simeon's revenge on those that raped his sister, Dinah, as an analogue to the efforts needed to destroy the Assyrians.[23] She knows that things are in God's hands, so she petitions him to break down the Assyrian's strength and to prevent them from carrying out their intention to destroy the temple. For her role, she asks specifically for "strong hands to do what I plan. By the deceit of my lips strike down the slave with the prince and the prince with his servant; crush their arrogance by the hand of a woman" (9:9–10).[24] She continues her focus on her deceptive plan by asking God: "Make my deceitful words bring wound and bruise on those who have planned cruel things against your covenant, and against your sacred house, and against Mount Zion, and against the house your children possess" (9:13). She ends her prayer with the plea, "Let your whole nation and every tribe know and understand that you are God, the God of all power and might, and that there is no other who protects the people of Israel but you alone!" (9:14).

The next part of her plan requires physical preparation. "She removed the sackcloth she had been wearing, took off her widow's garments, bathed her body with water, and anointed herself in the festive attire that she used to wear while her husband Manasseh was living. She put sandals on her feet, and put on her anklets, bracelets, rings, earrings, and all her other jewelry. Thus she made herself very beautiful, to entice the eyes of all the men who might see her" (10:3–4).[25] Judith also prepares a bag with simple, kosher food and gives it to her maid to carry as she accompanies her out of the village and toward the Assyrian camp.

Judith and her maid are quickly "captured" by an Assyrian patrol. When asked who she is and what she is doing, Judith lies: "I am a daughter of the Hebrews, but I am fleeing from them, for they are about to be handed over to you to be devoured. I am on my way to see Holofernes the commander of your army, to give him a true report; I will show him a way by which he can go and capture all the hill country without losing one of his men, captured or slain" (10:12–13). Admiring her beauty, the Assyrians hastily escort her to camp (with a hundred-man escort). Her arrival creates a great stir as reports of her beauty are passed from tent to tent. "They admired the Israelites, judging them by her. They said to one another, 'Who can despise these people, who have women like this among them? It is not wise to leave one of their men alive, for if we let them go they will be able to beguile the whole world!'" (10:19).[26]

Judith is brought into Holofernes's richly adorned tent, where he rests on a grand bed under a bejeweled canopy. Holofernes assures Judith that he will not harm her, and that in fact he has no intention of hurting anyone who submits to Nebuchadnezzar, but because Judith's people have resisted, they have brought upon themselves his retribution. Judith's response ironically uses the title "lord" for God, rather than Holofernes (as he understands it), and thus how the subsequent events will unfold depends upon perspective: "Accept the words of your slave, and let your servant speak in your presence. I will say nothing false to my lord this night.[27] If you follow out the words of your servant, God will accomplish something through you, and my lord will not fail to achieve his purposes" (11:5–6). Judith next flatters Holofernes, claiming that "we have heard of your wisdom and skill, and it is reported throughout the whole world that you alone are the best in the whole kingdom, the most informed and the most astounding in military strategy" (11:8).[28]

Judith also advises Holofernes to not dismiss Achior's earlier counsel regarding how the Israelites can be conquered. She affirms, "Indeed our nation cannot be punished, nor can the sword prevail against them, unless they sin against their God" (11:10). Judith explains that the Israelites are about to sin because of their desperate condition: they are planning to eat the first fruits and tithes reserved for the temple. As a result, Judith fled from them, and she says, in another ironic statement, "God has sent me to accomplish with you things that will astonish the whole world wherever people shall hear about them" (11:16). Judith then lays out her plan: she will remain with Holofernes, but go out every night into the valley to pray to God. "He will tell me when they have committed their sins. Then I will come and tell you, so that you may go out with your whole army, and not one of them will be able to withstand you.[29] Then I will lead you through Judea, until you come to Jerusalem; there I will set your throne. You will drive them like sheep that have no shepherd, and no dog will so much as growl at you. For this was told me to give me foreknowledge; it was announced to me, and I was sent to tell you" (11:17–19).

Holofernes and his servants like what they hear.[30] They marvel, "No other woman from one end of the earth to the other looks so beautiful or speaks so wisely!" (11:21). Holofernes then assures Judith, "If you do as you have said, your God shall be my God, and you shall live in the palace of King Nebuchadnezzar and be renowned throughout the whole world" (11:23).

Holofernes has the final preparations made for an intimate dinner, but Judith explains that she cannot partake of his Gentile food, but must eat from the food she brought herself.[31] When Holofernes asks what she will do if she runs out of food, Judith responds with another ironic statement: "As surely as you live, my lord, your servant will not use up the supplies I have with me before the Lord carries out by my hand what he has determined" (12:4). For three days Judith is allowed to do as she has proposed: she eats her own food and prays in the valley without anyone hindering her.

On the fourth day, Holofernes feels antsy and does not want to be mocked for not seducing Judith.[32] When the servant summons Judith, she replies with another ironic statement, "Who am I to refuse my Lord? Whatever pleases him I will do at once, and it will be a joy to me until the day of my death" (12:14). The moment has seemingly arrived and "Judith came in and lay down. Holofernes' heart was ravished with her and his passion was aroused, for he had been waiting for an opportunity to seduce her from the day he first saw her" (12:16).[33] They both begin drinking (Judith from her supply), and Holofernes drinks a great quantity of his wine, "much more than he had ever drunk in any one day since he was born" (12:20).

After dismissing all attendants, the couple is finally alone in Holofernes's tent, but then Holofernes passes out on his bed "dead drunk" (13:2). Judith petitions the Lord for strength, and then retrieves Holofernes's sword hanging nearby. "She came close to his bed, took hold of the hair of his head . . . then she struck his neck twice with all her might, and cut off his head.[34] Next she rolled his body off the bed and pulled down the canopy from the posts. Soon afterward she went out and gave Holofernes' head to her maid, who placed it in her food bag. Then the two of them went out together, as they were accustomed to do for prayer. They passed through the camp, circled around the valley, and went up the mountain to Bethulia, and came to its gates" (13:7–10).

Judith cries out for the gatekeepers to open the gates, and when the villagers hear her voice, they run toward the gate. Judith exclaims, "Praise God, who has not withdrawn his mercy from the house of Israel, but has destroyed our enemies by my hand this very night!" (13:14).[35] She pulls out the mighty general's head from her bag and states, "The Lord has struck him down by the hand of a woman. As the Lord lives, who has protected me in the way I went, I swear that it was my face that seduced him to his destruction, and that he committed no sin with me, to defile and shame me" (13:16). All the people bow down and worship God. Uzziah exclaims, "O daughter, you are blessed by the Most High God above all other women on earth . . . Your praise will never depart from the hearts of those who remember the power of God. May God grant this to be a perpetual honor to you, and may he reward you with blessings, because you risked your own life when our nation was brought low, and you averted our ruin, walking in the straight path before our God" (13:19–20).

Judith commands them to hang Holofernes's head from the parapet of the wall and prepare themselves to march against the Assyrians at daybreak. "Perhaps the most striking reversal [of traditional gender roles] appears in 14:1–5, where Judith replaces Joakim as the military strategist and commander, giving the orders for the counterattack."[36] She predicts that when they rush into the tent of Holofernes and find him dead, then panic will come over them and they will flee. But before those commands are carried out, she tells them to bring Achior to her so that he can "see and recognize the man who despised the house of Israel and sent him to us as if to his death" (14:6). When Achior comes and sees the head of Holofernes, he faints.[37] "When they raised him up he threw himself at Judith's feet, and did obeisance to her, and said, 'Blessed are you in every tent of Judah! In every nation those who hear your name will be alarmed. Now tell me what you have done during these days'" (14:7–8). So Judith recounts her actions, and when she finishes the people shout and make a joyful noise, and Achior converts to the God of Israel on the spot and is circumcised.[38]

The next day proceeds just as Judith had predicted: Holofernes's chief servant finds his master's body lying on the floor with his head missing. "He cried out with a loud voice and wept and groaned and shouted, and tore his clothes. Then he went to the tent where Judith had stayed, and when he did not find her, he rushed out to the people and shouted, 'The slaves have tricked us! One Hebrew woman has brought disgrace on the house of King Nebuchadnezzar. Look, Holofernes is lying on the ground, and his head is missing!'" (14:16–18). The crying and shouting spreads among the Assyrian army leaders, and soon all the men in the tents flee by every path out of the camp. The waiting Israelite army quickly falls upon them and destroys them.

Following the military victory, the high priest and elders from Jerusalem come to see all that happened and bless Judith. "You have done all this with your own hand; you have done great good to Israel, and God is well pleased with it. May the Almighty Lord bless you forever!" (15:10). For thirty days, the people plunder the Assyrian camp, and Judith receives all the silver dinnerware, beds, bowls, and furniture from Holofernes's tent, which she piously loads on carts to take up to Jerusalem and dedicate to God. Great rejoicing breaks out, especially among the women. "All the women of Israel gathered to see her, and blessed her, and some of them performed a dance in her honor. She took ivy-wreathed wands in her hands and distributed them to the women who were with her, and she and those who were with her crowned themselves with olive wreaths. She went before all the people in the dance, leading all the women, while all the men of Israel followed, bearing their arms and wearing garlands and singing hymns" (15:12–13).[39]

The last chapter of Judith (similar to that of Tobit) is a thanksgiving psalm the people sing as they make their way up to Jerusalem, praising God for his mercy and recounting his assistance in their trials. It emphasizes the fact that a woman, not one of their mighty ones, was God's instrument of destruction: "Her sandal ravished his eyes, her beauty captivated his mind, and the sword severed his neck!" (16:9). The hymn praises the greatness of God and those who fear him, and it ends with a warning to those who may try to oppose God: "Woe to the nations that rise up against my people! The Lord Almighty will take vengeance on them in the day of judgment; he will send fire and worms into their flesh;[40] they shall weep in pain forever" (16:17). When the celebratory party reaches Jerusalem, they purify themselves and bring forth their offerings to God and worship him. "For three months the people continued feasting in Jerusalem before the sanctuary, and Judith remained with them" (16:20). Following the lengthy celebration, everyone returns home and Judith lives out the rest of her life on her estate, being honored throughout the whole country.[41] Although many desired to marry her, she remained a widow until her death at age 105, when she was buried next to her husband Manasseh.

The closing verse testifies of her lasting impact: "no one ever again spread terror among the Israelites during the lifetime of Judith, or for a long time after her death" (16:25).

Legacy

Despite the popularity of Judith's story in antiquity, it was not an authoritative text for the Jews. This is a little puzzling. As one scholar put it, why was Judith, which "had all the essentials of Palestinian Judaism (i.e. God, prayer, dietary scrupulousness, sacrifice, Temple, Jerusalem[)]" excluded from the canon; while the book of Esther (which doesn't even mention God) was chosen for inclusion?[42] It is likely that a number of factors combined to make Judith unsuitable for complete Jewish acceptance: its blatant factual inaccuracies, its unorthodox portrayal of women, its portrayal of Achior's conversion, and its late date of composition were all probable factors in its exclusion.[43] Despite being noncanonical, the book of Judith became popular among medieval Jews through its supposed connections to the festival of Hanukkah.[44]

Christians received the book of Judith through the Septuagint translation, and the story proved to be as popular among Christian readers as it was among the Jews. Many early Christian authors praised Judith in their writings and cited her story frequently.[45] However, the fact that Judith was not considered scripture by the Jews made some Christian leaders wary of accepting it into their Bibles. It was consistently heralded as canonical by the Roman Catholic Church,[46] but others (particularly later Protestants) were less convinced. European artists and writers, unconcerned with the scriptural status of the story, created numerous paintings, plays, and poems about Judith and her exploits. Christians who didn't encounter Judith in their Bible were well-acquainted with her from grim paintings of the decapitation of Holofernes.[47]

CONCLUSION

The book of Judith is remarkable for its focus on a woman as the heroine—one perhaps even greater than Esther, since Judith literally had to take matters into her own hands in order to bring about Israelite salvation. It is therefore fitting that the book's name and main character mean "Jewess," as a Jewish woman succeeds where the men fall short. But Judith's deceitful words and actions led later readers to often exclude it from the canon,[48] similar to Esther's questionable canonical status among the Dead Sea Scrolls (see the earlier chapter on Greek Additions to Esther). But there is no other version of Judith like in the case of Esther, where another version was produced to resolve interpretative issues. The story's many historical inaccuracies push it into the realm of fiction and leave the reader wondering what the author's intentions were in writing this story. Perhaps this story was like other parables or tales of fictional characters (like the fictional but instructive Parable of the Good Samaritan) that inspire hope and courage in trying times and teach important lessons in memorable fashion. Although Judith may not have been a historical woman from a small village in Samaria who literally defeated an Assyrian army singlehandedly, her legendary exploits could be retold and celebrated by countless women and men through the ages to find emotional relief from dominant imperial rule. The story's frequent ironic statements and situations provide an entertaining venue for presenting another account of mortal instruments helping Israel triumph.

Since the book of Judith seems to be of such a fictive nature, perhaps it is better to think of it as a type of parable meant to share a primary message, but not to examine its details for historicity. As such, it is another story that reminds the reader that God can do the seemingly impossible when faith is placed in him. In this story, Judith becomes the instrument to deliver her people from their threatening situation. Being a widow, she is one of the last people one would expect to be able to pull off such a military victory, but her story is another reminder that God can work through even the least vessels to accomplish his purposes: "By small and simple things are great things brought to pass; and small means in many instances doth confound the wise" (Alma 37:6). Her past righteousness and faithfulness have prepared her to do what is needed to protect her people. Judith is another story that demonstrates the principle of great things coming from small and simple things, and it is enjoyable to sit back and read its entertaining twists, turns, and irony as the plot unfolds.

NOTES

1. "The text of Judith survives chiefly in the Septuagint tradition, in three distinct editions . . . The differences, which tend to be minor, are not due to new examinations of the Hebrew or to different underlying Hebrew manuscripts. Jerome created his Vulgate version by emending the Old Latin in light of an Aramaic version known to him (but evidently not a direct witness to the original). Jerome himself does not pretend to give a precise or careful translation; his goal is to give 'sense for sense, more than word for word.' The Sahidic (Coptic), Syriac, and Ethiopic are translations of the Septuagint, and the Hebrew versions are later compositions based on Greek or Latin translations . . . The result is that, ultimately, our only reliable access to the original text of Judith is through the Septuagint tradition." deSilva, *Introducing the Apocrypha*, 90.

2. "What the feminist novelist Rebecca West described as 'the obviously gorgeous theme of Judith' has fascinated the western world. Over the centuries, it has remained more consistently popular and influential than anyone now imagines. Representations of Judith have been ubiquitous in all the arts: there are literally thousands of them. In literature there are epics, plays, novels and poems. The story's sensational aspects have been almost obsessively reproduced by numerous artists in the visual and plastic media. It has also been filmed, set to music, illustrated and lampooned. Unnervingly, it has even been consciously re-enacted in real life. The Book of Judith has had a profound and lasting impact upon

Western culture." Margarita Stoker, *Judith: Sexual Warrior* (New Haven: Yale University Press, 1998), 2.

3. Indeed, irony is so central to the book of Judith that Casey Moore stated: "Failure to recognize irony as *the* quintessential characteristic of the book is the primary reason for so many of the misinterpretations of it and may just be the clue to many of its historical, geographical, and moral problems." Casey Moore, "Why Wasn't the Book of Judith Included in the Hebrew Bible?" in *"No One Spoke Ill of Her:" Essays on Judith* (ed. James C. VanderKam, Atlanta: Scholars Press, 1992), 65. For an additional discussion on the irony and humor found in Judith, see Gruen, *Diaspora*, 158–170.

4. "The writer made use of historical figures in writing his story, but the transparent deviations from historical precision lead one to think that he was less interested in historical figures and places than his more immediate goal of teaching a lesson." VanderKam, *Introduction to Early Judaism*, 74–75.

5. "Writing in Hebrew or Aramaic, Jewish authors of the Hellenistic age continued to conform to the literary conventions of their ancestors . . . Esther, Judith, 1 Maccabees, and later on the *Seder Olam Rabbah* and *Megillat Antiochus*, following the example of the historical books of the Bible, were published anonymously." Bickermann, *The Jews*, 202.

6. Judith's rigorous fasting, her adherence to ritual purity laws, and her prayer practices are cited by Larry Helyer as possible evidence of Pharisaic influence. "One of the difficult issues in historical research of early Judaism and Christianity has been an accurate reconstruction of Pharisaism. Judith is valuable in this connection because it seems to portray an earlier phase of Pharisaism than we see in the NT and later rabbinic sources. We may be justified in speaking of pre-Pharisaism in Judith." Helyer, *Exploring Jewish Literature*, 170.

7. Many textual features "have made experts think of Maccabean times (that is, after 167 BCE [BC]). Among these are: (a) worship of the divine king Nebuchadnezzar which echoes a practice in Hellenistic times when the ruler cult was widespread (see 3:8, for example), although it is attested for earlier periods. (see Isa. 14, Ezek. 28.); (b) the defiling of the Jeruslem temple feared by the Jews which reminds one of what Seleucid forces did to the temple from 167–164 BCE [BC] (4:12; 9:8); and (c) aspects of the story (especially Holofernes's fate) that parallel the battle between Judas Maccabeus and the Seleucid general Nicanor who had threatened the temple and was later decapitated (1 Macc. 7:33–50; his army, like that of Holofernes, panicked when he was the first to fall)." VanderKam, *Introduction to Early Judaism*, 72.

8. "[S]ome aspects of the story fit nicely into the Persian period. This would include such features as the names Holofernes and Bogoas, the recent return of the Jews to their land (Jdt 4:3), a possible reflex of the Persian title 'satrap' (Jdt 2:14), and the symbolism of earth and water for submission (Jdt 2:7). A compromise position suggests that an earlier Persian period tale has been reused and updated in the aftermath of the Maccabean revolt." Helyer, *Exploring Jewish Literature*, 167.

9. "The book of Judith is a literary work of considerable artistic merit. Chapters 1–7, which many consider to provide an imbalance of useless information overload, actually constitute the first half of a carefully crafted literary diptych, in which the second part (chaps. 8–16) resolves events and issues presented in the first part, and in which each of the two parts contains a threefold, thematically unified chiastic structure within itself. Another aspect of the author's literary artistry is the sophisticated manner in which the author depicts Judith and Achior as counterparts to one another. The use of multifaceted humor, including irony and absurdity, is also an important part of the author's literary artistry." Nickelsburg, *Jewish Literature*, 99.

10. "Like modern action movies, Judith leaps immediately into a rousing action scene that is only preparatory to the longer military campaigns to follow. The presence of a 'chapter 1,' set chronologically well before the main action of the story, is not unusual in the literature of this period (see, e.g., Esther 1, Tobit 1, Matthew 1–2, and Luke 1–2). The function of this introduction is not simply to engage the reader with exciting action—although that is an important element of popular literature; the carefully orchestrated rising action serves to dramatize, first, that Nebuchadnezzar is apparently invincible, since even the great king Arphaxad is defeated by him, and second, that Nebuchadnezzar is bent on world domination and will not stop his expansion until the entire subcontinent is under his control." Lawrence M. Wills, *The Book of Judith* (NIB IV; Nashville: Abingdon Press, 1999), 1095.

11. Once again, the nonsensical path of the Assyrians' march suggests that the historical details of the story were never intended to be taken seriously.

12. "For the ancient author to have established the general historical period for the events of his story by saying that it happened 'a short time' after the Return (i.e., shortly after 538 B.C.) and 'just recently' after the reconsecration of the Temple (i.e., sometime after 515 B.C.) is very curious, especially since elsewhere in his account the author offers an extended yet reasonably coherent history of his people (see Jdt 5:6–19; 8:26–27; 9:2–4)." Casey A. Moore, *Judith* (Anchor Bible 40; Garden City: Doubleday, 1985), 147.

13. "Bethulia's strategic importance for the capture of Jerusalem—whatever Bethulia's location, if it existed at all, it had no such significance in 'real life'—results from the influence of the stirring tale of the battle of Thermopylae (Herodotus, *Historiae* 7.176, 201–233), where a brave band of Spartan soldiers held off Xerxes' army long enough for the Athenians to mobilize and defeat them. Here the 'set up' is undertaken to highlight Judith's heroism and not that of the whole town or its armed men." deSilva, *Introducing the Apocrypha*, 98.

14. "The city name Bethulia is an example of how the author proceeds. There is no city by this name in any historical record, and the position given it in the book would be more appropriate for a site that would be guarding the city of Samaria than for one protecting Jerusalem. The name may well be symbolic: it could reflect the Hebrew term for virgin (*betulah*). Bethulia would, then, be a representation of Israel, the virgin Israel whom the enemy desired to ravage, just as Holofernes wanted to have Judith, a name that means 'Jewess.' As God saved Judith, so he saved Bethulia = the virgin Israel from enemy hands." VanderKam, *Introduction to Early Judaism*, 75.

15. "It is not only the men and women who are draped in sackcloth, but also the children, resident aliens, slaves, and cattle! Is this a symbol of the completeness of Israel's penitence, or is it intended to be as humorous to the ancient reader as it is to the modern? [Toni] Craven, probably correctly, takes it to be the latter, as we find the same motif used at Jonah 3:8, most likely also in a humorous way." Wills, *Judith*, 1114.

16. For an Ammonite, Achoir certainly displays an impressive knowledge of Israelite history, as well as a healthy regard for the justice of Israel's God! Several scholars have noted the unique role that Achior plays throughout the story of Judith. Adolfo Roitman insightfully points out that the almost-pious Gentile is "designed thematically as well as functionally in the mirror image of Judith, being a kind of double or 'alter-ego'. In some way, the Ammonite leader is the masculine/pagan version of the feminine/Jewish Judith." Adolfo D. Roitman, "Achior in the Book of Judith: His Role and Significance," in *"No One Spoke Ill of Her:" Essays on Judith* (ed. James C. VanderKam, Atlanta: Scholars Press, 1992), 38.

17. In 6:2, Holofernes dismissively asks Achior, "What God is there except Nebuchadnezzar?" Casey Moore states that "this question is more than just one expression of Holofernes' characteristic bluster: it is *the* question posed by Judith itself, primarily because of the actions of such historical villains such as Antiochus IV Epiphanes . . . [Toni Craven] rightly perceived that 'the question which subtly motivates the entire narrative is who is most powerful: Nebuchadnezzar or Yahweh." Moore, *Judith*, 166–67.

18. In the ancient world (and particularly in the arid Near East), cutting off a city's access to food and water was an effective method for either hastening the surrender of an enemy city or at least weakening it before an assault. The Judahite king Hezekiah, anticipating such a strategy by the approaching Assyrian invaders in the late eighth century BC, blocked up the springs outside the walls of Jerusalem and rerouted the waters of the Gihon spring through an artificial tunnel into the city, so that Jerusalem would have ample water during a siege (see 2 Chronicles 32:2–4).

19. "The name 'Judith' is the feminine equivalent of 'Judah' or 'Judas,' from which the province name 'Judea' is derived . . . It is from the word 'Judean' that the English word 'Jew' ultimately derives; her name thus means 'Jewess.' Assuming that the name was invented for the character, it could have been chosen to be emblematic of the ideal heroine—that is, it communicates the fact that the Jews would be saved by a heroic 'Jewess.' It is also possible that it evokes the name of one of the heroes of the Maccabean revolt, Judah the Maccabee. This seems even more likely when we consider the close parallels between Judah the Maccabee's defeat of Nicanor (1 Macc 7:47; 2 Macc 15:35)." Wills, *Judith*, 1132.

20. "While the Torah grants no succession rights to the widow, the Jews in Elephantine stipulated at the time of the marriage that either spouse could inherit from the other if there were no children. Two centuries later, Judith's husband left her his whole estate unconditionally, and before she died she disposed of her goods in her own right. The Book of Judith is Maccabean, but even in pre-Maccabean times Ben Sira had spoken of women who inherited their husbands' (or fathers') property." Bickerman, *The Jews*, 197.

21. deSilva, *Introducing the Apocrypha*, 108.

22. "There is a close Greek parallel to this motif, the Lindus chronicle, in which the Greek city of Lindus, besieged by Darius of Persia, prays to Athena to bring rain within five days. Rain does come, and Darius realizes that Lindus enjoys divine protection and passes it by. This is clearly intended to be a positive assessment of the city's prayer. The author of Judith has taken this tradition and challenged it: Fervent prayer is not sufficient before God, but a strict humility before God's decrees is called for." Wills, *Judith*, 1137.

23. Judith's mention of the rape of Dinah and its aftermath is significant to Judith's unfolding story. Just as Simeon and Levi used trickery to lower the guard of the men of Shechem (Gen 34:13–17) and then struck in a moment of weakness (Gen 34:25–26), Judith will also deceive the Assyrians and then attack when her assailant is incapacitated. Benedikt Otzen also notes that this reference leads the reader to view "Dinah as an

antitype to Judith: Dinah was raped by the heathen, while Judith keeps her virtue in spite of heavy attacks upon it." Otzen, *Judith and Tobit*, 74.

24. "Judith emphasizes that unlike the warriors Simeon and Levi, revenge in this case is left in the hands of a widow (v.4). She returns to this theme in v. 9, and in v. 10 entreats God to destroy Holofernes and his army by the hand of a female. Judith here picks up another theme from the book of Judges, for at Judg 9:53 Abimelech is shamed because he is mortally wounded by a woman and is later known for this (2 Sam 11:21). In a world conscious of honor and shame, for a warrior to be killed by a woman was a great shame." Wills, *Tobit*, 1144.

25. "Judith's great beauty, breath-taking and thought-depriving for every man who would now see her, is a *Leitmotif* for the rest of the chapter. Bethulia's sentries (v 10), the Assyrian outpost (v 14), the entire Assyrian camp (10:18), including its highest officers and general (10:23)—all are struck by Judith's beauty. Dancy thinks there is a touch of the storyteller's humor in all this: 'strong' men, young and old, significant and insignificant, they all fall immediately victim to this 'defenseless' widow." Moore, *Judith*, 201.

26. "The soldiers draw the conclusion that the audience would want them to draw: that Israelite women—and therefore men as well—are superior to any on earth. This means of affirming ethnic superiority is typical of much of the writing of this period, both in the dominant Greek and Roman culture, and of the various indigenous peoples. It is found in a very similar way in *Joseph and Aseneth* 1:4–5, where it is said that Aseneth was 'tall and comely, and more beautiful than any young woman on earth. Indeed, she bore little resemblance at all to Egyptian women, but was in every way more like the women of the Hebrews: as tall as Sarah, as comely as Rebecca, as beautiful as Rachel.'" Wills, *Judith*, 1150–51.

27. "With her opening words, Judith deliberately used the ambiguous term 'lord,' which can be interpreted as referring to the general (and so Holofernes obviously understood it) or to God, inasmuch as Judith would not lie to the Lord. Judith used this ambiguous word several times in her first interview with Holofernes. To say that she preferred to equivocate rather than deliberately to lie is to miss the point. Humor, not moral compunctions, dictated the author's choice of words here; for Judith had no compunctions against lying to Holofernes (see her petition in 9:13 for 'a beguiling tongue'). Rather, the author delighted in the irony of it all; here, for instance, so powerful and confident is Holofernes that it never occurred to him to look behind the face of this beautiful woman." Moore, *Judith*, 208.

28. "Playing up to Holofernes's arrogant pretensions, Judith addresses him as if he were the king himself (11:8, 19). Her conversation is a string

of lies, half-truths, and double entendres. Dazzled by Judith's beauty, Holofernes 'loses his head before it has been cut off.'" Nickelsburg, *Jewish Literature*, 98.

29. David deSilva notes that Judith "resembles Themistocles, the Athenian naval commander who sends word to the Persian fleet commanders that he is favorable to their cause, luring them to the battle of Salamis, where the Persians were defeated (Herodotus, *Historiae* 8.75–90). This also attests incidentally to the acceptable use of deceit to defeat one's enemies and to lure them into a position of weakness." deSilva, *Introducing the Apocrypha*, 98.

30. "In the ensuing conversation the ambiguous remarks of Judith are over the head of Holofernes, who is totally obsessed by his sensuality and vanity. For example when Judith (11.16) says, 'God has sent me to accomplish with you things that will astonish the whole world', Holofernes is so delighted that he, in spite of his intention to make Nebuchadnezzar the only god of the whole world, at once promises to acknowledge Judith's God. The Jewish reader would find this both ludicrous and contemptible." Otzen, *Tobit and Judith*, 118–19.

31. Commenting on the issues faced by Jews dining among Gentiles, Elias Bickerman noted that "it was the religious use of food that disqualified the pagan table for the Jew. The Law prohibits the consumption of anything that has been offered as a sacrifice to idols. But at that time a meal was inseparable from cult: any meat that was available usually came from an animal that had been sacrificed; the first fruits of field and tree were offered by Jews to the Lord but by pagans to false gods; thus consecrating the entire crop; a cake made of the same dough as the bread on the table had been presented to the domestic spirits, and the wine served for libations. Moreover, a grace was said before every meal. Therefore there was no way that Jews who partook of a heathen meal could avoid exposing themselves to the germs of idolatrous impurity . . . [Thus] Judith brings not only wine but even bread and figs to Holofernes' tent and has her meals prepared by her Jewish maid. Thus the precept ascribed to Abraham in Jubilees, not to eat with the gentiles, must already have been followed by the Jews in the third century B.C.E. [BC] In this way, as Tacitus says, the Jews became 'separated at table.'" Bickerman, *The Jews*, 249.

32. Although Holofernes is in the position of power in this situation, he nevertheless sends his servant to "go and persuade the Hebrew woman . . . to join us" (12:13), as if afraid of offending her. "That Judith remains in control of Holofernes and the other persons around her is seen in the odd combination of phrases used by Holofernes: 'Go and persuade her,' 'it would be a disgrace,' 'if we do not seduce her, she will laugh at us.'

On the one hand, Holofernes displays the bravado of one who thinks he will soon have sex with Judith, whether she is agreeable or not; on the other hand, he awaits her word and has yet to say no to a single one of her unusual requests." Wills, *Judith*, 1158.

33. The combined themes of sensuality and death in this text are commonly combined elements in ancient literature, "and the author of the book of Judith has, at least, met with it in the Old Testament, where it is a favorite topos. Most scholars juxtapose Judith and Jael, several have seen a relationship to the story of Sampson and Delilah, and not to forget, the book of Judith itself draws our attention to the tale of the rape of Dinah and the gruesome revenge of her brothers. Also the story of Susanna is a tale of sexuality and death, and so is the book of Esther, in so far as the king evidentially is concerned that Haman will rape Esther and immediately has him executed (Est. 7.8–10)." Otzen, *Tobit and Judith*, 110.

34. "Among the biblical passages that have likely influenced the author of Judith is the struggle between David and Goliath (1 Samuel 17). In preparation for his encounters with Goliath, David takes off the armor of Saul, which is a symbol of strength, and chooses the weapon of the weak: five smooth stones taken from a riverbed. Thus he affirms the power of the weak just as Judith does. He places the stones in his pouch as he marches out, just as Judith has placed in her pouch her kosher food, a necessary 'weapon' for her stay in Holofernes' camp. Finally, David's utterance to Goliath is similar to Judith's language, although David has no need for double entendre: 'This very day the Lord will deliver you into my hand, and I will strike you down and cut off your head' (1 Sam 17:46 NRSV). David first strikes Goliath in the head with a stone to subdue him, then, lacking a sword of his own, David, like Judith, stands over his adversary, takes his sword, and cuts off his head. When the enemy forces saw that their leader had been beheaded, they fled." Wills, *Judith*, 1162.

35. "The expression 'by the hand of Judith' is a [recurrent theme] in the book of Judith. Patrick Skehan has examined the occurrences of the expression (nearly a dozen) in the book of Judith. He traces it back to the Old Testament, not least to a text that we have met several times as a source-text for the book of Judith: Exodus 1–15. Just as God uses Moses' hand, when Israel is delivered, so he uses Judith's hand to free his people. Both Moses and Judith are in post-exilic times seen as outstanding examples of Jewish piety and as the elect ones used by God as his instruments." Otzen, *Tobit and Judith*, 103.

36. deSilva, *Introducing the Apocrypha*, 105.

37. "Achior's reaction is dramatic, even more dramatic than that of the Bethulians in 13:17. However, he escaped from close contact with

Holofernes and had known the man face-to-face. In addition, it dramatizes the fulfillment of Holofernes' foolhardy prediction that 'you shall not see my face again from this day until I take revenge on this race' (6:5). It is very ironic that Achior immediately faints at the sight of Holofernes' head, since Judith had been so bold and nerveless both in taking it and handling it." Wills, *Judith*, 1167.

38. Achior was an Ammonite, so technically his conversion was against the Law of Moses, which forbade any Ammonites from joining the House of Israel. (See Deuteronomy 23:3).

39. "There is a strong tradition in Israel of women dancing and singing victory songs and dances. The song of Miriam at Exod 15:21 is sung after the pharaoh and his troops are drowned in the Red Sea . . . More typical of the victory songs is probably the song sung by the women after David slew Goliath (1 Sam 18:6): 'The woman came out of all the towns of Israel, singing and dancing . . . with tambourines, with songs of joy, and with musical instruments' (NRSV). The tambourine is also known from ancient depictions found in archaeological excavations; it was a small hand drum without the metal rattles found on modern tambourines." Wills, *Judith*, 1174.

40. "According to 2 Macc 9:9, the body of Antiochus IV Epiphanes, Israel's arch-villain, 'swarmed with worms' even while he was still alive, all of which *may* have been an example of the type of punishment included in the phrase 'day of judgment.'" Moore, *Judith*, 252.

41. Some modern commentators, particularly those who examine the text from the perspective of feminist theory, criticize Judith's 'retirement' from public life as a resubmission to the cultural norms of female domesticity that she so spectacularly overcame in the preceding chapters. Amy-Jill Levine postulates that, in Israel's patriarchal society, Judith's bold actions could not "be allowed to continue unchecked" lest they upset proper gender roles. "Only by remaining unique and apart [could] Judith be tolerated, domesticated and even treasured by Israelite society." Amy-Jill Levine, "Sacrifice and Salvation: Otherness and Domestication in the Book of Judith," in *A Feminist Companion to Esther, Judith, and Susanna* (ed. Athalya Brenner, Sheffield: Sheffield Academic Press, 1995), 218–19. In contrast, one may see in Judith's quiet retirement a great measure of humility—a trait which fits the book's descriptions of her piety. She reflects the lives of many ordinary people throughout history who performed herculean service, and then gave God the glory and humbly shunned the limelight.

42. Moore, *Judith*, 86.

43. For a good discussion of the reasons behind Judith's unfitness for the Jewish canon, see Casey Moore, "Why Wasn't the Book of Judith

Included in the Hebrew Bible?" in *"No One Spoke Ill of Her:" Essays on Judith* (ed. James C. VanderKam, Atlanta: Scholars Press, 1992), 61–71.

44. "Judith grew in popularity in the post-talmudic age as the story came to be closely associated with Hanukkah and thus the subject of several different midrashim connected with that festival. Her story was told in tandem with the victories of Judah, her male namesake. Jewish art also attests to her growing popularity during the medieval period." deSilva, *Introducing the Apocrypha*, 107.

45. "Clement of Rome cites Judith, together with Esther, as an example of a woman receiving power 'by the favor of God' to do 'manly things' (= 'courageous things'; the Greek etymology of *andreia*, 'courage,' is noteworthy), praising her for embracing personal danger for the love of her people (*1 Clement* 55.4–5). Judith's prayer addresses God as 'God of the lowly, help of the oppressed, upholder of the weak' (9:11), a phrase that Origen recontextualizes in *Commentarii in evangelium Joannis* 2.22.16. Origen further regards Judith's necessary use of falsehood as a model for those who are pressed of necessity into dissimulation (*Stromata* 6, quoted in Jerome, *Adversus Rufinum libri III* 1.474). Clement of Alexandria derives the proverb "Whoever is near the Lord is full of stripes" (*Stromata* 2.7) from Jdt. 8.27, 'The Lord scourges those who are close to him.'" deSilva, *Introducing the Apocrypha*, 108.

46. "In sum, in the West, the book was nearly always regarded as canonical, while in the Eastern Church it was generally denied canonical status." Moore, *Judith*, 90.

47. For a thorough examination of how Judith has been portrayed in art throughout the ages, see Margarita Stoker, *Judith: Sexual Warrior* (New Haven: Yale University Press, 1998).

48. "[Judith's] use of deceit, and specifically of her sexuality, will seem offensive to modern sensibilities. For the author it is the opposite. Judith wisely chooses the weapon in her arsenal that is appropriate to her enemy's weakness. She plays his game, knowing that he will lose. In so doing she makes fools out of a whole army of men and humiliates their general." Nickelsburg, *Jewish Literature*, 99.

11

---

1 Maccabees

1 Maccabees is the most historical book in the Apocrypha, recounting some of the key Jewish events from the second century BC. It follows in the style and genre of the books of 1 and 2 Samuel and 1 and 2 Kings in the Old Testament. "The author has given many signals to the reader that he or she is reading 'history' in the use of precise dates, the inclusion of state documents and records, and the general verisimilitude of the events narrated. These signals also mark the historical writings of Josephus and Greek historians."[1] Many of its stories were later retold by the Jewish historian Josephus in his history of the Jews. 1 Maccabees shares the vital account of the Maccabean Revolt and the subsequent establishment of the Jewish festival of Hanukkah. It is sometimes called "dynastic propaganda" because it also relates the events of three generations of the Hasmonean (Maccabee) family. It was almost certainly originally written in Hebrew, although only the Greek translation has been found.[2] So although 1 Maccabees is no longer part of the Jewish scriptural canon, it provides influential models of resistance to Gentile persecution and the reasons for the Jews' observance of this most important post–Old Testament festival.

Background

1 Maccabees begins with the conquest of the Near East region by Alexander the Great, a young Macedonian king, around 333 BC, but its real focus is on the historical events between 175 and 104 BC. The text first sets the stage with Alexander, who "fought many battles, conquered strongholds, and put to death the kings of the earth . . . He gathered a very strong army and ruled over countries, nations, and princes, and they became tributary to him" (1:2–4). This sweeping statement is not hyperbole because after Alexander's relentless military campaigning had ended, he was the ruler of Macedon, Greece, Egypt, and Persia. At Alexander's sudden death in 323 BC, his conquered territories were divided among his generals. "Then his officers began to rule, each in his own place. They all put on crowns after his death, and so did their descendants after them for many years; and they caused many evils on the earth" (1:8–9). The evil deeds of one such descendant (and the Jews' response to them) become the focus of 1 Maccabees.

One of Alexander's generals, Seleucus, ruled from Syria; another, Ptolemy, ruled from Egypt. Judea, stuck in between Egypt and Syria, became the battleground between these two competing Greek empires. After initially being under Ptolemaic rule, Judea was taken over by the Seleucids in 198 BC. However, Seleucid fortunes changed in a disastrous loss to the emerging Romans in 190 BC. The Seleucids not only lost territory to the Romans, but were also forced to pay them a hefty annual tribute, leaving the Seleucid rulers searching for targets to plunder to maintain payments. When Antiochus IV Epiphanes ("God manifest") took the Seleucid throne around 175 BC, he wanted to take over Egypt and thereby gain enough wealth to easily cover the tribute to Rome. 1 Maccabees recounts his successful foray into Egypt (1:17–19) until Rome warned Antiochus IV that if he annexed Egypt, they would break their treaty and attack him.[3] Antiochus IV withdrew his plans to annex Egypt and instead turned his sights to Jerusalem.

The first chapter of 1 Maccabees describes some of the effects of Greek conquest and influence on Jerusalem and the Jewish people. An effect of Alexander the Great's conquest of the region was the acceleration of the phenomenon called Hellenism, whereby Greek language, thought, art, and religion were blended with the local cultures of the Near East and Eastern Mediterranean. The Jewish people around Jerusalem chose from among three options when dealing with Hellenism: adopt it, adapt it, or resist it. (It is similar to the issue we face today with the "world": How do we live *in* the world without being *of* the world?) Some Jews, particularly the political elites, became so zealous in their adoption of Hellenism that they built a gymnasium in Jerusalem near the temple which promoted Greek forms of education and recreation—including exercising in the nude. These Gentile influences subsequently led some Jews to remove the marks of their circumcision and abandon their holy covenant (1:15).[4] Others, particularly the lower classes, kept their distance from most aspects of Hellenistic culture. They clung to the traditional Jewish life of their ancestors despite the rapid changes occurring around them. The divide between the Hellenistic elites and the traditionalists grew ever wider as the Seleucids became increasingly involved in Jewish affairs.

Antiochus IV's presence and impact in Jerusalem increased as he "arrogantly entered the sanctuary [temple] and took the golden altar, the lampstand for the light, and all its utensils. He took also the table for the bread of the Presence, the cups for drink offerings, the bowls, the golden censers, the curtain, the crowns, and the gold decoration on the front of the temple; he stripped it all off" (1:21–22).[5] Two years later, the chief collector of tribute returned to Jerusalem with a military force, plundered the city, and tore down houses and surrounding walls. They built up a fortress, called the Acra, to garrison their troops overlooking the temple. This Gentile citadel became a thorn in the Jews' side for many years.[6]

The king then made a new decree, probably under the influence of the Jewish Hellenizers, who may have encouraged him to force their fellow Jews to abandon some of their religious customs so that they would be more like their Gentile neighbors. He declared that the Jews must abandon their worship practices such as Sabbath observance, sacrifices, and circumcision so that all the people in the empire could be "one people" (1:41–42).[7] They "erected a desolating sacrilege on the [temple] altar of burnt offering. They also built altars in the surrounding towns of Judah, and offered incense at the doors of the houses and in the streets.[8] The books of the law that they found they tore to pieces and burned with fire. Anyone found possessing the book of the covenant, or anyone who adhered to the law, was condemned to death by decree of the king" (1:54–57). In order to avoid punishment, some Jews immediately followed the king's commands, while others tried to secretly remain faithful to their covenants. Those caught maintaining their Jewish worship were tortured and even put to death. "Many in Israel stood firm and were resolved in their hearts not to eat unclean food. They chose to die rather than to be defiled by food or to profane the holy covenant; and they did die" (1:62–63).

RISE OF THE MACCABEES

Chapter 2 begins the tale of the rise of the Maccabees over the Seleucids. It first introduces the Jewish family led by Mattathias, a priest, and his five sons: John, Simon, Judas Maccabeus (where the name Maccabees comes from; it seems to be a nickname for something like "hammer," an indication of this son's personality), Eleazar, and Jonathan. One of Mattathias's forefathers was named Hashmonia, so the Maccabees are also referred to as the Hasmoneans. They lived in a small village in the hill country named Modein, lying between Jerusalem and the Mediterranean. Mattathias was distraught by the Gentiles' corruption of Jerusalem. One day, Antiochus's officers arrive in Modein to enforce the king's decrees prohibiting Jewish worship and promoting Gentile worship instead. Because he is a respected elder in the town, Mattathias is approached by the officers to be the example of obedience to the king. He and his sons are promised wealth and honor if they obey. 1 Maccabees 2:18 contains the officer's promise to Mattathias that his actions will earn him a place "among the friends of the king." This was not a vague promise of a favored status, but rather a guarantee of a specific, prestigious rank. "The Friends of the King had the privileges of members of the royal court. They were entitled to wear purple broad-brimmed Macedonian hats and purple robes," which were marks of royalty in the Near Eastern world.[9]

Mattathias strongly replies, "Even if all the nations that live under the rule of the king obey him, and have chosen to obey his commandments, everyone of them abandoning the religion of their ancestors, I and my sons and my brothers will continue to live by the covenant of our ancestors. Far be it from us to desert the law and the ordinances" (2:19–21). At that moment, another Jew steps forward to offer sacrifice on the altar according to the king's command. Mattathias "burned with zeal and his heart was stirred. He gave vent to righteous anger; he ran and killed him on the altar. At the same time he killed the king's officer who was forcing them to sacrifice, and he tore down the altar" (2:24–25). Mattathias's actions were modeled on the Hebrew Bible story of Phinehas, a righteous priest who zealously speared an idolatrous couple and turned the Lord's wrath away from the Israelites (Numbers 25:6–15).[10] With this bold act, Mattathias effectively begins the Maccabean revolt.

Mattathias then invites all who are zealous for the law and support the covenant to go out with him to the hills.[11] "Then he and his sons fled to the hills and left all that they had in the town" (2:28). One group, the Hasideans, is specifically singled out for joining their cause. The Hasideans ("the pious") wanted to preserve the religious law, so despite their misgivings with the violent actions of the revolt, they probably saw this as the best avenue to defend the law. Their participation also gave greater religious legitimacy to the Maccabees.[12] The hills become the staging ground for guerilla-type warfare against Seleucid military forces, and the brothers become the backbone for the resistance to the Gentiles and Gentile sympathizers. It is little wonder that, almost two thousand years later, the Maccabees served as role models in the Jewish effort to form the State of Israel over seventy years ago. Today they are still seen as a symbol of resistance for Jews (and as symbols of vigorous athleticism—many professional basketball teams in Israel are named *Maccabees*).

But even after Mattathias's actions, not all Jews choose to militarily resist the king's decree and instead choose to suffer martyrdom while remaining faithful to the covenant. Immediately after the Maccabees flee to the hills to take up the cause, the text recounts the tragic story of another group who tried to hide in the Judean wilderness. The king's officers and troops hear of their hiding places and pursue them. A showdown occurs on the Sabbath day when this group of Jews will not obey the king's commands, especially because it would profane the Sabbath day. Similarly, because it is the Sabbath day, when the Seleucids attack, the Jews do nothing to defend themselves but instead proclaim, "Let us all die in our innocence; heaven and earth testify for us that you are killing us unjustly" (2:37). In a short time they are all killed.[13]

When Mattathias and his followers hear of the tragedy, they mourn for the martyrs and determine that they will not idly sit back on Sabbath days, or they will quickly perish.[14] Instead, they will fight against anyone that comes against them, even on the Sabbath—a momentous decision to subordinate the Sabbath to their revolt (and a decision not made by a prophet or high priest).

The initial targets of the Maccabean revolt were actually their fellow compatriots who complied with the king's decree. 1 Maccabees recounts the attacks against sinners and renegades, forcing the survivors to flee to the Gentiles for safety (2:44). "And Mattathias and his friends went around and tore down the altars; they forcibly circumcised all the uncircumcised boys that they found within the borders of Israel. They hunted down the arrogant, and the work prospered in their hands. They rescued the law out of the hands of the Gentiles and kings, and they never let the sinner gain the upper hand" (2:45–48).

A year or so after the beginning of the revolt, Mattathias is on his deathbed. As part of his last counsel to his sons, he encourages them to continue the resistance and "show zeal for the law, and give your lives for the covenant of our ancestors" (2:50).[15] To encourage them, he recounts the valiant deeds of some of their forefathers: Abraham, Joseph, Phinehas, Joshua, Caleb, King David, Elijah, Daniel, and Daniel's three friends Hananiah, Mishael, and Azariah (the Hebrew names for Shadrach, Meshach, and Abed-Nego). Mattathias then "transfers" the leadership of the revolt to two of his sons: Simon as the chief administrator and Judas as the military commander. Mattathias admonishes them to "pay back the Gentiles in full" (2:68), and then he blesses his sons and dies in 166 BC.[16]

REDEDICATION OF THE TEMPLE—HANUKKAH

Chapters 3 and 4 recount many battles between the small band of Jewish warriors led by Judas Maccabeus and various Seleucid military commanders. The conflict escalates with each Jewish victory as higher-ranking Seleucid military officials are summoned to lead an increasingly larger army.[17] From his Syrian capital, King Antiochus grows angrier and wants to rid himself of this Jewish problem, but realizes he can't commit all his financial resources to this conflict without severe repercussions down the road. He turns his attention toward Persia to find opportunities to plunder there, leaving his most trusted officials behind to lead the other half of his forces and secure the victory. At first the large Seleucid army frightens the smaller Jewish forces, but Judas rallies their courage and leads them in battle. Like Captain Moroni, Judas exhorts his men to trust in heaven's help: "It is not on the size of the army that victory in battle depends, but strength comes from Heaven. They come against us in great insolence and lawlessness to destroy us and our wives and our children, and to despoil us; but we fight for our lives and our laws, He himself will crush them before us; as for you, do not be afraid of them" (3:19–22).[18]

The people spiritually prepare themselves for battle by fasting, reading the law, gathering offerings, and praying to heaven to ask where they should bring their offerings and priesthood vestments if the temple is profaned. Meanwhile, Judas organizes the forces, prepares them with weapons, and insists "it is better for us to die in battle than to see the misfortunes of our nation and of the sanctuary. But as his will in heaven may be, so shall he do" (3:59–60).[19] He also hearkens back to the miracle of the Exodus, when their ancestors were saved at the Red Sea, and encourages his small band to again cry to Heaven "to see whether he will favor us and remember his covenant with our ancestors and crush this army before us today. Then all the Gentiles will know that there is one who redeems and saves Israel" (4:10–11). Judas is successful in that battle and in the next when an even larger army attacks, forcing the Seleucids to regroup in Antioch and thereby leaving Jerusalem in Judas's hands.

A bleak portrayal of Jerusalem's condition is described when the Maccabean forces first enter the city. "They saw the sanctuary desolate, the altar profaned, and the gates burned. In the courts they saw bushes sprung up as in a thicket, or as on one of the mountains. They saw also the chambers of the priests in ruins. Then they tore their clothes and mourned with great lamentation; they sprinkled themselves with ashes and fell face down on the ground. And when the signal was given with the trumpets, they cried out to Heaven" (4:38–40). The cleaning of the temple and its grounds begins under the leadership of "blameless priests devoted to the law" (4:42). "They deliberated what to do about the altar of burnt offering, which had been profaned.[20] And they thought it best to tear it down, so that it would not be a lasting shame to them that the Gentiles had defiled it. So they tore down the altar, and stored the stones in a convenient place on the temple hill until a prophet should come to tell what to do with them" (4:44–46). They rebuild the altar with unhewn stones in accordance with the requirements of the Law of Moses, rebuild the sanctuary and the interior of the temple, and consecrate the courts. "They made new holy vessels, and brought the lampstand, the altar of incense, and the table into the temple. They placed the bread on the table and hung up the curtains. Thus they finished all the work they had undertaken" (4:49–51).

The next morning, they offer the morning sacrifice on the new altar as the Law directs and begin an eight-day celebration for the dedication of the altar. "Then Judas and his brothers and all the assembly of Israel determined that every year at that season the days of dedication of the altar should be observed with joy and gladness for eight days, beginning with the twenty-fifth day of the month of Chislev" (4:59). Thus the festival of Hanukkah, or dedi-cation, is instituted in 164 BC and has been observed ever since. The eight-day festival seems to be patterned after Hezekiah's recon-secration of the temple when it had been profaned in his day (see 2 Chronicles 29:17) and is celebrated like the Feast of Tabernacles, which they had not been able to celebrate a few months earlier because of the conflict, "with great gladness and with the bearing of the branches of palms and of other trees."[21] Because of all the illumination from the celebrations, it is also referred to as the Feast of Lights.[22]

Later Jewish accounts in the Talmud attribute the eight days to a miracle of the consecrated oil. When they first regain control of the Temple, the Jews are faced with a dilemma: they have only one day's worth of oil to burn in the candelabrum (menorah) in the Temple courtyard, and it takes seven days to produce and conse-crate more. Should they light the one day's worth at the beginning, letting the menorah return to darkness for the period needed to consecrate more oil? Or should they wait until the last day of the consecration period and then light the menorah, continuing with replenished oil from that time forward? They decide to light the menorah on the first day and the oil miraculously continues to burn for seven days; thus, the lighting of the menorah becomes a symbolic reminder of this miraculous period.[23] Regardless of its true origins, Hanukkah has become a symbol of God's assistance in dire circumstances and the rejoicing associated with the rededication of the Temple.

REIGN OF THE HASMONEANS

Unfortunately, the rest of 1 Maccabees is not as glorious as the first. The Hasmoneans go on ruthless offensives against the Hellenizers, neighboring peoples, and anyone who does not support their cause. It is during this period that many non-Jewish inhabitants of the Holy Land are (forcibly) converted to Judaism, most notably the Idumeans from which Herod the Great later descended. Despite gaining control of the Temple in Jerusalem, the Jews cannot initially dislodge the Seleucid garrison in their midst; the Acra (or citadel) that housed the foreign forces proves to be impenetrable. Seleucid rulers continually fight to regain complete authority over Judea. Several setbacks for the Maccabees occur that lead to the deaths of some of the brothers. In one of the later battles, Eleazar is crushed to death by an elephant carrying soldiers that collapses on top of him after he stabs it from beneath (6:46).[24] After more victories, vengeful attacks, and an alliance with the growing Roman Empire,[25] Judas also is killed in battle when many soldiers in his forces flee at the approaching Seleucid army. The military leadership passes to his brother Jonathan (9:28–31).[26]

Hasmonean history becomes intricately intertwined with Seleucid politics as various pretenders to the throne of Judea or to the office of high priest seek Seleucid assistance for their causes. One such individual, Alcimus, is given the position of high priest despite not being from a legitimate high priestly family. He uses his influence to promote Hellenism and tear down traditional beliefs and practices. Judas said of Alcimus that he and his associates did more damage among the Israelites than the Gentiles (7:23). Fortunately, when Alcimus begins to tear down the wall of the inner court of the sanctuary—the work of the prophets Haggai and Zechariah— he is stricken, paralyzed, and dies in great agony (9:54–56).[27] But shortly thereafter, the high priesthood is offered to Jonathan, one of the Hasmoneans, by one of the Seleucid kings as part of a peace treaty.[28] Now the family that had revolted against the Seleucids is becoming part of their inner circle, "a king's Friend," and reliant on Seleucid support for legitimacy. Yet in the swirling intrigue of Seleucid politics, Jonathan is betrayed by one aspirant to the throne and captured in the city of Ptolemais (12:46–48). Jonathan is later killed as a hostage (13:23).

Simon becomes the last brother standing and naturally takes over both as high priest and leader of anti-Seleucid resistance. Simon strengthens the strongholds of Judea and stores up food for inevitable sieges. He finally secures victory over the Acra, or citadel, in Jerusalem that had garrisoned foreign troops for decades. He then turns over military leadership to his son, John Hyrcanus, who later reigns as high priest from 134–104 BC. 1 Maccabees comes to an end with Simon's death, when he is killed in treachery at a banquet in Jericho held in his honor.[29] Many challengers want to seize the opportunity of Simon's death to take over the land, but Simon's son, John Hyrcanus, fights to maintain power. 1 Maccabees finishes with an allusion to John's efforts preserved in another record of the continuation of the Hasmonean rule: "The rest of the acts of John and his wars and the brave deeds that he did, and the building of the walls that he completed, and his achievements, are written in the annals of his high priesthood, from the time that he became high priest after his father" (16:23–24).

Thus the Maccabees, who had been heroic in resisting evil and restoring the temple to its glory, become caught up in the power struggles around them, eventually leading them to accommodation with the evil that they had fought against earlier.[30] They who had restored the sanctity of the temple inappropriately take the office of the high priest and rule as many of the neighboring worldly kings around them. So the tragedy of 1 Maccabees is not just in the severe persecution and martyrdom that many Jews face at the hands of their enemies, but in the later vengeful, contentious history of the Hasmoneans that turns the heroes into questionable role models.

CONCLUSION

The forms of Jewish resistance modeled in 1 Maccabees can also be seen in the plaza outside the modern Holocaust Museum, Yad Vashem, in Jerusalem, where visitors find two large murals depicting Jewish responses to Nazi aggression and the horrors of the Holocaust.[31] One with grand, strong figures shows the valiant resisters who led the uprising in the Warsaw ghetto. The other shows a march of meek, submissive Jews being herded away to death camps by overseeing soldiers. These murals capture the poignant issue of how one can respond to extreme persecution that puts one's religious traditions and very life in jeopardy. Which is the correct response: fight for one's life or submit to the captor's will? Death could result in either case, but one does not usually know that when first making the decision.

In the immediate post-Holocaust world, many death camp survivors were ashamed for having submitted to the demands of their persecutors rather than resist (although most resisters did not survive). But after several decades, many Jews recognized the courage and contribution of these survivors and how their response preserved many faithful Jews. If all had violently resisted, then probably many more would have been killed.

1 Maccabees also confronts the issue of how to respond to extreme persecution and may have even served as inspiration for those facing Nazi persecution. Some Jews in the second century BC chose to resist through strong, violent military clashes, while others

submissively responded with martyrdom. In either case, both can be honored for remaining faithful to the covenant and resisting the evil decree, while those who complied with the king's decree became the true enemy. While Latter-day Saints may not celebrate Hanukkah or have faced the same situation that early Jews did at the hands of the Seleucids, they have had episodes of extreme persecution in their own Latter-day Saint tradition. These episodes of persecution forced early saints to confront the issue of how to respond. Some chose to violently resist, such as at Haun's Mill, but this response did not bring much change and often led to their deaths. Most chose to submit to the persecutors' demands by abandoning their hard-earned fields and homes and leaving for other destinations in search of freedom from persecution. This pattern was repeated several times until they finally found refuge in the Salt Lake Valley. Their meek and courageous response preserved the cause and left them to live another day. Their responses took a lot of courage and faith that somehow things would work out. We can look up to and honor those who remained faithful to their covenants rather than give in to the easier path of abandoning their beliefs and assimilating with their non-LDS neighbors.

In our own day and age, we are faced with the issue of being surrounded by the world and its various views and philosophies. Religious freedom is increasingly under attack, forcing challenging situations for how to remain faithful to one's beliefs and practice one's tenets in a pluralistic society. We hope that circumstances will not deteriorate to the point of severe, violent persecution, but if so, how will we respond? Will we respond with Captain Moroni–like zeal, gathering like-minded individuals to militarily support and defend our cause? Or will we submit to the powers that be and live for another day that we hope will lead to better religious conditions in the future? Accommodation to the surrounding world is always a challenge; there usually needs to be enough accommodation to get along, but not too much to lose our own identity and be too restricted in our religious worship.

But with whatever we face, perhaps the most important question is whether we will remain strong and loyal to our covenants in the midst of the worldly pressure and avoid the temptations to assimilate to the world around us.

NOTES

1. deSilva, *Introducing the Apocrypha*, 248.
2. For example, Grabbe, "Apocrypha," 19.
3. "[The Roman general] Popillius informed the proud king that the Roman senate ordered him to withdraw from Egypt at once or face the displeasure of Rome. Antiochus answered that he would consider Rome's request. But the general wasn't satisfied. With remarkable disdain for the prestige of a foreign monarch, he took his staff and drew a circle in the sand around King Antiochus. Then, he said to the king, 'You may consider as long as you like—but Rome requires your answer before you leave that circle.' Antiochus was outraged—but he was also helpless. He'd recently been a captive in Rome, and he knew that his kingdom wasn't yet in any position to win a war with the mighty Republic. His only choice was to withdraw." Anthony J. Tomasino, *Judaism Before Jesus: The Ideas and Events that Shaped the New Testament World* (Downers Grove, IL: InterVarsity Press, 2003), 134.
4. "The gymnasium was built on the Temple hill, below the fortress, and crowds of young men . . . among them some priests who had abandoned their more decorous Temple duties for the lure of naked athletics (in particular discus throwing), now began to exercise with the enthusiasm of converts. For many the urge to break away from the isolation imposed by strict Judaism had become very strong. However, these impassioned would-be Greeks had one embarrassing problem to overcome: the highly un-Greek fact of their circumcision. In one scholar's delicate phrase, they 'employed artificial means to efface it.' Just how they 'concealed' or even 'removed' evidence of the *mohel*'s knife is not at all clear. All we know is that surprising number of people did so." Peter Green, *Alexander to Actium: The Historical Evolution of the Hellenistic Age* (Berkeley: University of California Press, 1990), 510.

5. Antiochus IV "was, as always, short of money, and the object of his visit was to raise some quick loot. The plundering of sanctuaries had become a common habit since Antiochus II had embarked on it, and Epiphanes himself was no stranger to the practice . . . There was no open uprising at the time, but Antiochus's actions left a legacy of deep hatred and resentment behind, and not only among strict traditionalists: what the king regarded as no more than catching up on arrears of tribute, and, thus, his royal prerogative, appeared in Jewish eyes as plain sacrilege." Green, *Alexander to Actium*, 512.

6. There are no clear remains from this once-prominent fortress, and its former location in Jerusalem is a matter of scholarly debate. For a discussion on the location of the Acra and other features of the ancient Temple Mount, see Leen Ritmeyer, "Locating the Original Temple Mount," *Biblical Archaeology Review* 18, no. 2 (Mar/Apr 1992): 24–45, 64–65.

7. There is a great deal of scholarly debate over the real motivations for Antiochus's repression of Jewish religion. The rationale alluded to in the text, that Antiochus desired greater unity in his empire, does not adequately explain why he took such drastic steps to stamp out Judaism—a policy that contrasts greatly with the religious tolerance common in Hellenistic kingdoms. "This act of the king, which seems to have been contrary to his normal policy in dealing with subject peoples, amounted to a prohibition of the Jewish religion on pain of death. Why did a seemingly enlightened monarch take so radical a step? The reasons that motivated Antiochus have been debated at length, but it is clear at least that Jerusalem had been a trouble spot for some time and that he regarded the unusual religion of the Jews as the heart of the problem." James C. VanderKam, *An Introduction to Early Judaism* (Grand Rapids, MI: Eerdmans Publishing, 2001), 20.

8. "A great deal of energy has been spent trying to pinpoint exactly what cult was imposed upon Jerusalem by Antiochus IV. The sources tell us that the temple was dedicated to Zeus Olympios (2 Macc 6:2), that a desolating sacrilege and an altar were placed on top of the altar of burnt offering in the temple courtyard (1 Macc 1:54, 59; 4:43–44), and that both the king's birthday and the feast day of the god Dionysus were celebrated monthly (2 Macc 6:7) . . . Rather than the imposition of the worship of one god in place of Yahweh, it seems that the worship of many gods, including Dionysus and Zeus Olympios, took place. Thus regular paganism, characterized by the worship of many gods and goddesses, was introduced." Robert Doran, *The First Book of Maccabees* (NIB IV; Nashville: Abingdon Press, 1996), 11.

9. Jonathan A. Goldstein, *1 Maccabees* (Anchor Bible 41; Garden City: Doubleday, 1976), 232.

10. The author's purposeful linking of Phinehas and Mattathias was likely done to magnify Mattathias through association with this well-known Israelite hero. Both Phinehas and Mattathias are described as priests. Both of them decisively strike against sinful idolaters. Both of them are described specifically as "zealous" for the Lord (Numbers 25:11; 1 Maccabees 2:24). And both of them are given a family legacy for their actions: Phinehas's posterity is given the priesthood, and Mattathias becomes the head of a new dynasty of Jewish rulers.

11. Latter-day Saint readers can identify many similarities between the actions of Mattathias and Captain Moroni in the Book of Mormon. Like Mattathias, Moroni expressed anger towards an oppressive threat (Amalickiah and his forces), he calls his people to be true to their covenants with God, and induces many men to take up arms in response to his pleas. (Particularly compare Alma 46 with 1 Maccabees 2.)

12. "[The text] suggests that the Hasideans were a well-known group, but their exact identity has evoked much scholarly debate. Are they to be connected with "the wise ones" of Daniel 11:33 or with those described allegorically in 1 Enoch 90:6–9? Are they to be linked with the Essenes or to the Pharisees? The term "Hasidean itself draws upon traditional terminology, where those loyal to God are referred to as *hasidim* . . . [They are] a distinguished people, and their willingness to offer their own lives for the sake of the law responds to Mattathias's call to all who are zealous for the law to follow him (2:27). In 1 Maccabees, then, the Hasideans are neither pacifist nor apocalyptic, but important folk devoted to the law." Doran, *The First Book of Maccabees*, 47.

13. The story of these Jewish martyrs bears striking resemblance to that of the Anti-Nephi-Lehi converts in the Book of Mormon, who refuse to take up arms against their Lamanite assailants. Their motivations are similar: the persecuted Jews refuse to break the Mosaic covenant and decide to "die in [their] innocence" (1 Maccabees 2:37); likewise, the Anti-Nephi-Lehies refuse to break the covenant of nonviolence that they made with God, "vouching and covenanting with God, that rather than shed the blood of their brethren they would give up their own lives" (Alma 24:18). Even the number of casualties is similar: 1 Maccabees 2:38 lists the number of slain Jews as one thousand, and Alma 24:22 gives a casualty count of one thousand and five.

14. "[The Jewish revolutionary] Bar-Kochva has cogently pointed out that previously there had not been any ban against warfare on the Sabbath, otherwise Jews could not have served in Hellenistic armies (as they certainly did). Nonetheless, the emphasis in both this and the previous

passage is on defense on the Sabbath in particular (2:32, 34, 38, 41), not just on any day; there were many who opposed any kind of warfare on the Sabbath. The pseudepigraphic book of *Jubilees* states that anyone who made war on the Sabbath should die, a position maintained by some into the first century CE [AD]. Allowing oneself to be killed by refusing to fight on the Sabbath was considered a pious act." Doran, *The First Book of Maccabees*, NIB IV:47.

15. Mattathias's deathbed speech to his sons echoes similar speeches given by other prominent Israelite leaders throughout the Hebrew Bible. Characters such as Jacob (Genesis 49), Moses (Deuteronomy 33), Joshua (Joshua 23), Samuel (1 Samuel 12), and David (1 Kings 2) blessed, counseled, and prophesied to their people shortly before their deaths. The use of formulaic phrases common to these other speeches indicates that the author of 1 Maccabees meant to explicitly link Mattathias to these venerated Israelite patriarchs. (See Doran, *The First Book of Maccabees*, NIB IV:49–50.) This motif of a farewell speech, particularly from fathers to sons, is well attested in the Book of Mormon as well: Lehi (2 Nephi 1–3), King Benjamin (Mosiah 1–5), Mosiah (Mosiah 29), Alma the Younger (Alma 36–42), and Mormon (Mormon 7) give similar discourses.

16. Mattathias's traditional tomb outside of Modein can still be visited today.

17. "With the assumption of military command by [Mattathias's] son Judas Maccabaeus insurrection entered a new phase: it became a highly politicized revolutionary war, challenging the Seleucid regime and aiming, ultimately, at complete independence for the Jewish *ethnos*. Judas was a natural general, who welded a heterogeneous mass of untrained followers, in a remarkably brief space of time, into a formidable fighting force, over six thousand strong. He not only showed a flair for guerilla tactics, but proved himself capable of winning pitched battles." Green, *Alexander to Actium*, 518.

18. "The author devotes 40 percent of his history to an account of the exploits of Judas . . . [But] our author does not simply sing the praises of a great hero. Judas's victories are possible only through divine help. He enters battle with prayer (3:46; 4:30–33; 5:33; 7:30–42) and celebrates victory by praising God (4:24,33,55). His exhortations to his army remind them of other times in the past when God supported Israel against overwhelming odds (4:8–9, 30; 7:41). "It is not on the size of the army that victory in battle depends, but strength comes from heaven" (3:18–19). Some of the descriptions of Judas's wars make clear that he was following the ancient practices of holy warfare. Our author believes that through Judas "the savior of Israel" (9:21) God "the savior of Israel" (4:30) delivered God's people." Nickelsburg, *Jewish Literature*, 104–105.

19. In this and other passages throughout 1 Maccabees, the author avoids direct references to God. "He is reticent about using the holy names of 'God' and 'Lord,' always employing in their stead a surrogate like 'Heaven,' or using simply the second or third person pronoun in referring to the Deity (for example, 'They [i.e. Judas and his men] sang hymns and praises to Heaven, for his mercy is good and everlasting,' 4:24). Since the Pharisees were likewise scrupulous in thus avoiding the possibility of profaning the name of God, it has sometimes been thought that our author was a member of this party." Bruce M. Metzger, *An Introduction to the Apocrypha* (New York: Oxford University Press, 1957), 131.

20. The quandary alluded to here was sparked by seemingly contradictory laws given in Deuteronomy about the treatment of altars. While Deuteronomy 12:2–3 commands the Israelites to destroy any pagan altars found in their lands, verse 4 states that the same action should not be taken against the Lord's altar. So what was to be done with an altar that had been dedicated to Jehovah, yet had been used for pagan sacrifices? In an attempt to obey both of the Mosaic mandates, the altar was not completely destroyed (as was the customary treatment for a heathen altar), but was merely dismantled and relocated, awaiting a prophet to provide clarification on what should be done with its stones. (See Goldstein, *1 Maccabees*, 285.)

21. LDS Bible Dictionary, 644.

22. According to John 10:22–39, some tried to stone Jesus during a later observance of this festival while he walked through Solomon's porch near the temple. "This festival stirred patriotic feelings among the Jewish people then, and it continues to do so today. The exploits of the Maccabees were rehearsed and hopes for the coming Messiah renewed. It is no surprise that in John's Gospel, on the occasion of Hanukkah (Jn 10:22), the religious authorities huddled around Jesus asked him a very apropos question. 'How long will you keep us in suspense? If you are the Messiah, tell us plainly' (Jn 10:24). His answer, according to John's Gospel, was unequivocal (Jn 10:25), but they did not believe him (Jn 10:31). He simply did not fit the expectations created by the Maccabean legacy." Helyer, *Exploring Jewish Literature,* 158.

23. The incident is recorded in the Babylonian Talmud as follows: "When the Temple was rededicated it was discovered that the oil for the lamp in the Sanctuary had been desecrated by the invaders. After a diligent search, however, a single cruse of undefiled oil sealed by the High Priest was found. In it was oil enough for the lamp to burn but a single day. Then a miracle was wrought for the Maccabees; the oil was multiplied so that it proved to be sufficient to burn for eight days. (*b. Sabb* 23.b)" Quoted in Helyer, *Exploring Jewish Literature,* 158. Another allusion

to the miraculous preservation of the oil can be found in the popular dreidel game played during Hanukkah. The four sides of the dreidel bear the Hebrew letters נ (Nun), ג (Gimel), ה (Hey), and ש (Shin), which are the first letters of the words in the Hebrew saying "A great miracle happened there." Metzger, *An Introduction to the Apocrypha*, 137.

24. The account of Eleazar's heroic death reads as follows: "Now Eleazar, called Avaran, saw that one of the animals was equipped with royal armor. It was taller than all the others, and he supposed the king was on it. So he gave his life to save his people and win for himself an everlasting name. He courageously ran into the midst of the phalanx to reach it; he killed men right and left, and they parted before him on both sides. He got under the elephant, stabbed it from beneath, and killed it; but it fell to the ground upon him and he died" (6:43–46).

25. 1 Maccabees 8 includes a glowing evaluation of the Roman state as well as a description of a Jewish diplomatic mission sent to the Senate to seek an alliance. It's possible that the Hasmoneans did seek an alliance with Rome, but no other record of this diplomatic mission or letter has been discovered. Regardless, the author of 1 Maccabees obviously had a very optimistic perspective on future Jewish-Roman relations—a hope that would prove tragically naïve in the centuries to come.

26. "When the Jewish troops saw the great Syrian host drawing near, they appealed to Judas to flee—but he would have none of it. Confident in his God, expecting a miracle, he refused to be intimidated by the Syrian numerical superiority. But his soldiers weren't quite so faithful. Many of them deserted, until his army dwindled to only eight hundred. Still, Judas refused to back down the fight. He encouraged the irresolute, 'If this is where we're to meet our end, then let us meet it bravely.' There at Elasa the armies met, but the short conflict can hardly be called a battle. Judas was killed early in the skirmish, and the rest of his army scattered. His brothers Jonathan and Simon gathered up his body and carried it away for burial in the family tomb at Modein." Tomasino, *Judaism Before Jesus*, 153.

27. Disease in the ancient world was often seen as a sign of divine judgment, and many ancient authors were quick to provide the lurid details of the deaths of hated figures. Luke, for example, shares the cautionary tale of the impious Herod, who failed to give God glory and was "eaten by worms" (Acts 12:21–23).

28. While the author of 1 Maccabees appears to have no problem with the Hasmoneans claiming the office of high priest, many Jews were outraged that a non-Zadokite would dare take this priesthood title. "In fact, the Pharisaic, Sadducean and Essene movements, which generated years of sectarian strife among the Jewish people during the Second Temple

period, probably go back to this fateful decision." Helyer, *Exploring Jewish Literature*, 154. Many scholars believe that the "Wicked Priest" vilified in the Dead Sea scrolls may refer to Jonathan or Simon, the first of the Hasmoneans to usurp the high priesthood; their impious actions may have led the "Teacher of Righteousness" to form the community at Qumran.

29. "Now Simon was visiting the towns of the country and attending to their needs, and he went down to Jericho with his sons Mattathias and Judas, in the one hundred seventy-seventh year, in the eleventh month, which is the month of Shebat. The son of Abubus received them treacherously in the little stronghold called Dok, which he had built; he gave them a great banquet, and hid men there. When Simon and his sons were drunk, Ptolemy and his men rose up, took their weapons, rushed in against Simon in the banquet hall and killed him and his two sons, as well as some of his servants. So he committed an act of great treachery and returned evil for good." (1 Maccabees 16: 14–17)

30. Robert Doran insightfully states that "the narrative of 1 Maccabees seems to end where it had begun. As the 'lawless renegades' had sought Seleucid intervention at the beginning of the story to bring about their control of Judea, so now within the Hasmonean family there are strife and fighting for control of Judea, and one side seeks the support of the Seleucids to gain control." From *The First Book of Maccabees. NIB* 4:178.

31. A debt of gratitude is expressed to Ophir Yarden, adjunct faculty member at the BYU Jerusalem Center for Near Eastern Studies, for his explanations of these murals at Yad Vashem.

12

2 MACCABEES

2 MACCABEES IS ANOTHER BOOK ABOUT THE MACCABEAN REVOLT and covers some of the same events as 1 Maccabees, but it focuses on events in Jerusalem and a shorter time period: 180–161 BC (basically paralleling 1 Maccabees 1–8). It follows the style of 1 Maccabees, but the reworked material contains more direct references to divine assistance and clearly explains the heavenly rationale for why events happened the way they did. In this fashion, 2 Maccabees emphasizes how Jews cannot change their own lives if not for God's intervention (whereas 1 Maccabees highlights how Jews could change their own lives). 2 Maccabees is sometimes described as "temple propaganda" because of its focus on the reconquest and defense of the temple, or "pathetic history" because of its appeal to the emotions (*pathē* in Greek).[1] It claims to be an abridgment of a five-volume work by Jason of Cyrene, but nothing of this original text remains. That it is an abridgment is sometimes revealed "by the fact that a few times (4:45; 8:33; 10:37; 12:36) new characters are mentioned as if they are known to the reader. Various indications show that the abridger—who also addresses the readers in a few theological excurses (5:17–20; 6:12–17; cf. 4:16–17)—undertook some very substantial editing."[2] Although fully part of the Catholic Bible, "there is little trace of any Jews reading 2 Maccabees prior to the modern period" except in the cases of 4 Maccabees and

the tenth-century author of *Josippon*.[3] 2 Maccabees fits comfortably within its Hellenistic environment as the author argues that "the Jews are a civilized and respectable people organized around a *polis*, the central bearer of Greek culture. . . . That is, good Jews are a type of good Greeks."[4] Examples abound throughout the work, especially in changes from 1 Maccabees, which emphasize the author's goal to situate the Jews within Hellenistic society.

2 Maccabees is found in many miniscule Greek manuscripts as well as in the Alexandrinus and Venetus manuscripts of the Septuagint. The most important translation is into Old Latin with additional ones into Syriac and Armenian. It was probably written shortly after the death of Nicanor because that battle plays such a prominent role in the story and led to the formation of a festival to celebrate this victory (yet this victory waned in importance after subsequent events). Thus, some place its composition between 160 and 124 BC in a process that adapted the main body of the tale to a Jerusalem/Palestinian context and then added the initial letters to encourage Hanukkah observance.

2 Maccabees is basically divided into two halves: the first half on the persecutions and subsequent martyrdoms of the Jews at the hands of the Greek Seleucid rulers due to the institutionalized Hellenization in Jerusalem, and the second half on the military exploits of Judas Maccabeus. Overall, 2 Maccabees emphasizes the principle that history is unfolding according to God's plan, which includes periods of trial and persecution followed by deliverance and heavenly assistance. It also includes two letters from the Jewish community in Palestine to the Jewish community in Egypt encouraging them to celebrate the festival of Hanukkah. The two letters at the beginning of 2 Maccabees are out of chronological order, given that they encourage observance of a festival that would not be instituted until after the events portrayed later in the book. During the last centuries BC, a large Jewish community grew in Egypt, particularly Alexandria. The two letters are addressed to these Diaspora Jews. Besides sending their greetings, the Jews

in Jerusalem and Judea share that they are praying for them and asking God's blessings to be with them (1:1–9). They exhort the Egyptian Jews to remember the covenant made with Abraham, Isaac, and Jacob and urge them to keep the festival of Hanukkah on the twenty-fifth of Chislev.[5]

The second letter (1:10–2:18) gives more justification for why Hanukkah should be celebrated even though it was not prescribed by Moses nor found in the Hebrew Bible. Hanukkah, following the pattern of the rededication of the temple under Nehemiah, celebrates the purification of the temple after the victories over the Seleucid forces. The letter recounts a miracle: when the Jews were taken into Babylonian exile, a portion of the altar's fire from the first temple was preserved. Although the fire eventually extinguished in a dry cistern, it left behind a black liquid that they were able to put on the sacrificial wood during the time of Nehemiah. When the sun came out, it ignited the liquid and the flame consumed the sacrifice. In the second letter, they also petition for God's help to gather the scattered Israelites from among the Gentiles to plant them in his holy place. The letter also mentions the prophet Jeremiah taking the tent (tabernacle) and the Ark of the Covenant with him to Mount Nebo so they would not fall into Babylonian hands. This incident is quoted in an early 1832 LDS periodical, *The Evening and the Morning Star*,[6] in one of the first examples of quoting from the Apocrypha in Church literature (discussed previously in chapter 2). It relates how during the Babylonian attack Jeremiah took "the tent and the ark and the altar of incense" to Mount Nebo where they were sealed up in a cave-dwelling. Jeremiah declared that the place would remain unknown until the time God gathers his people again and discloses the location.

The second letter in 2 Maccabees ends with the plea, "Will you therefore please keep the days [of Hanukkah]? It is God who has saved all his people, and has returned the inheritance to all, and the kingship and the priesthood and the consecration, as he promised through the law. We have hope in God that he will soon have mercy on us and will gather us from everywhere under heaven into his holy place, for he has rescued us from great evils and has purified the place" (2:16–18).

The rest of chapter 2 serves as a preface and summary of the actual account of the Maccabees. The text emphasizes that it will describe "the appearances that came from heaven to those who fought bravely for Judaism" (2:21) and how they regained possession of the temple and liberated Jerusalem (2:22). The preface also explains the difficulty of condensing these acts into a single book with the aim to "please those who wish to read, to make it easy for those who are inclined to memorize, and to profit all readers" (2:25). For the editor, this task is no easy matter and "calls for sweat and loss of sleep" (2:26). These sentiments are somewhat similar to what Mormon and Moroni wrote about their editorial efforts in which they had to reduce their record from multiple other records, leaving not even 1/100th part of what could have been written (see Words of Mormon 1:5), and the concern they felt for how their record would be received by others (see Ether 12:23–25).

Persecution and Martyrdom

The first half of the story of 2 Maccabees focuses on the persecution of the Jews during the second century BC and the attendant martyrdom of many faithful. The story begins with Simon, the captain of the temple, having a disagreement with the high priest. Since Simon could not win the argument, he spitefully tells one of the Seleucid governors that the temple treasury is full and that it can be handed over to the king. Shortly thereafter, Heliodorus, a representative of the Seleucid king, enters the holy temple complex against the priests' and people's wishes. However, just as Heliodorus enters the treasury, "a magnificently caparisoned horse, with a rider of frightening mien; . . . rushed furiously at Heliodorus and struck at him with its front hoofs. Its rider was seen to have armor and weapons of God. Two young men also appeared to him, remarkably strong, gloriously beautiful and splendidly dressed, who stood on either side of him and flogged him continuously, inflicting many blows on him" (3:25–26). Heliodorus blacks out and has to be carried away by his men on a stretcher. The people rejoice at the divinely orchestrated turn of events and all come to recognize the sovereign power of God. Meanwhile, the high priest worries there will be severe repercussions on the Jewish people so he offers prayers and sacrifice for Heliodorus's recovery. Consequently, the two glorious figures reappear to Heliodorus and tell him, "Be very grateful to the high priest Onias, since for his sake the Lord has granted you your life. And see that you, who have been flogged by heaven, report to all people the majestic power of God" (3:33–34). Heliodorus recovers, makes sacrifices to God, and bears "testimony to all concerning the deeds of the supreme God, which he had seen with his own eyes" (3:36). When Heliodorus meets with the Seleucid king and the king asks who he should send in his place, Heliodorus warns him that it is doubtful whoever is sent will survive for "there is certainly some power of God about the place. For he who has his dwelling in heaven watches over that place himself and brings it aid, and he strikes and destroys those who come to do it injury" (3:38–39).

Chapter 4 recounts the efforts by some Jews to Hellenize their compatriots. Jason, who becomes the new high priest after usurping the position from his brother Onias, promises the Seleucid king a large sum of money "if permission were given to establish by his authority a gymnasium and a body of youth for it, and to enroll the people of Jerusalem as citizens of Antioch. When the king assented and Jason came to office, he at once shifted his compatriots over to the Greek way of life" (4:9–10). 2 Maccabees goes on to lament, "There was such an extreme of Hellenization and increase in the adoption of foreign ways because of the surpassing wickedness of Jason, who was ungodly and no true high priest" (4:13). The priests serving in the temple are so distracted by nearby Greek activities, such as wrestling, that they hurry through their sacrificial service in order to participate. They disdain "the honors prized by their ancestors" and instead value the "Greek forms of prestige" (4:15). The rest of the chapter shares some of the treacherous exploits of Menelaus, the brother of Simon mentioned above. Through the theft of golden temple vessels, bribery, and murder, he is able to take over the high priesthood and amass power. Overall, this chapter is a strong condemnation of Menelaus's pagan introductions into the Jewish society and corruption of Jewish worship.

Chapter 5 recounts the disastrous rebellion Jason initiates when he believes a false rumor that the Seleucid ruler, Antiochus, has died in Egypt. Jason is willing to fight against anyone, including his own Jewish brethren, who attempt to stop him, "not realizing that success at the cost of one's kindred is the greatest misfortune" (5:6). Jason is ultimately unsuccessful and meets a miserable death after being chased by one enemy after another. Because of the rebellion, a Seleucid army is sent, over 80,000 people are killed, and at least that many are sold into slavery (5:14). The temple is targeted for plunder because, as the text points out, "the Lord was angered for a little while because of the sins of those who lived in the city, and that this was the reason he was disregarding the holy place" (5:17). 2 Maccabees also explains that "the Lord did not choose the nation for the sake of the holy place, but the place for the sake of the nation. Therefore the place itself shared in the misfortunes that befell the nation and afterward participated in its benefits" (5:19–20). In retaliation for the rebellion, a surprise attack is carried out on the Sabbath against the Jews. Judas Maccabeus and a small band escape and live in the wild, avoiding death and pagan defilement while awaiting the right moment to revolt.

The next chapter refers to the decree attempting to ban Jewish religious law and practice. The desecration of the temple increases as persecution intensifies against those who try to maintain their worship. As is common for the author of 2 Maccabees, a rationale for this dire predicament is given:

> Now I urge those who read this book not to be depressed by such calamities, but to recognize that these punishments were designed not to destroy but to discipline our people. In fact, it is a sign of great kindness not to let the impious alone for long, but to punish them immediately. For in the case of the other nations the Lord waits patiently to punish them until they have reached the full measure of their sins; but he does not deal in this way with us . . . Although he disciplines us with calamities, he does not forsake his own people. (6:12–16)

The author then recounts the martyrdom of the old scribe, Eleazar. Several times the author editorializes on the nobleness of Eleazar's faithfulness and how his martyrdom should serve as a model for others—which undoubtedly influenced later Jewish and Christian martyrs familiar with these accounts. First, Eleazar spits out the swine flesh he is being forced to eat, "as all ought to go, who have the courage to refuse things that it is not right to taste, even for the natural love of life" (6:20). When he is urged to simply pretend to eat the prohibited flesh, he refuses on the grounds that such a pretense is not worthy and could lead others astray who may not know he has not eaten. Instead, Eleazar wants to leave behind "a noble example of how to die a good death willingly and nobly for the revered and holy laws" (6:28). After being placed on the rack, Eleazar cries out, "in my soul I am glad to suffer these things because I fear him [God]" (6:30). "So in this way he died, leaving in his death an example of nobility and a memorial of courage, not only to the young but to the great body of his nation" (6:31).

Chapter 7 recounts the martyrdom of a mother and her seven sons (a story which becomes the principal subject of 4 Maccabees, another Maccabean text that is not found in the Apocrypha). This family resists the prohibitions against their worship and encourages one another to die nobly rather than succumb to evil designs. Successive brief statements and gruesome descriptions about the death of each son are given in the text. Here a brief synopsis of each son's last words or feelings is given:

1. "We are ready to die rather than transgress the laws of our ancestors" (7:2).
2. "You dismiss us from this present life, but the King of the universe will raise us up to an everlasting renewal of life, because we have died for his laws" (7:9).
3. "He regarded his sufferings as nothing" (7:12).
4. "One cannot but choose to die at the hands of mortals and to cherish the hope God gives of being raised again by him. But for you there will be no resurrection to life!" (7:13).
5. "Do not think that God has forsaken our people. Keep on, and see how his mighty power will torture you and your descendants!" (7:16–17).
6. "We are suffering these things on our own account, because of our sins against our own God . . . But do not think that you will go unpunished for having tried to fight against God!" (7:18–19).
7. "If our living Lord is angry for a little while, to rebuke and discipline us, he will again be reconciled with his own servants. . . . You have not yet escaped the judgment of the almighty, all-seeing God. For our brothers after enduring a brief suffering have drunk of ever-flowing life, under God's covenant; but you, by the judgment of God, will receive just punishment for your arrogance. I, like my brothers, give up body and life for the laws of our ancestors, appealing to God to show mercy soon to our nation and by trials and plagues to make you confess that he alone is God, and through me and my brothers to bring to an end the wrath of the Almighty that has justly fallen on our whole nation" (7:33, 35–38).

The text points out that the last son "died in his integrity, putting his whole trust in the Lord" (7:40). Meanwhile, the mother stands as a witness to her seven sons' martyrdoms. She is described as "admirable and worthy of honorable memory . . . she bore it with good courage because of her hope in the Lord" (7:20). She encourages each son to remain faithful, especially the last, in their own language so the Greeks will not understand them. She believes that just as it is miraculous how each of them formerly grew within her womb and became living beings, God would give them life and breath again for their faithfulness. In the end, she dies after her sons.

Maccabean Revolt

After the background material and stories of persecution and martyrdom, 2 Maccabees turns to the Maccabean Revolt. Not only is the revolt a turning point in the Jews' resistance to the Seleucids, but also God's wrath turns to mercy as he now assists their endeavors. Despite Seleucid generals being sent "to wipe out the whole race of Judea" (8:9) and sell the Jews into slavery, God is on their side and brings them through their trials. Similar to other scriptural texts (Daniel 9:19), the Jews plead for God's assistance for the sake of the covenants he has made with their ancestors and for his name's sake. Hearkening back to the time God destroyed 185,000 Assyrians besieging Jerusalem (2 Kings 19:35), the Jews take courage and prepare to defend themselves with God as their ally (8:21, 24). Their first victory happens the day before the Sabbath, allowing them to keep the Sabbath and give praise and gratitude to God who allotted the victory to them "as the beginning of mercy" (8:27). After the Sabbath, they share their spoils with the needy and persecuted; a pattern that continues in their subsequent clashes. The Seleucid general Nicanor, who has been forced to flee, comes to acknowledge that the Jews have a "Defender" and are therefore "invulnerable, because they followed the laws ordained by him" (8:36).

Chapter 9 describes how the Seleucid ruler Antiochus is struck with a grave illness. In his desperate condition, Antiochus turns to the Lord and acknowledges God's sovereignty over even a king like himself (9:12). Antiochus makes vows to stop the persecution of Jews and liberate Jerusalem and make its inhabitants free citizens. In fact, he even promises to become a Jew and travel around proclaiming the power of God. But when his illness does not subside, he writes a letter to the Jewish people encouraging their loyalty to his son upon his impending death.

Following Antiochus's death, Judas Maccabeus and his followers recover the temple and the city (10:1). The text briefly relates their purification of the sacred precincts and their sacrificial offerings after a two-year hiatus. They then inaugurate the festival of Hanukkah in similar fashion to their celebration of the festival of booths. What one would think would be the climax of the work and thus deserving of the most attention is instead briefly narrated as the story moves on to the subsequent political intrigues of the region.

The last five and a half chapters of 2 Maccabees give an overview of the various political competitions among the leaders of the region—Seleucid rulers, governors, and usurpers; Egyptian (Ptolemaic) leaders; Jewish leaders such as high priests; and members of the Maccabean family. The Maccabees are regularly seen petitioning God for help and guidance, so interspersed among various battles are manifestations of heavenly aid often in the form of angelic forces supporting the Maccabees and leading them to victories (see 10:29–31; 11:8–12). The Jewish people suffered under their own corrupt leadership as the high priesthood frequently changed hands, usually to the highest bidder (11:3); thus, not all the Maccabees' compatriots supported their cause. Consequently, there are frequent actions taken by the Maccabees against those not loyal to their cause (see 10:21–23). The writer takes frequent opportunity to praise the Maccabees' efforts and defend their often brutal actions.

2 Maccabees ends with a final battle between Judas Maccabeus and Nicanor. Nicanor wishes to attack on the Sabbath day, but his forces try to persuade him that he needs to obey the sovereign in heaven. Meanwhile, Judas "did not cease to trust with all confidence that he would get help from the Lord" (15:7). Judas rallies his troops to look for the victory that God will give them, encouraging them with words from the law and the prophets. Judas also

relates a vision he receives where the former high priest, Onias, is praying with outstretched hands for the Jews when a heavenly figure of marvelous majesty and authority appears. That figure is Jeremiah, who gives Judas a golden sword with which to strike down his adversaries (16:14–16). The Jewish forces become determined to defend Jerusalem, the temple, and their families. After a final petition for God's assistance, they meet the enemy forces on the field of battle "fighting with their hands and praying to God in their hearts" (15:27). The Jews are successful, Nicanor dies, and Judas hangs Nicanor's severed head from the citadel, "a clear and conspicuous sign to everyone of the help of the Lord" (15:35). The writer ends his story here, announcing that from that time Jerusalem "has been in the possession of the Hebrews" (15:37).

Conclusion

2 Maccabees provides another version of the events associated with the Maccabean Revolt. Somewhat surprisingly, it deals very little with the actual revolt that regained control of the Jerusalem Temple, but focuses instead on the persecution and martyrdoms leading up to it, and the battles after it as the Maccabees sought to establish their control of the region. The turning point comes when God is no longer chastising his people—allowing them to face trials of persecution and the loss of their core religious practices—but comes to their aid and restores the religious and political glory of Israel. Throughout the text, Judas Maccabeus is the hero who receives heavenly assistance and leads the fledgling forces against much larger, experienced, and better-equipped armies. Somewhat like Captain Moroni in Alma, Judas rallies the people to defend their worship and families by turning to God and seeking his deliverance.

Similar to some of the other Apocrypha books I have discussed, 2 Maccabees shares the principle of periods of trial and persecution followed by deliverance and heavenly assistance. It seems these patterns continue in our day as we face trials that shall be but for a moment. We are reminded again that though God may discipline us with calamities and hardships, he will never forsake us. The faithfulness with which some of the figures in this text face their tribulations were models for early Christians and can continue to be so for us today. Like the account about Eleazar's martyrdom, the prophet Abinadi in the Book of Mormon suffered a similar fate at the hands of King Noah's court. When pressured to recall his words against the king and his people, Abinadi responds, "I will not recall the words which I have spoken unto you concerning this people, for they are true; and that ye may know of their surety I have suffered myself that I have fallen into your hands. Yea, and I will suffer even until death, and I will not recall my words, and they shall stand as a testimony against you. And if ye slay me ye will shed innocent blood, and this shall also stand as a testimony against you at the last day" (Mosiah 17:9–10). Abinadi's words almost lead to his release, but ultimately he is put to death "because he would not deny the commandments of God, having sealed the truth of his words by his death" (Mosiah 17:20). Will we likewise have the resolve to not deny the commandments of God and our spiritual experiences, but remain steadfast throughout whatever we may face in our lives?

NOTES

1. Daniel J. Harrington, "Apocrypha, Old Testament," in *The Eerdmans Dictionary of Early Judaism*, ed. John J. Collins and Daniel C. Harlow (Grand Rapids and Cambridge: William B. Eerdmans Publishing Company, 2010), 349.
2. Daniel R. Schwartz, "Maccabees, Second Book of," in *The Eerdmans Dictionary of Early Judaism*, 906.

3. Schwartz, "Maccabees, Second Book of," 905.
4. Schwartz, "Maccabees, Second Book of," 905. Schwartz goes on to argue the book's background in the diaspora through four main points: (1) Gentiles, especially the kings, are usually good and respect the Jews; (2) the temple and sacrificial cult are of lesser interest; (3) martyrdom is very important because they likely would not be able to fight in the Diaspora; (4) nothing really changes in the book, so the beginning is like the end, whereas 1 Maccabees emphasizes how much the Hasmoneans *changed* things (905–906).
5. The text calls it the "festival of booths," which usually refers to the Feast of Tabernacles, but the dating of the festival as well as its context indicate they are really talking about Hanukkah. They may be saying "festival of booths" because when the Maccabees first initiated Hanukkah, they were belatedly celebrating the Feast of Tabernacles because they were involved in the revolt when the festival should have been held.
6. "Hosea Chapter III," *The Evening and the Morning Star*, Vol. 1, No. 2 (July 1832): 14.

13

WISDOM OF SOLOMON

BACKGROUND

MANY CULTURES IN THE ANCIENT NEAR EAST, SUCH AS IN EGYPT, Mesopotamia, and Israel, wrote traditional wisdom sayings in texts we classify together as wisdom literature. The Bible includes three collections of such wisdom texts, Proverbs, Job, and Ecclesiastes, while the Apocrypha includes two examples: the Wisdom of Solomon and the Wisdom of Jesus ben Sirach. The purpose of wisdom texts, as their name implies, is to pass on wisdom from teachers to students/disciples or from parents to children. As a genre, these texts encourage the pursuit of knowledge so that one can achieve a successful and fulfilling life. The varied topics of wisdom literature are often practical, such as advice about marriage, raising children, ethics, occupations, and so forth. A common feature found particularly among Jewish wisdom literature is the personification of wisdom as a female figure that is highly praised and desired. Within Judaism, the study of scripture or religious law (Torah) is the usual path to greater wisdom.

The Wisdom of Solomon in the Apocrypha is an ideal example of wisdom literature and one of the few examples of Jewish wisdom literature originally written in Greek. Its complete form is found in the great uncials Sinaiticus, Alexandrinus, and Vaticanus. The Old Latin translation seems to come from North Africa in the second century AD, and this version was probably used by Jerome for the Vulgate without revision.[1] A Syriac version also derives from the Greek with some corrections based on the Old Latin. Even though Solomon's name is never used, tradition ascribes the sayings to Solomon particularly because his petition for wisdom seems to be reflected in chapters 7–9. In reality, however, the Wisdom of Solomon was likely written in Alexandria, a Greek-speaking Jewish community in Egypt.[2] It shows influence from the surrounding Greek culture by focusing on common philosophical concepts and the cardinal virtues popular in Greek philosophical discourse. One of the purposes of this text may have been to encourage Jews living among Greeks to believe that their wisdom is superior to that of their neighbors.[3] The Wisdom of Solomon is dependent on the Septuagint version of the Bible and follows a similar style of poetic parallelism.

Some see three major sections in the Wisdom of Solomon.[4] The first section (chapters 1–5; sometimes called the Book of Eschatology) treats the doctrine of immortality and encourages righteous living in order to be later found among the holy ones in heaven. It is addressed to the "rulers of the earth." The second section (chapters 6–9; sometimes called the Book of Wisdom) highlights a personified Wisdom and explores her attributes. Wisdom is seen as one of the saviors of Israel's ancestors. The last section (chapters 11–19; sometimes called the Book of History), besides making occasional attacks on idolatry, illustrates Wisdom's power with examples from ancient Israelite history such as the Exodus and the contrast between God's treatment of the Egyptians with that of the Israelites. This section is a midrash (exposition) on the Exodus from Egypt and recounts Wisdom's activity among the early figures of the Old Testament (comparable with the lists of the "great men of Israel" such as found in Ben Sira 44–50). God's power and redemption are emphasized as the Israelites are blessed and the Egyptians defeated. The contrast with the Egyptians is "in the form of a *synkrisis*, a set of antitheses contrasting the sufferings of the Egyptians in the plagues with the benefits to the Israelites. It was a form highly developed in the Graeco-Roman literary context."[5]

"There is no evidence that the Wisdom of Solomon ever had canonical status in any Jewish group" and "no evidence of the work is found at Qumran."[6] However, it did have mixed acceptance among early Christian groups and writers (positive: Tertullian and Clement of Alexandria; negative: Origen and Jerome). It became part of the Roman Catholic and Greek Orthodox canons, and selections from the Wisdom of Solomon became widely quoted in Orthodox Christian liturgy, particularly associated with commemorations of various New Testament figures like John the Baptist and later Orthodox saints. In fact, the Wisdom of Solomon is the second most quoted Old Testament book in Orthodox liturgy after Psalms. The prevalent use of the Wisdom of Solomon has helped the Apocrypha remain a significant part of the Orthodox canon.

The Wisdom of Solomon is "probably the best example of a writing in the Apocrypha that attempts in one way or another to interpret preexisting biblical texts."[7] Since the Wisdom of Solomon is not narrative prose, it is more difficult to summarize its content. To glimpse some of the content of this text, I will examine various topics of the Wisdom of Solomon and group verses together under those topics. Through these topics, we can see the recounting of some scriptural stories, especially around the Exodus, and we can appreciate the valuable wisdom principles being presented.

Topics

Wisdom

The primary topic of this text, as its name suggests, is wisdom. The Wisdom of Solomon not only gives lengthy descriptions of wisdom and her value, but also raises wisdom to a personified figure nearly on par with God. She is a female figure who is "more beautiful than the sun, and excels every constellation of the stars" (7:29). She is God's creative agent and teaches the Stoic cardinal virtues of self-control, prudence, justice, and courage (8:4–7). One passage logically shows how the pursuit of wisdom leads to a heavenly kingdom: "The beginning of wisdom is the most sincere desire for instruction, and concern for instruction is love of her, and love of her is the keeping of her laws, and giving heed to her laws is assurance of immortality, and immortality brings one near to God; so the desire for wisdom leads to a kingdom" (6:17–20). Chapters 7 and 8 describe Solomon's pursuit for wisdom (without naming him specifically) and give further descriptions of her qualities and characteristics (7:22–8:8). In the end, Solomon acknowledges that wisdom is a gift from God, so he makes a petition to receive her (8:21–9:4).

The creative power of wisdom is sometimes coupled with God's *word*—the creative agent revealed in the beginning of the Gospel of John as Jesus. "O God . . . [you] who have made all things by your word, and by your wisdom have formed humankind" (9:1–2). Later on, God's word, or *logos*, was the stern warrior who carried out destruction on the firstborn in the tenth plague in Egypt (18:15–16). In speaking of the creation, the Wisdom of Solomon praises God for his all-powerful hand "which created the world out of formless matter" (11:17), an acknowledgment that creation was not *ex nihilo*. Another aspect of creation that the Wisdom of Solomon describes is that God's creations testify of him and show that he is the true god (as opposed to the idols of the wicked, who cannot create). God is acknowledged as the author of beauty "for from the greatness and beauty of created things comes a corresponding perception of their Creator" (13:5). Having power over the elements, God is able to use his creations for his own purposes. "For creation, serving you who made it, exerts itself to punish the unrighteous, and in kindness relaxes on behalf of those who trust in you" (16:25). A vivid example of this is when he parted the Red Sea for the Israelites to "experience [or accomplish] an incredible journey" (19:5). "For the whole creation in its nature was fashioned anew, complying with your commands, so that your children might be kept unharmed . . . dry land emerging where water had stood before, an unhindered way out of the Red Sea, and a grassy plain out of the raging waves" (19:6–7).

Chapter 10 begins a lengthy section that reviews many examples of when wisdom saved various individuals from destruction. Adam, Noah, Abraham, Lot, Jacob, Joseph, and especially Moses were beneficiaries of divine help through wisdom. The events of the Exodus under Moses's leadership and the subsequent conquest of Canaan are reviewed in the next several chapters to highlight how the Israelites were blessed through wisdom and God's mighty hand while the Egyptians, Canaanites, and other foes were destroyed, sometimes by the very creatures they worshipped, because they lacked wisdom. God is viewed as the savior of the Israelites most pointedly in the recollection of the episode of poisonous serpents afflicting the Israelites. "They were troubled for a little while as a warning, and received a symbol of deliverance to remind them of your law's command. For the one who turned toward it was saved, not by the thing that was beheld, but by you, the Savior of all . . . it was your word, O Lord, that heals all people" (16:6–7, 12). The connection between the brazen serpent and the Savior (Christ) is also clearly found in the Book of Mormon where the brazen serpent was lifted up as a type of

Christ so that those who had faith enough to look could live (see Helaman 8:14–15 and Alma 33:19–22).

God's Judgment

The Wisdom of Solomon teaches that God's judgment looks on the inside of an individual (similar to 1 Samuel 15). "God is a witness of their inmost feelings, and a true observer of their hearts" (1:6). The means whereby God can judge everyone is similar to the LDS concept of the Light of Christ that is in everything. "The spirit of the Lord has filled the world, and that which holds all things together knows what is said" (1:7).

The Wisdom of Solomon warns the unrighteous that they are on the wrong path, which, if pursued, will lead them to eternal destruction. The unrighteous have the unsound philosophy that there is no immortality after this life, so the focus should be on the here and now (similar to the "eat, drink, and be merry philosophy" discussed in the Book of Mormon). "Come, therefore, let us enjoy the good things that exist, and make use of the creation to the full as in youth. Let us take our fill of costly wine and perfumes, and let no flower of spring pass us by. Let us crown ourselves with rosebuds before they wither. Let none of us fail to share in our revelry; everywhere let us leave signs of enjoyment, because this is our portion, and this is our lot" (2:6–9). In a later passage, talking specifically about wicked idolaters, it states, "they considered our existence an idle game, and life a festival held for profit, for they say one must get money however one can, even by base means" (15:12). The passage in chapter 2 then goes on to share all the ways they could do wickedness against others, especially against the righteous, for their own gain (2:10–16). One of their worst plots against the righteous was to kill them because, they reasoned, if God is their father, then he will help and deliver them (2:17–20). This logic is the same evil reasoning that Satan used against Jesus when tempting him to leap from the pinnacle of the temple, and the same malicious taunt that came from opponents as Jesus hung on the cross.

Teaching a similar concept to the Parable of the Sower, the Wisdom of Solomon discusses the deep roots of virtue which are absent among the ungodly. As such, "none of their illegitimate seedlings will strike a deep root or take a firm hold. For even if they put forth boughs for a while, standing insecurely they will be shaken by the wind, and by the violence of the winds they will be uprooted" (4:3–4). The unrighteous do not have the depth of spirituality needed to survive the trials that come.

The Wisdom of Solomon points out that the true test for the righteous does not come from the wicked, but from God. Even if the righteous suffer and seem to be punished in this life, "their hope is full of immortality. Having been disciplined a little, they will receive great good, because God tested them and found them worthy of himself; like gold in the furnace he tried them" (3:4–6). Because of their faithfulness in the face of severe derision and persecution, the righteous will govern nations and rule over peoples "and the Lord will reign over them forever" (3:8). A later section gives more symbolic language of the eternal rewards of reigning and protection for the righteous. "They will receive a glorious crown and a beautiful diadem from the hand of the Lord, because with his right hand he will cover them, and with his arm he will shield them" (5:16). The Lord's protection of the righteous is given in language made familiar by the great apostle, Paul (see Ephesians 6:14–17). "The Lord will take his zeal as his whole armor, and will arm all creation to repel his enemies; he will put on righteousness as a breastplate, and wear impartial justice as a helmet; he will take holiness as an invincible shield, and sharpen stern wrath for a sword, and creation will join with him to fight against his frenzied foes" (5:17–20).

The Wisdom of Solomon alludes to Enoch and his incredible experience of being translated and gives some reasons for their experience. "There were some who pleased God and were loved by him, and while living among sinners were taken up. They were caught up so that evil might not change their understanding or guile deceive their souls" (4:10).

The Final Judgment is a favored topic of the Wisdom of Solomon. In it, the righteous will stand with confidence while the wicked will shake with dreadful fear (5:1–2). It is at this point that the unrighteous will be filled with remorse, express dismay at their situation, and regret how they treated the righteous who now stand saved (5:3–8). They realize that by spending their mortal life in wicked pursuits, they are left with nothing to show for it (5:9–12). One especially poignant, self-reflective passage captures their pitiful state: "'We also, as soon as we were born, ceased to be, and we had no sign of virtue to show, but were consumed in our wickedness.' Because the hope of the ungodly is like thistledown carried by the wind, and like a light frost driven away by a storm; it is dispersed like smoke before the wind, and it passes like the remembrance of a guest who stays but a day" (5:13–14).

Leadership

The Wisdom of Solomon specifically targets the unrighteous among the kings, judges, and rulers of the earth. They are warned that their dominion was given them by the Lord and he will judge them accordingly (6:3–5). The text also acknowledges the greatness of God; as Creator, he "will not stand in awe of anyone, or show deference to greatness; because he himself made both small and great, and he takes thought for all alike" (6:6–7). In another passage, it encourages the pursuit of wisdom in order to reign forever (see 6:21).

Gratitude

God's kindness over his people is illustrated through his gift of manna in the wilderness. It is called the "food of angels" and without toil God "supplied them from heaven with bread ready to eat, providing every pleasure and suited to every taste. For your sustenance manifested your sweetness toward your children; and the bread, ministering to the desire of the one who took it, was changed to suit everyone's liking" (16:20–21). But besides keeping the Israelites alive, manna also taught them an important lesson about gratitude since they had to rise early in the morning to gather it before the sun melted it. It was an object lesson "to make it known that one must rise before the sun to give you thanks, and must pray to you at the dawning of the light; for the hope of an ungrateful person will melt like wintry frost, and flow away like waste water" (16:28–29; see also D&C 59:21 about the seriousness of ingratitude).

PREMORTAL LIFE

There are brief references in the Wisdom of Solomon to the premortal existence of the soul. Unlike the Platonic philosophy of its day, however, the Wisdom of Solomon teaches that this soul is born into an undefiled body. Solomon's birth is described as follows: "As a child I was naturally gifted, and a good soul fell to my lot; or rather, being good, I entered an undefiled body" (8:19–20). Yet later, the text talks about the perishable body that weighs down the soul and burdens the thoughtful mind, so perhaps it is acknowledging the hindering effects of the natural man after childhood (9:15). In a later passage railing on idol makers, it talks about their limited mortality and their future death "when the time comes to return the souls that were borrowed" (15:8). Likewise, "a human being made them [idols], and one whose spirit is borrowed formed them" (15:16). They have "failed to know the one who formed them and inspired them with active souls and breathed a living spirit into them" (15:11).

Conscience

A concept similar to the LDS belief in the Light of Christ is shared at the beginning of chapter 12 as an influence or conscience in all things. Gentle corrections for those that err help them to learn from their mistakes and eventually be freed from wickedness. "For your immortal spirit is in all things. Therefore you correct little by little those who trespass, and you remind and warn them of the things through which they sin, so that they may be freed from wickedness and put their trust in you, O Lord" (12:1–2). The "spirit of the Lord" is also described as filling the world, holding all things together, and knowing what is said so those "who utter unrighteous things will not escape notice" (1:7).[8]

Opportunity to Repent

Another theme found throughout the Wisdom of Solomon is the notion that God will delay his destructive punishment of sinners so that they may have time to repent. "But judging them little by little you gave them an opportunity to repent" (12:10); "granting them time and opportunity to give up their wickedness" (12:20); "you are merciful to all, for you can do all things, and you overlook people's sins, so that they may repent" (11:23); "you have filled your children with good hope, because you give repentance for sins" (12:19). The Bible and the Book of Mormon both share this notion of God granting an opportunity for mortals to repent so that they can be better prepared for the final judgment. In relation to the Fall of Adam and Eve, 2 Nephi 2:21 teaches that "the days of the children of men were prolonged, according to the will of God, that they might repent while in the flesh; wherefore, their state became a state of probation, and their time was lengthened." Repeatedly the Lord says he takes no pleasure in the death of the wicked, but rather that that wicked repent and live, implying that he gives them opportunities for repentance before death (see Ezekiel 18:23, 32; 33:11).

IDOLATRY

The Wisdom of Solomon's attack on idolaters is noticeable. Among the idolaters, those that worship forms of nature are the least culpable because at least they are seeing the power and beauty of God's creations, but instead of these natural forces, they should acknowledge the true Creator behind them (13:1–9). Stronger rebuke is given to those who seek assistance from lifeless images like we saw previously in Bel and the Dragon and the Letter of Jeremiah (which shares a lot with the canonical book of Jeremiah): "For health he appeals to a thing that is weak; for life he prays to a thing that is dead; for aid he entreats a thing that is utterly inexperienced; for a prosperous journey, a thing that cannot take a step; for money-making and work and success with his hands he asks strength of a thing whose hands have no strength" (13:18–19). Instead it is the Father's providence that should be recognized and accepted (14:3–5). Idols are snares and traps for human souls and the beginning of fornication and corruption "for they did not exist from the beginning, nor will they last forever. For through human vanity they entered the world, and therefore their speedy end has been planned" (14:13–14).

PROVIDENCE

The Wisdom of Solomon abruptly ends with the message of God's providence over his people: "For in everything, O Lord, you have exalted and glorified your people, and you have not neglected to help them at all times and in all places" (19:22).

Conclusion

Besides the parallels with LDS thought and principles highlighted above, particularly with the notion of premortal souls and a concept of everyone having a type of conscience (the Light of Christ), the Wisdom of Solomon is instructive as a wisdom text admonishing us to pursue valuable wisdom that can be carried beyond the veil. While it can be challenging to read a wisdom text from cover to cover because it usually lacks a narrative, reading a little a day can uplift us, guide us, and "keep the devil away" (as my father would say about reading a Psalm a day). Like the Wisdom of Solomon, restored scriptures give both admonitions to seek wisdom as well as warnings against the wisdom of the world. Alma encourages his son, Helaman, to learn wisdom in his youth (see Alma 37:35), Saints are encouraged to seek wisdom, not riches (see D&C 6:7), and we are admonished to teach one another words of wisdom (D&C 88:118). Righteous knowledge and wisdom should be our never-ending pursuit in mortality. Solomon and others are examples from the scriptures of those who pursued this uplifting wisdom. The Wisdom of Solomon repeatedly admonishes its readers to seek after this higher wisdom so they will not be trapped by the false teachings of the world. The Wisdom of Solomon also emphasizes that one aspect of wisdom is knowing that *now* is the time to repent while the Lord allows us an opportunity. Ultimately, wisdom is a gift from God for which we should be grateful, along with his mercy and tender oversight of his children. Through the attainment of wisdom, one can achieve immortality and live with the Lord forever.

NOTES

1. Joseph Reider, *The Book of Wisdom. An English Translation with Introduction and Commentary* (New York: Harper & Brothers, 1957), 6.
2. For an overview of the possible author/community that produced this text, see Reider, *The Book of Wisdom*, vii–ix and 15–22.
3. For other possible motives for this text, including as a response to Ecclesiastes or as a proselyting tract, see Reider, *The Book of Wisdom*, 9–11. For a recent, strong collection of essays related to the Wisdom of Solomon, see *Studies in the Book of Wisdom. Supplements to the Journal for the Study of Judaism. Vol 142*, ed. Geza G. Xeravits and Jozsef Zsengeller (Leiden/Boston: Brill, 2010).
4. For example, Lester L. Grabbe, *Wisdom of Solomon. Guides to Apocrypha and Pseudepigrapha* (Sheffield: Sheffield Academic Press, 1997), 13–17.
5. Grabbe, "Apocrypha," 20. For his more detailed work on this specific text, see Grabbe, *Wisdom of Solomon*.
6. Grabbe, *Wisdom of Solomon*, 28.
7. Grabbe, "Apocrypha," 20.
8. There is also a passage that uses the word "conscience" to describe the guilty feelings the wicked will have. Incidentally, this passage is the only place where the word "conscience" is used in the Septuagint. "For wickedness is a cowardly thing, condemned by its own testimony; distressed by conscience, it has always exaggerated [or anticipated] the difficulties" (17:11).

14

ECCLESIASTICUS, THE WISDOM OF JESUS BEN SIRA, OR SIRACH

BACKGROUND

ANOTHER WISDOM TEXT THAT BECAME VERY POPULAR AMONG Jews and Christians goes by several names: Ecclesiasticus (Latin), Wisdom of Jesus Ben Sira (Hebrew), or the shortened version Sirach (Greek). It is one of the rare texts in the Apocrypha that gives an attribution of its authorship. Jesus (the Greek form of Joshua), son of Eleazar, son of Sirach, was a scribe or sage living in Jerusalem just before 200 BC. He wrote down wisdom sayings in Hebrew that were part of the training in his scribal school in Jerusalem. About sixty-five or seventy years later, his grandson translated these sayings into Greek "for those who want to follow the Law but live 'abroad.'" Reading the grandson's preface reminds one of Mormon's and Moroni's feelings of concern that their editorial work and writing may prove inadequate.

The title *Ecclesiasticus* was used in many Latin texts such as the Vulgate and means "the Church's book," perhaps indicating its common use in early Christian communities. Rabbis quoted from Sirach, sometimes even with the formula usually reserved for scripture even though technically Sirach was never part of the Jewish canon and usually came with warnings against giving the book too much authority. Manuscripts of Sirach have been found in both Hebrew and Greek.[1] Some small fragments of Sirach were found among the Dead Sea Scrolls (2Q18 [from 6:14–15 or 1:19–20 and 6:20–31]; 11Q5 21:1–22:1 [from Sirach 51]) and from discarded Masada texts (fragmentary text of 39:27–44:17).[2] Hebrew medieval manuscripts of Sirach were also discovered at the Cairo Synagogue's Geniza that match closely with the Masada fragments. Altogether, about 68% of the Greek text of Sirach is extant in Hebrew manuscripts. "The Greek tradition also has one unique characteristic. All of the extant Greek manuscripts have a textual displacement where 30.25–33.13a and 33.13b–36.16a have exchanged places. This is most likely the result of the transposition of leaves of a Greek manuscript, but it also means that every Greek manuscript in existence derives ultimately from this one exemplar."[3] There is also a Syriac translation of Sirach which was probably translated before the early fourth century AD by Ebionite Christians based on a text with influence from the Greek.[4]

Since this is like a "lifetime scrapbook" of a teacher, it contains a variety of material.[5] Yet still, rather than a collection of separate proverbs, Sirach has woven together its many sayings into somewhat lengthy poems, often with the same number of lines as the number of letters in the Hebrew alphabet (the last chapter, for example, is an acrostic). One verse, also found in rabbinical material, may sum up much of Sirach's content: "By three things the world is sustained: by the Law, by the (Temple-) Service, and by deeds of loving-kindness" (7:17; cf. Aboth 4:4. See also Aboth 1:2). Sirach is an important witness to some of the changes occurring during Second Temple Judaism as the Old Testament was being formalized and a new mainstream tradition, the rabbinic movement, was beginning. Thus Sirach "provides an admirable link between the Old Testament and the later Judaism appearing in the New Testament."[6] .

Topics

Like most ancient wisdom texts, such as the Book of Proverbs, Sirach gives wise sayings and exhortations on a wide variety of topics and is especially noteworthy for his exploration of the relationship between the Jewish law (Torah) and wisdom.[7] I will highlight some of the major topics his statements treat, particularly those that might be interesting to an LDS audience. They are shared with the hope that they will entice you to read through these wise and pithy verses on your own and find those sayings that appeal to you.

Wisdom

It should come as no surprise that this text includes a lot of sayings and exhortations about wisdom. Although the text occasionally shares the view of personified wisdom so prevalent in the Wisdom of Solomon, here the focus on wisdom is more related to the study of scripture and gaining wisdom of God's ways. In the prologue of the text, Sirach's grandson points out that his grandfather was "led to write something pertaining to instruction and wisdom, so that by becoming familiar also with his book those who love learning might make even greater progress in living according to the law." For Sirach, wisdom is from the Lord who created her and "poured her out upon all his works" and "he lavished her upon those who love him" (1:1, 9–10). More specifically, wisdom was given to the House of Israel and ministered before the Lord in the tabernacle and found rest in Jerusalem (24:8, 10–11).

The pursuit of wisdom should be a lifelong endeavor: "My child, from your youth choose discipline, and when you have gray hair you will still find wisdom. Come to her like one who plows and sows, and wait for her good harvest. For when you cultivate her you will toil but little, and soon you will eat of her produce" (6:18–19). Wisdom herself invites others to eat their fill of her fruits: "For the memory of me is sweeter than honey, and the possession of me sweeter than the honeycomb. Those who eat of me will hunger for more, and those who drink of me will thirst for more. Whoever obeys me will not be put to shame, and those who work with me will not sin" (24:20–22). Sirach likens the pursuit of wisdom to hunting, lying in wait, listening, and camping—all so that one can find her and be near her (14:22–25). He also says we should meditate, reason, reflect, and ponder on wisdom so that we can both achieve wisdom ourselves and also place our children under her shelter (14:20–21, 26). The rewards of wisdom are spelled out in one section: "Wisdom teaches her children and gives help to those who seek her. Whoever loves her loves life, and those who seek her from early morning are filled with joy. Whoever holds her fast inherits glory, and the Lord blesses the place she enters. Those who serve her minister to the Holy One; the Lord loves those who love her" (4:11–14). "Wealth and wages make life sweet, but better than either is finding a treasure. Children and the building of a city establish one's name, but better than either is the one who finds wisdom" (40:18–19).

In his closing benediction and epilogue, Sirach recounts his efforts to seek wisdom. "While I was still young, before I went on my travels, I sought wisdom openly in my prayer. Before the temple I asked for her, and I will search for her until the end. From the first blossom to the ripening grape my heart delighted in her; my foot walked on the straight path; from my youth I followed her steps" (51:13–15). Sirach recognized and was grateful for the many blessings wisdom had brought him in his life and encouraged all to acquire wisdom for themselves, not through money but through strict dedication.

Almsgiving

There are lengthy exhortations on the purpose of almsgiving and the blessings that come from it, which is described as the chief expression of kindness (and Sirach equates kindness with righteousness). Almsgiving atones for sins and can help oneself in the future in case one falls on hard times and needs help (3:30). Sirach addresses the common awkward moment of encountering someone in need. "Do not cheat the poor of their living, and do not keep needy eyes waiting . . . do not add to the troubles of the desperate, or delay giving to the needy" (4:1, 3). One should not avert their eyes from the poor (4:5), but rather "return their greeting politely" (4:8). "Be patient with someone in humble circumstances, and do not keep him waiting for your alms. Help the poor for the commandment's sake, and in their need do not send them away empty-handed" (29:8–9). Succinctly, "do not let your hand be stretched out to receive and closed when it is time to give" (4:31). "Stretch out your hand to the poor, so that your blessing may be complete" (7:32). Besides giving temporal support, Sirach encourages others to lend emotional support: "Do not avoid those who weep, but mourn with those who mourn. Do not hesitate to visit the sick, because for such deeds you will be loved" (7:34–35). Likewise, God helps those with needs, whatever they might be. "There are others who are slow and need help, who lack strength and abound in poverty; but the eyes of the Lord look kindly upon them; he lifts them out of their lowly condition and raises up their heads to the amazement of the many" (11:12–13). It is particularly vital to help the orphan and widow so that one can become "like a son of the Most High, and he will love you more than does your mother" (4:10). "Kindness is like a garden of blessings, and almsgiving endures forever" (40:17).

AGENCY

Although Sirach is clear that God is over everything and has foreknowledge of all, he teaches that that does not absolve us from our responsibility to choose the right. "Do not say, 'It was the Lord's doing that I fell away'; for he does not do what he hates. Do not say, 'It was he who led me astray'; for he has no need of the sinful. . . . It was he who created humankind in the beginning, and he left them in the power of their own free choice. If you choose, you can keep the commandments, and to act faithfully is a matter of your own choice" (15:11–12, 14–15). Similar to Nephi (see 2 Nephi 2:27–29), Sirach emphasizes that each person has the choice between life and death (15:17) and he uses the metaphor of having fire and water placed before us and we can reach out our hand for whichever one we choose (15:16).

ANGER

Avoidance of anger is another common exhortation in Sirach. "Unjust anger cannot be justified" and will lead to ruin (1:22). "Refrain from strife, and your sins will be fewer; for the hot-tempered kindle strife, and the sinner disrupts friendships and sows discord among those who are at peace" (28:8–9). We can choose what we will do in moments of potential strife, and that choice affects subsequent events: "If you blow on a spark, it will glow; if you spit on it, it will be put out; yet both come out of your mouth" (28:12). Those who are patient in trying times, however, will "stay calm until the right moment, and then cheerfulness comes back to them" (1:23).

APPEARANCE

Just as the prophet Samuel learned not to judge by appearance (see 1 Samuel 16:7), Sirach teaches that we cannot always judge things by the outside. "Do not praise individuals for their good looks, or loathe anyone because of appearance alone. The bee is small among flying creatures, but what it produces is the best of sweet things" (11:2–3).

Courage to Speak Out

One of the challenges of wisdom is that one can have knowledge that should be shared, yet one can feel reticent about sharing that wisdom with others. Sirach exhorts those with wisdom not to hide their wisdom, but rather share it "for wisdom becomes known through speech, and education through the words of the tongue" (4:24).

Rather than speaking out rashly, one should be deliberate in answering. "If you know what to say, answer your neighbor; but if not, put your hand over your mouth" (5:11–12). In another passage, Sirach again highlights the wisdom of knowing when to speak and knowing when to remain silent. "Some people keep silent because they have nothing to say, while others keep silent because they know when to speak. The wise remain silent until the right moment, but a boasting fool misses the right moment" (20:6–7)

Eternal Perspective

In order to live a just life, Sirach suggests considering the end of one's life because it can motivate one to avoid sin (see 7:36). A deterrent to sin is the final punishment of the sinner. He acknowledges that sinners may appear to have a good life now, but states that it will not last. "Do not envy the success of sinners, for you do not know what their end will be like. Do not delight in what pleases the ungodly; remember that they will not be held guiltless all their lives" (9:11–12). Perhaps it is helpful to remember the counsel of Paul to the Corinthians that keeping an eternal perspective can help us through our times of trial and affliction. "For our light affliction, which is but for a moment, worketh for us a far more exceeding and eternal weight of glory" (2 Corinthians 4:17).

Righteous Examples

Near the end of his text, Sirach holds up many individuals from Israelite history as righteous examples and role models for his readers, showing his knowledge of most of the current Old Testament (the Pentateuch, Prophets, and Chronicles). The focus on Israel's sacred history is unique for wisdom literature, but Sirach found these scriptural figures' faithfulness to covenant worthy to emulate. Some of the individuals highlighted include Enoch, Noah, Abraham, Isaac, Jacob, Moses, Joshua, Samuel, David, Solomon, Elijah, Elisha, Hezekiah, and Josiah. Besides mentioning their names, vignettes about their faithfulness are recounted and some of their sins are related, but always with the intention to encourage the reader to be faithful and honor these precious ancestors (chapters 44–49). One illustration follows: "Enoch pleased the Lord and was taken up, an example of repentance to all generations" (44:16).

Families

Focusing on the fifth commandment, Sirach reviews the importance of children's obedience to their parents. "Those who honor their father atone for sins, and those who respect their mother are like those who lay up treasure. Those who honor their father will have joy in their own children, and when they pray they will be heard" (3:3–5). "With all your heart honor your father, and do not forget the birth pangs of your mother. Remember that it was of your parents you were born; how can you repay what they have given to you?" (7:27–28). Particularly important is the need to care for elderly parents: "My child, help your father in his old age, and do not grieve him as long as he lives; even if his mind fails, be patient with him; because you have all your faculties do not despise him. For kindness to a father will not be forgotten, and will be credited to you against your sins" (3:12–14). He also points out the strength of father's blessings (3:9) and that "the glory of one's father is one's own glory" (3:11). Sirach admonishes strict discipline from an early age and especially guarding daughters' chastity; the father–daughter relationship receives special attention, as Sirach highlights the anxiety and concern that naturally comes with this relationship (7:23–24). He warns that "an unbroken horse turns out stubborn, and an unchecked son turns out headstrong" (30:8). "A daughter is a secret anxiety to her father, and worry over her robs him of sleep; when she is young, for fear she may not marry, or if married, for fear she may be disliked" (42:9). "Give a daughter in marriage, and complete a great task; but give her to a sensible man" (7:25).

There are also entire sections devoted to wives that highlight both the positive characteristics of a righteous wife and the perils of a wicked one. "Happy is the husband of a good wife; the number of his days will be doubled. A loyal wife brings joy to her husband, and he will complete his years in peace. A good wife is a great blessing; she will be granted among the blessings of the man who fears the Lord. . . . A wife's charm delights her husband, and her skill puts flesh on his bones. . . . Like the sun rising in the heights of the Lord, so is the beauty of a good wife in her well-ordered home" (26:1–3, 13, 16). On the flip side, "a bad wife is a chafing yoke; taking hold of her is like grasping a scorpion" (26:7).

Fear of the Lord

Throughout Sirach, wisdom is often coupled with the biblical notion of the "fear of God," which denotes obedience and reverence toward God, sometimes out of a sense of fear of God's judgment. But this notion should not be construed as negative, for as Sirach points out, "the fear of the Lord is glory and exultation and gladness and a crown of rejoicing. The fear of the Lord delights the heart, and gives gladness and joy and long life. Those who fear the Lord will have a happy end; on the day of their death they will be blessed" (1:11–13).[8] In one passage, the fear of the Lord is viewed not only as the beginning of wisdom, but the fullness, crown, and root of wisdom (1:14, 16, 18, 20). In another verse, "the whole of wisdom is fear of the Lord" (19:20). Sirach outlines some of the blessings that can come to those who fear the Lord. "Happy is the soul that fears the Lord! To whom does he look? And who is his support? The eyes of the Lord are on those who love him, a mighty shield and strong support, a shelter from scorching wind and a shade from noonday sun, a guard against stumbling and a help against falling. He lifts up the soul and makes the eyes sparkle; he gives health and life and blessing" (34:17–20). Simply stated, "if you desire wisdom, keep the commandments, and the Lord will lavish her upon you. For the fear of the Lord is wisdom and discipline, fidelity and humility are his delight" (1:26–27). Since the time of creation, the Lord has put the fear of him into humans' hearts (17:8). One who fears the Lord is greater than rulers. "The prince and the judge and the ruler are honored, but none of them is greater than the one who fears the Lord" (10:24). "Better are the God-fearing who lack understanding than the highly intelligent who transgress the law" (19:24). "Riches and strength build up confidence, but the fear of the Lord is better than either. There is no want in the fear of the Lord, and with it there is no need to seek for help. The fear of the Lord is like a garden of blessing, and covers a person better than any glory" (40:26–27). "How great is the one who finds wisdom! But none is superior to the one who fears the Lord. Fear of the Lord surpasses everything; to whom can we compare the one who has it?" (25:10–11).

Foolishness

The opposite of wisdom is foolishness, so it is not surprising that Sirach frequently talks about fools and contrasts the wise with the foolish. "The knowledge of the wise will increase like a flood, and their counsel like a life-giving spring. The mind of a fool is like a broken jar; it can hold no knowledge. When an intelligent person hears a wise saying, he praises it and adds to it; when a fool hears it, he laughs at it and throws it behind his back" (21:13–15). Sirach emphasizes the importance of learning by contrasting how a foolish person thinks it is simply a burden. "To a senseless person education is fetters on his feet, and like manacles on his right hand" (21:19). Fools seem to speak without thinking, while the wise always focus on thoughtful comments. "The mind of fools is in their mouth, but the mouth of the wise is in their mind" (21:26). Sirach can also be quite blunt on the "risk" of being around foolish, stupid people too much. "Sand, salt, and a piece of iron are easier to bear than a stupid person" (22:15). "Among stupid people limit your time, but among thoughtful people linger on" (27:12).

FORGIVENESS

Sirach teaches the principle that our sins are forgiven when we learn to forgive another (see Matthew 6:12, 15). "Forgive your neighbor the wrong he has done, and then your sins will be pardoned when you pray. Does anyone harbor anger against another, and expect healing from the Lord? If one has no mercy toward another like himself, can he then seek pardon for his own sins?" (28:2–4). He also acknowledges that forgiveness often requires a higher order of thinking that sees a bigger picture. "Remember the covenant of the Most High, and overlook faults" (28:7).

FOREKNOWLEDGE

Sirach teaches that God knew everything even before creation. This knowledge allows him to understand everything and everyone in their current conditions. "Before the universe was created, it was known to him, and so it is since its completion" (23:20). "He searches out the abyss and the human heart; he understands their innermost secrets. For the Most High knows all that may be known; he sees from of old the things that are to come. . . . No thought escapes him, and nothing is hidden from him" (42:18, 20). Because God has all knowledge, he can reveal some of that knowledge to mortals. "He discloses what has been and what is to be, and he reveals the traces of hidden things" (42:19).

FRIENDSHIP

Good friends are vital for living a good life, while evil acquaintances can lead one astray. Sirach encourages good friends and spells out how one can gain them, but he also warns against rushing into friendship too quickly: he advocates "testing" the friendship to ensure it is sincere, uplifting, and without ulterior motive. "Pleasant speech multiplies friends . . . let those who are friendly with you be many, . . . when you gain friends, gain them through testing, and do not trust them hastily. For there are friends who are such when it suits them, but they will not stand by you in time of trouble" (6:5–8). Continuing on the topic of fair-weather friends, Sirach explains that "there are friends who sit at your table, but they will not stand by you in time of trouble. When you are prosperous, they become your second self, and lord it over your servants; but if you are brought low, they turn against you, and hide themselves from you" (6:10–12). Sirach singles out the rich as potentially treacherous friendships because "a rich person will exploit you if you can be of use to him, but if you are in need he will abandon you. . . . When he needs you he will deceive you, and will smile at you and encourage you; he will speak to you kindly and say, 'What do you need?' He will embarrass you with his delicacies, until he has drained you two or three times, and finally he will laugh at you" (13:4–7). Even "enemies" can appear friendly when one prospers, "but in adversity even one's friend disappears" (12:9).

Even worse, some friends turn into enemies: "Every friend says, 'I too am a friend'; but some friends are friends only in name. Is it not a sorrow like that for death itself when a dear friend turns into an enemy?" (37:1–2). Faithful friends, however, "are a sturdy shelter: whoever finds one has found a treasure. Faithful friends are beyond price; no amount can balance their worth" (6:14–15). He warns to "not abandon old friends, for new ones cannot equal them. A new friend is like new wine; when it has aged, you can drink it with pleasure" (9:10). The key, according to Sirach, is to find your friends though the fear of the Lord since as someone is, so their friends will be also (6:16–17).

There is also a responsibility to maintain that friendship through trust and honesty. Sirach highlights the dangers of betraying secrets from a friend, because once that trust is gone, it is like a bird that has escaped and cannot be recaptured. "Whoever betrays secrets destroys confidence, and will never find a congenial friend. Love your friend and keep faith with him; but if you betray his secrets, do not follow after him. For as a person destroys his enemy, so you have destroyed the friendship of your neighbor" (27:16–18). In another passage, Sirach holds out hope for reconciliation with friends in cases of threats or evil speaking against friends: "but as for reviling, arrogance, disclosure of secrets, or a treacherous blow—in these cases any friend will take to flight" (22:21–22).

GOSSIP

Sirach gives strong admonition against gossip through some clever descriptions. "Never repeat a conversation, and you will lose nothing at all. With friend or foe do not report it, and unless it would be a sin for you, do not reveal it; for someone may have heard you and watched you, and in time will hate you. Have you heard something? Let it die with you. Be brave, it will not make you burst! Having heard something, the fool suffers birth pangs like a woman in labor with a child. Like an arrow stuck in a person's thigh, so is gossip inside a fool" (19:7–12). The solution to hearing false rumors or hurtful things is to confront the person you've heard something about and see if it is true. "Question a friend; perhaps he did not do it; or if he did, so that he may not do it again. Question a neighbor; perhaps he did not say it; or if he said it, so that he may not repeat it. Question a friend, for often it is slander; so do not believe everything you hear" (19:13–15).

Happiness

Happiness should be a goal in life, and our countenance, reflecting our inner state, reveals whether we are or not. "The heart changes the countenance, either for good or for evil. The sign of a happy heart is a cheerful face" (13:25–26). Sirach encourages us to enjoy the journey because at the end of life we leave behind our fruit of labors for others. "Do not deprive yourself of a day's enjoyment; do not let your share of desired good pass by you" (14:14). Sirach also warns against allowing sadness and stress to overtake us. "Do not give yourself over to sorrow, and do not distress yourself deliberately. A joyful heart is life itself, and rejoicing lengthens one's life span. Indulge yourself and take comfort, and remove sorrow far from you, for sorrow has destroyed many, and no advantage ever comes from it" (30:21–23).

Honesty

Not surprisingly, Sirach condemns lying and promotes honesty. He exhorts, "refuse to utter any lie, for it is a habit that results in no good" (7:14). "A lie is an ugly blot on a person . . . a thief is preferable to a habitual liar, but the lot of both is ruin" (20:24–25). "A slip on the pavement is better than a slip of the tongue; the downfall of the wicked will occur just as speedily" (20:18). "Birds roost with their own kind, so honesty comes home to those who practice it" (27:9).

In one section of things that people should *not* be ashamed of doing, Sirach highlights many honest characteristics and practices. He includes not being ashamed of maintaining honest business records and accurate scales and measurements (42:3–4). He advocates not being ashamed "of the law of the Most High and his covenant, and of rendering judgment to acquit the ungodly" (42:2).

Humility

One principle that can help someone remain humble is to remember their proper relationship to God's greatness, greater than mortals' understanding. "Do not boast about wearing fine clothes, and do not exalt yourself when you are honored; for the works of the Lord are wonderful, and his works are concealed from humankind" (11:4). Sirach acknowledges the truth that arrogance is not enjoyed or accepted by either God or mortals. "Arrogance is hateful to the Lord and to mortals" (10:7). He also outlines the path toward pride, which begins with forsaking God and embracing sin. "The beginning of human pride is to forsake the Lord; the heart has withdrawn from its Maker. For the beginning of pride is sin, and the one who clings to it pours out abominations" (10:12–13).

Hypocrisy

When one is trying to follow the Lord, complete sincerity is required. One is exhorted not to approach the Lord with a divided mind (1:28) and woe is given "to the sinner who walks a double path" (2:12). People who are two-faced and duplicitous cannot be trusted and should be avoided. "Whoever winks the eye plots mischief, and those who know him will keep their distance. In your presence his mouth is all sweetness, and he admires your words; but later he will twist his speech and with your own words he will trip you up" (27:22–23). When we are hypocritical, we leave our secure moorings and become tossed about by the waves of life and falsehood. "The wise will not hate the law, but the one who is hypocritical about it is like a boat in a storm" (33:2).

JUDGMENT AND MERCY

Although God is merciful, he is also a God of justice. "He is mighty to forgive—but he also pours out wrath. Great as is his mercy, so also is his chastisement; he judges a person according to his or her deeds" (16:11–12). We can trust that God will reward us with the consequences of our decisions and actions. "Everyone receives in accordance with his or her deeds" (16:14). Sirach simply, yet beautifully, captures the blessing of God's mercy in the midst of our afflictions and its answer to our needs. "His mercy is as welcome in time of distress as clouds of rain in time of drought" (35:26).

LEADERSHIP

Sirach includes a section of exhortations directed to leaders. "A wise magistrate educates his people, and the rule of an intelligent person is well ordered. As the people's judge is, so are his officials; as the ruler of the city is, so are all its inhabitants. An undisciplined king ruins his people . . . The government of the earth is in the hand of the Lord, and over it he will raise up the right leader for the time" (10:1–4). These sentiments are similar to King Mosiah's about the value of a righteous king and the dangers of a wicked one who causes much iniquity to occur (see Mosiah 29:13, 17–18).

LOVE THE LORD

Sirach emphasizes the importance of the first great commandment. Besides admonishing one to fear the Lord, he encourages others to love their Maker with all their might (7:29–30). But besides loving the Lord himself, we should love his ministers and revere his priests and bring them the appropriate offerings to sustain them (7:29–31).

Moderation

Latter-day Saints are frequently taught moderation in all things, which seems to agree with some of Sirach's teachings. "In everything you do be moderate" (31:22). "Do not be greedy for every delicacy, and do not eat without restraint; for overeating brings sickness, and gluttony leads to nausea" (37:30–31). Wisdom texts commonly extol the virtue of self-control against the vices and passions of the flesh. Sirach is no different. "Do not follow your base desires, but restrain your appetites. If you allow your soul to take pleasure in base desire, it will make you the laughingstock of your enemies" (18:30–31). Self-control extends to avoiding materialism and buying things on credit: "Do not revel in great luxury, or you may become impoverished by its expense. Do not become a beggar by feasting with borrowed money, when you have nothing in your purse. The one who does this will not become rich" (18:32–19:1). Sirach counsels against two common excesses for men: wine and women. "Wine and women lead intelligent men astray" (19:2). Instead, the key to self-control is obedience and fear of the Lord. "Whoever keeps the law controls his thoughts, and the fulfillment of the fear of the Lord is wisdom" (21:11).

Mysteries of God

In one brief section, the text warns against seeking things that are beyond our mortal understanding for it can lead one astray (3:24). "Neither seek what is too difficult for you, nor investigate what is beyond your power. Reflect upon what you have been commanded, for what is hidden is not your concern" (3:21–22).

Opposites

Similar to Lehi's teaching in the Book of Mormon about opposition (see 2 Nephi 2:11), Sirach points out this eternal principle. "Good is the opposite of evil, and life the opposite of death; so the sinner is the opposite of the godly. Look at all the works of the Most High; they come in pairs, one the opposite of the other" (33:14–15). "All things come in pairs, one opposite the other, and he has made nothing incomplete. Each supplements the virtues of the other" (42:24).

Prayer

"Do not grow weary when you pray" (7:10). "Do not repeat yourself when you pray" (7:14). "The one whose service is pleasing to the Lord will be accepted, and his prayer will reach to the clouds. The prayer of the humble pierces the clouds, and it will not rest until it reaches its goal; it will not desist until the Most High responds and does justice for the righteous, and executes judgment" (35:20–22). Even more than trusting in our own heart and mind, which are almost always better than mortal counselors around us, Sirach urges "above all pray to the Most High that he may direct your way in truth" (37:15). Just as sin and healing are sometimes linked in the New Testament, Sirach urges that when one is ill, "do not delay, but pray to the Lord, and he will heal you. Give up your faults and direct your hands rightly, and cleanse your heart from all sin" (38:9–10). Sirach praises physicians for their services and sees their skill as a manifestation of God's mighty works, making the simple claim that "there may come a time when recovery lies in the hands of physicians, for they too pray to the Lord that he grant them success in diagnosis and in healing, for the sake of preserving life" (38:13–14).

Repentance

Repeatedly, Sirach encourages the sinner to repent, confess, and make amends for misdeeds. He discourages those who think that since nothing bad has happened it doesn't matter if they have sinned. In reality, they have only been spared this long because the

Lord is slow to anger. He also warns, "do not be so confident of forgiveness that you add sin to sin. Do not say, 'His mercy is great, he will forgive the multitude of my sins,' for both mercy and wrath are with him, and his anger will rest on sinners. Do not delay to turn back to the Lord, and do not postpone it from day to day; for suddenly the wrath of the Lord will come upon you" (5:5–7). Avoiding sin in the first place is of prime importance. "To keep from wickedness is pleasing to the Lord, and to forsake unrighteousness is an atonement" (35:5). "Flee from sin as from a snake; for if you approach sin, it will bite you. Its teeth are lion's teeth, and can destroy human lives" (21:2).

The promise is held out that "to those who repent he grants a return, and he encourages those who are losing hope. Turn back to the Lord and forsake your sins; pray in his presence and lessen your offense. Return to the Most High and turn away from iniquity, and hate intensely what he abhors" (17:24–26). "How great is the mercy of the Lord, and his forgiveness for those who return to him!" (17:29). "The compassion of the Lord is for every living thing. He rebukes and trains and teaches them, and turns them back, as a shepherd his flock" (18:13). Simply, one should not be ashamed to confess one's sins (4:26), and one should forsake one's sins for good: "do not commit a sin twice; not even for one will you go unpunished" (7:8). Also on the note of the need to forsake one's sin: "So if one fasts for his sins, and goes again and does the same things, who will listen to his prayer? And what has he gained by humbling himself?" (34:31).

RICHES

"Riches are good if they are free from sin; poverty is evil only in the opinion of the ungodly" (13:24). "Treat yourself well, according to your means, and present worthy offerings to the Lord" (14:11). However, if riches become too much the focus, they can lead to one's downfall. "One who loves gold will not be justified; one who pursues money will be led astray by it. Many have come to ruin because of gold, and their destruction has met them face to face. It is a stumbling block to those who are avid for it, and every fool will be taken captive by it. Blessed is the rich person who is found blameless, and who does not go after gold" (31:5–8).

Self-Esteem

It can be easy for mortals to feel insignificant in the midst of a vast universe, yet Sirach admonishes, "Do not say, 'I am hidden from the Lord, and who from on high has me in mind? Among so many people I am unknown, for what am I in a boundless creation?' . . . Such are the thoughts of one devoid of understanding" (16:17, 23). Self-esteem is part of living a good, healthy life, but it should be tempered with humility. "Honor yourself with humility, and give yourself the esteem you deserve. Who will acquit those who condemn themselves? And who will honor those who dishonor themselves" (10:28–29).

Trials

Like many wisdom texts, Sirach points out the necessity and value of trials in our lives—this life is for testing and through trials we become refined. "Accept whatever befalls you, and in times of humiliation be patient. For gold is tested in the fire, and those found acceptable, in the furnace of humiliation" (2:4–5). But promises are also given for the faithful: "trust in him, and he will help you; make your ways straight, and hope in him" (2:6). For, the text goes on, "consider the generations of old and see: has anyone trusted in the Lord and been disappointed? Or has anyone persevered in the fear of the Lord and been forsaken? Or has anyone called upon him and been neglected? For the Lord is compassionate and merciful; he forgives sins and saves in time of distress" (2:10). In another passage, comfort is promised in trials to those who fear the Lord:

"No evil will befall the one who fears the Lord, but in trials such a one will be rescued again and again" (33:1). Even Wisdom will bring trials upon people until she trusts them. Once they pass the tests, she will return to them, gladden them, and reveal her secrets to them (4:17–18). If, however, they go astray in the midst of their trials, Wisdom "will forsake them, and hand them over to their ruin" (4:19).

Virtue

Wisdom literature commonly exhorts its listeners/readers to live a virtuous life. It warns against passion, which can tear a person apart and destroy them while making them the laughingstock of their enemies (6:2–4). More directly, it commands "never dine with another man's wife, or revel with her at wine; or your heart may turn aside to her, and in blood you may be plunged into destruction" (9:9). "The human body is a fleeting thing, but a virtuous name will never be blotted out. Have regard for your name, since it will outlive you longer than a thousand hoards of gold. The days of a good life are numbered, but a good name lasts forever" (41:11–13).

Work

Sirach encourages hard labor or farm work because it was created by the Most High (7:15). Rather than thinking that others, especially sinners, have an easy life, we should just keep working forward. "Stand by your agreement and attend to it, and grow old in your work. Do not wonder at the works of a sinner, but trust in the Lord and keep at your job" (11:20–21). "Hard work was created for everyone, and a heavy yoke is laid on the children of Adam, from the day they come from their mother's womb until the day they return to the mother of all the living" (40:1).

Conclusion

As seen above, Sirach covers a wide variety of topics as it encourages readers to draw closer to the Lord through seeking wisdom and instruction. Sirach is especially noteworthy for discussing the concept of fearing the Lord, a common concept found throughout scripture. We are encouraged to have reverence, honor, and deference to God. Righteous individuals who have manifested a fear of God over a fear of men are worthy of praise and give us motivation to do likewise. Besides the general helpful discussions about wisdom, especially in how it strengthens our relationship with God, there may be a few specific aspects of wisdom Sirach addresses that have particular relevance to Latter-day Saints. Sirach places a great responsibility on caring for the poor and at the least acknowledging them when we encounter them. It can be challenging to know how to assist those in need, especially if we do not have great extra abundance, but the principle of befriending and treating everyone as human seems to be shared by Sirach and King Benjamin in the Book of Mormon. In his masterful farewell speech, King Benjamin emphasizes the importance of assisting the poor, even to the point of acknowledging that retaining a remission of our sins can depend on it.

> And also, ye yourselves will succor those that stand in need of your succor; ye will administer of your substance unto him that standeth in need; and ye will not suffer that the beggar putteth up his petition to you in vain, and turn him out to perish.
>
> Perhaps thou shalt say: The man has brought upon himself his misery; therefore I will stay my hand, and will not give unto him of my food, nor impart unto him of my substance that he may not suffer, for his punishments are just—
>
> But I say unto you, O man, whosoever doeth this the same hath great cause to repent; and except he repenteth of that which he hath done he perisheth forever, and hath no interest in the kingdom of God. . . .

And again, I say unto the poor, ye who have not and yet have sufficient, that ye remain from day to day; I mean all you who deny the beggar, because ye have not; I would that ye say in your hearts that: I give not because I have not, but if I had I would give.

And now, if ye say this in your hearts ye remain guiltless, otherwise ye are condemned; and your condemnation is just for ye covet that which ye have not received.

And now, for the sake of these things which I have spoken unto you—that is, for the sake of retaining a remission of your sins from day to day, that ye may walk guiltless before God—I would that ye should impart of your substance to the poor, every man according to that which he hath, such as feeding the hungry, clothing the naked, visiting the sick and administering to their relief, both spiritually and temporally, according to their wants. (Mosiah 4:16–18, 24–26)

Sirach has several wisdom sayings related to the family and the importance of raising up children in righteousness. The LDS focus on family would certainly agree with many of these notions, and parents are continually encouraged to teach their children righteous principles so that they can become wise and govern themselves. Sirach reiterates the great need we have to repent and stresses the importance of not delaying it! Like Amulek and Alma taught in the Book of Mormon, now is the time of our probation, and we will be held accountable for what we have done and not done within our mortal experience (Alma 12:24). God allows us time to repent to help return us and keep us on the right track.

But not all of Sirach's teachings would agree with LDS teachings or modern sensibilities.[9] As Doctrine and Covenants 91 points out, there are things within the Apocrypha that are true, and there are things that are false. We could micro-apply that principle to the book of Sirach and avoid some of its false doctrine while also benefiting from its insightful wisdom.

Notes

1. For a detailed study of the relationship between the Hebrew and Greek Sirach manuscripts along with a study of translation techniques exhibited by Ben Sira's grandson, see Benjamin G. Wright, *No Small Difference. Sirach's Relationship to Its Hebrew Parent Text* (Atlanta: Scholars Press, 1989).

2. Information from Stuckenbruck, "Apocrypha and Pseudepigrapha," 150–151. For a detailed study of the Hebrew fragments found at Masada, see Yigael Yadin, *The Ben Sira Scroll from Masada* (Jerusalem: The Israel Exploration Society and the Shrine of the Book, 1965).

3. Wright, *No Small Difference*, 5. Jerome did not make a new Latin translation of Sirach for the Vulgate, but incorporated an Old Latin text that did not include this displacement, so it contains important evidence for another Greek translation tradition.

4. For further study of the texts and versions of Ben Sira, see *The Texts and Versions of the Book of Ben Sira. Transmission and Interpretation*, ed. Jean-Sébastien Rey and Jan Joosten. Supplements to the Journal for the Study of Judaism. Vol. 150 (Leiden, Boston: Brill, 2011). For additional studies on some of the translations as well as other issues of this text, see *Studies in the Book of Ben Sira. Papers of the Third International Conference on the Deuterocanonical Books*. Supplements to the Journal for the Study of Judaism. Vol. 127 (Leiden, Boston: Brill, 2008).

5. Analogy drawn from John G. Snaith, *Ecclesiasticus or The Wisdom of Jesus Son of Sirach* (Cambridge: Cambridge University Press, 1974), 3.

6. Snaith, *Ecclesiasticus*, 5.

7. For a collection of essays on the relationship between Ben Sira and early Jewish wisdom, see Benjamin G. Wright III, *Praise Israel for Wisdom and Instruction*. Supplements to the Journal for the Study of Judaism. Vol. 131 (Leiden, Boston: Brill, 2008). See also chapters 2 and 6 in Daniel J. Harrington, *Jesus Ben Sira of Jerusalem. A Biblical Guide to Living Wisely* (Collegeville, MN: A Michael Glazier Book, Liturgical Press, 2005).

8. One commentator stated it this way: "Ben Sira describes this phrase [fear of the Lord] as denoting a warm personal relationship of trust towards God which underlies all his advice and teaching on doctrinal and secular matters alike." See Snaith, *Ecclesiasticus*, 4.

9. Some of Sirach's counsel seems to run counter to our sense of propriety and seems to reflect a cultural difference between Sirach's day and our own, or it is an indication of his notions versus revealed truth. For example, in chapter 12, Sirach encourages selective alms. "Give to the

devout, but do not help the sinner. Do good to the humble, but do not give to the ungodly . . . for the Most High also hates sinners and will inflict punishment on the ungodly. Give to the one who is good, but do not help the sinner" (12:4–7). Sirach's feelings toward women would not be welcomed in today's society: "Better is the wickedness of a man than a woman who does good; it is woman who brings shame and disgrace. For from garments comes the moth, and from a woman comes woman's wickedness" (42:13–14). "A silent wife is a gift from the Lord" (26:14). Sirach encourages his readers to not be ashamed of frequent (physical) disciplining of children (and even drawing blood from the back of a wicked slave) (42:5; see also 33:25–33 about slavery). "Pamper a child, and he will terrorize you; play with him, and he will grieve you. Do not laugh with him, or you will have sorrow with him, and in the end you will gnash your teeth. . . . Bow down his neck in his youth, and beat his sides while he is young, or else he will become stubborn and disobey you, and you will have sorrow of soul from him. Discipline your son and make his yoke heavy" (30:9–10, 12–13). "He who loves his son will whip him often, so that he may rejoice at the way he turns out" (30:1). Sirach seems to preach against resurrection: "there is no coming back . . . remember his fate, for yours is like it; yesterday it was his, and today it is yours. When the dead is at rest, let his remembrance rest too, and be comforted for him when his spirit has departed" (38:21–23). Sirach seems to connect the creation of bad things to God: "From the beginning good things were created for the good, but for sinners good things and bad" (39:25).

AFTERWORD

THE APOCRYPHA CONSISTS OF A VARIETY OF TEXTS MAKING IT both interesting and challenging. Comprising wisdom literature, apocalypses, tales, and scriptural expansions, the Apocrypha runs the gamut of ancient religious literature. Its eclectic collection is reflected in how each book of the Apocrypha is handled in this work; varied approaches are used in different chapters because of the diverse styles of the texts. Yet despite their diversity, the texts give us a glimpse into the world of Second Temple Judaism and its Hellenistic influence. These texts are also important to understanding the historical background to Jesus and the early Christians and the concerns and aspirations of early Jews and Christians.

While Joseph Smith did not incorporate the Apocrypha as part of his JST project nor make it part of the LDS canon, he and other early Saints obviously knew about it and had some interaction with it. The revelation regarding the Apocrypha included in the Doctrine and Covenants (section 91) is helpful, but it can also be frustrating because it is so open-ended. The section acknowledges that there are many things in the Apocrypha that are true, but there are also things in it that are not true and are interpolations by the hands of men, yet it doesn't specify which is which within the individual texts themselves. I suppose that leaves the Apocrypha as an open invitation to explore on our own, through the guidance of the Spirit, to see what truth we find in it. Some doctrines and principles are consistent through time, and we can learn from their perspectives on them. Other aspects of the texts are tied more to their particular historical location, situation, and culture and may not have much relevance or agreement to the modern Latter-day Saint reader.

This book has been an attempt to introduce the contents of the Apocrypha so that the reader can gain basic confidence from this overview to search the passages to greater depths. I feel confident in the promise of Doctrine and Covenants 91:5 that "whoso is enlightened by the Spirit shall obtain benefit" from the Apocrypha. I encourage you to build on this introductory exploration of the Apocrypha and continue to glean from its many treasures.

ABOUT THE AUTHOR

JARED W. LUDLOW

JARED LUDLOW (JARED_LUDLOW@BYU.EDU) IS A PROFESSOR OF ancient scripture and ancient Near Eastern studies at Brigham Young University, where he has taught since 2006. Previously, he spent six years teaching religion and history at BYU–Hawaii. He has also taught two years at the BYU Jerusalem Center for Near Eastern Studies. Jared received his Bachelor's degree from BYU in Near Eastern studies, his Master's degree from the University of California–Berkeley in Biblical Hebrew, and his PhD in Near Eastern religions from UC–Berkeley and the Graduate Theological Union. His primary research interests are with texts related to ancient Judaism and early Christianity. He has published various articles and a book, *Abraham Meets Death: Narrative Humor in the Testament of Abraham* (Sheffield Academic Press/Continuum, 2002), on narratological topics. He is also the author of a world history textbook, *Revealing World History to 1500 CE* (Thinking Strings, 2016).